MW00445265

Treating Trauma from Sexual Betrayal

The Essential Tools for Healing

Dr. Kevin Skinner, LMFT, CSAT-S

Published by:

KSkinner Corp.

199 N. 290 W. ste. 150

Lindon, Utah 84042

Copyright 2017 by Kevin B. Skinner, Ph.D.

All rights reserved. No part of this book may be reprinted, reproduced, or utilized in any form or by any electronic, mechanical, or other means, now known or hereafter invented, including photocopying and recording, or in any information storage or retrieval system, without permission in writing from the publisher. Printed in United States.

Author's note: Throughout this book most of the stories of sexual betrayal come from women. I recognize that men also experience sexual betrayal trauma. Unfortunately, in the research sample of more than 5000 people, only 250 were men. The author believes that there is a great need for more research on men's responses after the discovery of sexual betrayal. Preliminary findings indicate that men too are experiencing trauma-like symptoms.

In order to protect the confidentiality of all clients and research participants, names and personal identifying information have been changed. In some cases, the author has also taken liberty to combine cases to illustrate specific points.

This book should not replace medical or professional advice.

Dedication

This book is dedicated to my wife, Katy, and our eight children, who have been very supportive as their husband and father has spent hours typing to create this book. They have been so patient and encouraging, especially when I have been unavailable. My wife has been by my side editing and cheering me on. She has also been my sounding board when the writing was difficult. I can't express how grateful I am for her loving support.

I would also like to express my gratitude to Caitlin Olsen, my primary editor. She has made this book better by providing me incredibly valuable feedback and insight. Thank you Caitlin.

I must also dedicate this book to all of the individuals who have shared their experiences with me as clients, as well as the thousands who have completed my online assessments. You have been my teachers. Truly this book is for you and because of you. You have shared your deepest hurts and pains with me, allowing me to get a small glimpse into your life. Thank you for being resilient and strong. You have taught me how to be strong while facing some of life's most difficult challenges. My life has been enriched because of you.

Contents

Introduction

In 2005, I received a phone call from a man who said he needed to meet with me; it was urgent. When Scott sat down in my office, he was scared. He looked at me and confided, "My wife is going crazy. She caught me viewing pornography and over the past few days she has done nothing but yell and scream at me. There is nothing I can say or do that will calm her down. Can you help her? Can you help us?"

When I met with his wife, I had very little experience working with individuals responding to their spouse's pornography use with such extreme emotions. During my years of graduate school, I had received very little training on how to treat this type of intense emotional response. I was not prepared to provide her good treatment.

Fortunately, a few weeks later, I was talking with a colleague of mine about this case.

My friend said, "I think the symptoms are very similar to posttraumatic stress disorder." After further evaluation, it became clear that she was indeed experiencing symptoms that matched posttraumatic stress disorder (PTSD).

Over the next few months, my study and understanding of what was happening increased. The more I learned, the more I began to see the depth of trauma my clients were experiencing. Indeed they were showing signs of posttraumatic stress. In an effort to understand the traumatic symptoms that were being seen in our offices, I teamed up with Drs. Shondell Knowlton and Jill Manning to write the first assessment of its kind that explored traumatic responses related to a partner's sexual behaviors.

Over the past decade, we have gathered more than 5000 responses from women and men who have experienced sexual betrayal in their relationship. As we initially began gathering data, I was stunned by the results. Survey after survey revealed elevated traumatic symptoms matching many PTSD criteria. Then, in 2006, the first study exploring the trauma that occurs in disclosure of sexual betrayal was published by Barbara Steffens and Robyn Rennie. They found that nearly 70% of their research participants were experiencing posttraumatic stress. (1) When I compared our results to theirs, there were many similarities. The primary difference was our assessment focused on specific responses after sexual betrayal (e.g. I have a hard time with media because so many things remind me of what my partner has done.), while Steffens and Rennie used a non-specific PTSD assessment.

Since partners reported that pornography was the most frequent way their spouses were sexually acting out (over 73%), I began to have other questions. Can a spouse's use of pornography trigger this type of intense response? Or is it something else that is happening in the relationship besides pornography? Drs. Shirley Glass and Susan Johnson were reporting that infidelity was triggering PTSD-like symptoms, but pornography too? (2,3)

If what we were finding was true, the Internet revolution of the mid-to-late 1990's was changing our entire society and most people had no idea. Over the past 20 years, the Internet has brought much advancement in how we live our lives, but the most sought-out Internet content -- pornography -- was altering our entire society.

Our results confirmed that sexual behavior outside of a committed relationship such as infidelity, visiting strip clubs, and countless other behaviors were indeed triggering PTSD symptoms. Since discovering those preliminary findings, I have spent much time learning about trauma and how to best treat it. I have had the privilege of working with many individuals and couples throughout the United States and Canada. I have trained leaders from various religious organizations. And currently, I am privileged to be one of the professional trainers for the International Institute for Trauma and Addiction Professionals (IITAP). IITAP trains professional therapists, religious leaders, and others seeking to understand addiction and trauma. The training I am responsible for focuses on helping clinicians treat trauma after sexual betrayal.

Unfortunately, educating the public and those who treat individuals dealing with sexual betrayal has been a very slow process. Even today, many individuals and professionals in our society struggle to accept that sexual behaviors can be addictive. Many of these same people also believe that viewing pornography is normal and that individuals are over-responding when they get upset when their partner views pornography. Others believe that infidelity is a normal behavior in committed relationships. Such arguments not only discount a betrayed partner's true emotions upon discovery, but also hinder the treatment process because many professionals cannot be properly trained if there is no such thing as sex addiction or if they are being told sexual behaviors outside of a committed relationship are common and should be expected.

The purpose of this book is two-fold. First, the stories of 5000 individuals who have completed my research survey on sexual betrayal have a very important message that needs to be told. The data tells their stories in a powerful way. What they are experiencing is posttraumatic stress and most of them do not know it. Second, individuals suffering from sexual betrayal need to know that there is help available and that healing is possible.

Book Outline

This book is divided into four sections. In the first part, the focus is on helping you understand why trauma is a normal response and how to assess your trauma. Specifically, the first chapter provides evidence to support posttraumatic stress as the right diagnosis for many individuals dealing with a partner's sexual betrayal. If you feel like you are going crazy or losing your mind, this chapter will help you understand that your response is much more common than you think.

In the second chapter, your level of posttraumatic stress is assessed along with each of the key criteria associated with it. You will be given access to the same assessment that thousands of individuals have completed, and you will be able to see your results and discover the areas in which you need support. This first step will help you understand the symptoms of trauma you are experiencing and you will be able to identify your personal level in all five categories.

The third chapter identifies how early life relationships and your current relationship interactions can combine to create complex trauma. In addition, you will explore how your partner's use of denial, deception, and blaming, commonly referred to as gaslighting, increases the trauma you may be experiencing.

Chapter Four focuses on how easy it is to get stuck in fight, flee, or freeze mode and explains the science of why this happens. It offers examples of how fight, flight, and freeze modes often manifest after sexual betrayal. Throughout the chapter, assignments are given to help you discover more about your response to sexual betrayal. The first four chapters are designed to help you understand that you are not going crazy, but are responding in a natural way to betrayal.

In the second part of the book, the focus turns to how to begin the healing process. In Chapter Five, there is a discussion on the disclosure process. Examples are given that illustrate the difference between a forced disclosure and self-disclosure. You will see how both forms of disclosure can trigger trauma when they are done poorly. In contrast, a well-planned disclosure can be the beginning step in the healing process.

Chapter Six focuses on the critical nature of establishing a safe environment for healing. An example is provided regarding how safety can be rebuilt using key principles, including no secrets and accountability. The chapter ends with core questions you will want to ask yourself about your relationship. If you don't know the answer to these questions, moving forward in your relationship will be very difficult.

In the seventh chapter, four specific reasons are provided for why people get stuck in trauma and how you can move forward. Specific attention is given to how you can start the process of shifting away from being stuck and toward taking meaningful action in your healing.

In Part Three, five chapters are devoted to helping you resolve each of the core criteria of posttraumatic stress. In Chapter Eight, the painful topic of sexual trauma that results from within your relationship is discussed. Three specific solutions are offered to help you begin taking action if you are experiencing this form of trauma.

If you keep replaying in your mind what your spouse has done, Chapter Nine is for you. You will learn how to resolve intrusive memories or thoughts that won't go away. Specific solutions are provided to help you deal with the intrusive memories that won't leave you alone.

Chapter Ten focuses on avoidance. Do you find that you are avoiding people, places, and activities that you used to enjoy? If so, you will learn helpful strategies for overcoming fears and worries that may be holding you back. This chapter ends by offering ideas to help you identify people that are understanding, provide you comfort, and are emotionally safe.

In the eleventh chapter, negative self-beliefs are addressed. One of the common side effects of sexual betrayal includes self-worth issues and alterations in mood that often accompany the discovery. In my research, I found that it is common for individuals to turn their trauma inward and blame themselves for their spouse's behaviors. This chapter provides three reasons why this occurs and offers specific solutions for how you can resolve these negative self-beliefs if this is happening to you.

If you find that you are more angry and upset than you have ever been in your life, it will be important for you to read Chapter Twelve. Part of healing and recovery is understanding how to deal with difficult emotions or behaviors (e.g. anger, fear, monitoring, etc.) that are common when sexual betrayal has occurred. When you experience these emotions or engage in these behaviors, it is usually because you are simply trying to protect yourself. Unfortunately, being stuck in protection mode wears you down and leaves you feeling overwhelmed. Two scientifically proven methods are provided so you can learn how to regulate these intense emotions.

In the fourth and final part, the focus is on helping you develop the essential tools for your healing. In Chapter Thirteen, self-compassion, the most important element of healing, is discussed. Try as you might to heal, without developing a sense of compassion for self, your healing will be limited. Based on current research, specific strategies for increasing self-compassion are offered.

In the fourteenth and final chapter, a model of the essential tools for healing is provided. A case study is discussed that will show you how implementing each part of the model into your life can aid in your healing. A step-by-step process of healing is shared.

I appreciate the chance to share with you what I have learned about the process of healing from sexual betrayal. My hope is that as you read this book you will receive insight that will inspire you to move forward. I believe healing is possible. I have seen it happen in my clients' lives as they have implemented the principles discussed in this book. The journey is not easy and it will be filled with many ups and downs. My desire is, as you apply the tools discussed in this book, you will discover your path to healing.

Let's get started!

Part One

Trauma: A Natural Response to Sexual Betrayal

Chapter One

The Creation of
Posttraumatic Stress

*We long for a deep connection that begins at birth and never ends. When the
love we desire is missing we search far and wide seeking what we lost.*

We are all born with a strong, natural desire to connect to other human beings.
Our first primary connection is with our mothers. We begin with staring into each
other's eyes, being held and cuddled, and making sweet playful noises ("Goochy,
goochy, goo!"). These seemingly simple behaviors begin our journey and exploration of connection in relationships. As we mature we continue to interact with
our environment, testing and determining how to interact with our peers. We learn
early who is safe and who is not so safe, who will meet our needs and who won't.

This process is well under way at birth and continues throughout our entire
lives. So how do we know if we are safe or not? Who we can trust or not trust? Or
whom to connect with and whom to avoid? What is the internal mechanism inside
of us that tells us how we should interact with the people around us? Fortunately,
we now know the answers to these questions.

Dr. Stephen Porges has found that our nervous system helps us determine
whether people are safe or not. He writes, "By processing information from the
environment through the senses, the nervous system continually evaluates risk.
I have coined the term neuroception to describe how neural circuits distinguish
whether situations or people are safe, dangerous, or life-threatening." (1) In essence, Dr. Porges has determined that our nervous system is constantly assessing
for our safety.

What's even more intriguing about this is that while we all desire connection,
our first and most basic instinct when interacting with new people is to hold back

and assess if we are in a safe environment or not. Once we determine we are safe, then and only then do we attempt to connect. As Dr. Porges writes, "What allows engagement behaviors to occur, while disabling the mechanisms of defense? To switch effectively from defensive to social engagement strategies, the nervous system must do two things: 1) assess risk, and 2) if the environment looks safe, inhibit the primitive defensive reactions to fight, flee, or freeze."

So what happens when we assess the risk in our interaction with others, but we cannot determine if we are safe or not? Or what happens when we let our guard down and attempt to connect with others but they betray that trust? When these things occur, we begin to question our ability to protect ourselves. We naturally pull back and stop trusting in them and we also stop trusting others in society.

In essence, when others betray our trust, we naturally move into protection mode and become more cautious so we don't experience the same hurt again. Consequently, the more pain and hurt we experience in life, the more skeptical and hesitant we become around others. This is a logical step we take to avoid being hurt over and over again.

Am I Safe with You?

Generally speaking, our ability to trust others stems from our formative years. Our relationships with our primary caregivers -- our parents -- are key to connecting with others as we grow and mature. When we learn early in life to have healthy relationships, our trust in others is usually high. When we experience neglect, abuse, rejection, or simply a lack of closeness, we begin to question our safety. Even growing up with good and caring parents is no guarantee that we will come out of our formative years without some scarring. There is no such thing as a perfect parent and as a result, parents can and do unintentionally struggle to meet all of their child's emotional needs. Unfortunately, far too many children grow up in homes that provide limited emotional support no matter the intention of the parents.

The following story illustrates key points about how difficult it can be to determine your safety in relationships. The story also demonstrates how seemingly good relationships can quickly become traumatizing. Finally, as you read this story, consider how Alecia's experience altered her belief about herself and others.

While growing up, Alecia's family moved around a lot. In elementary school, she learned to make friends quickly. However, after each move, those relationships abruptly ended. Entering junior high school, she had moved around so much that she didn't know anyone and she was starting over again. She made some friends, but these relationships seemed more superficial than real. In her junior year of high school, she met Matt who quickly became her "best friend." She was finally getting the attention for which she had longed.

Her parents did not know how to respond because she had never had a boyfriend. They warned her to be careful, but she felt like they did not trust or understand her. She had never had a close friend and Matt seemed to be a really good guy. When Alecia and Matt were together, they had a great time. She felt like they were really getting to know each other well. As time progressed, their relationship became more physical. Alecia felt uncomfortable, but she didn't want to say anything because they were such good friends. As they crossed more and more of her personal boundaries, she started expressing some of her concerns. They hadn't had sex, but he kept wanting more and more from her. Near the end of her junior year, Matt started pushing her to have sex with him. She was very hesitant because she was worried it would change their relationship, but he assured her that he loved her and that he was committed to their relationship. Finally, she gave in telling herself that she did love him and she didn't want him to pull away because she wouldn't have sex with him.

Unfortunately, once they had sex, things began to unravel. They began fighting more about small and petty things. He began controlling her by telling her to lie to her parents so they could spend more time together. He also told her to whom she could and couldn't talk. She didn't understand what was going on. Why was he changing? What was wrong?

A few months after their first sexual experience, Matt began pushing her to have sex with him more and more frequently. She felt like their relationship had become all about sex. When she started resisting sex, he became upset and told her he could get anyone and that she was lucky to have him. As a result, she gave in to his demands, but felt awful about herself and their relationship. He had limited her from developing other friendships and he was literally her only friend. She couldn't talk with anyone, including her parents.

Even as she sacrificed so much for the relationship, Matt was hurting her emotionally with his unkind words and controlling behaviors. Then everything changed. Matt got mad at her one night because she wanted to go and do something fun and all he wanted to do was have sex. He left her and went to a party. While there, he hooked up with another girl from school. A few days later Alecia heard rumors in the hallway about what Matt had done. When she confronted him, he brushed her aside and said, "I told you I could get anyone. I am done with you piece of trash."

She was devastated. He was the only person she had ever trusted and he had broken her heart. She began to feel like there was something wrong with her. She tried to talk with Matt but he was just punishing and critical of her. His final words to her were, "I'm not sure anyone will want you. You are so needy." Alecia felt broken and promised herself she would never be hurt like that again.

Over the next few months of her senior year she missed a lot of school and barely graduated. She was alone and felt like nobody cared about her. Her parents, while good people, were too busy with their own lives to realize that much had changed. When Alecia told her parents that her and Matt had broken up, they said, "Oh, good. We were worried things were getting too serious." She didn't confide in them again after that. She simply turned her attention to school and getting good grades. That seemed to be the only thing she could control. That too pleased her parents, but inside she felt like she was dying. When she graduated from high school she couldn't get to college fast enough.

When she went to college her her roommates thought she was extremely shy. They tried to get her to open up and have a little bit of fun. She was very reserved and they decided she must not like them. Throughout her first semester of college she began to open up a little to her roommates. She told them about Matt and they insisted that she get over him and start dating. In fact, they wanted to set her up with one of their friends with whom they went to high school.

They introduced her to Jerry. On the first date, Alecia put on a good face and pretended to be strong and confident. She had promised herself that she wasn't going to get hurt so she decided that when she was around guys she would be strong and show little interest. She had learned that neediness was a bad trait to have and the only way she could avoid that again was to be distant, almost cold. On their date, Jerry tried to get to know her, but she pretended to have very little interest in him. After the first date, Alecia's roommates asked what was wrong. She was not being herself. Alecia told them that nothing was wrong, she just didn't want Jerry to think she liked him.

They asked her, "Well, are you interested or not?" She said, "I think so. He is super cute, but I don't want to show too much interest in him. Guys don't like that." They gave her a puzzled look. She told them what Matt had said to her about being needy and that nobody would ever want her. For the first time ever, she was given what I call a "relationship gift." Her roommate said, "Are you kidding me? What a jerk. You are an amazing and wonderful person. Any guy would be lucky to date you." This caught Alecia off-guard and was the beginning of a big change in her.

After that conversation, Alecia felt more confident in her relationships. She began dressing up and showing more confidence around others. She thought she was finally over Matt. At this point, she met John. He swept her off her feet with his attention and kindness. He made her feel like she was all that mattered to him. Even though she felt like she was over Matt, she still held back some. Her fears hadn't completely gone away. John fought through her hesitancy and eventually she opened up to him. When they discussed past relationships she told him about what had happened with Matt. He said to her, "I would never treat you that way. What a jerk." When she asked about his previous relationships, he told her he'd been in two serious relationships. She asked what happened. He said, "I guess they just got bored with me." She tried to get more out of him, but he didn't say much more and they moved onto another subject.

As their relationship progressed, she insisted that they move slowly. She also began asking him some hard questions about his involvement with pornography, the extent of his sexual involvement in previous relationships, and if he would still love her if she wouldn't have sex with him until they were married. He told her that he had seen pornography in his past but it wasn't that big of a deal. He had had sex with two different women, and that he could wait if she really wanted to.

His openness about his past helped Alecia feel comfortable enough to move forward in their relationship. Over the next few months their relationship grew and they decided to get engaged. All was well until one evening when Alecia was at John's house decorating his room for his birthday party. She discovered something that bothered her. She bumped his computer mouse and it turned on. She was surprised when she looked at the browser and discovered one of the pages had pornography on it. She decided to look at his Internet search history. She discovered that he had been viewing many pornographic websites. She was shocked. He had told her it wasn't that big of a deal. In her mind that meant it was in the past.

That evening, instead of them celebrating his birthday, she confronted him with what she had found. He quickly denied it was his and said that his roommate sometimes used his computer. She wanted to believe him, but inside she was upset. Had he been lying to her? Was he who she thought he was? She was very confused. Over the next few days they fought about it. She didn't believe him and he insisted it was his roommates. Finally, he said, "Then why don't we just ask my roommate?" Alecia said, "Great idea!" At that point, John became a little anxious because he didn't think she would have the courage to do that. He then admitted that the pornography she found on his computer was his and that he had been viewing it periodically.

Alecia didn't know how to respond. She said, "I'm going to need to think about this. Don't contact me for a few days. I will contact you when I'm ready to talk about it."

Alecia was scared. Her fears about being hurt in another relationship made her pull back even more than others may have. For many days in a row John would call, but she wouldn't answer. She was upset and angry, sad and scared. She didn't know how to respond.

Finally, John visited her apartment and convinced her to go on a ride with him. She hesitantly agreed. While on their ride, John told her that he had viewed pornography only a few times since their relationship had begun and that if it bothered her that much, he would avoid it. He promised that it was over and he would stop viewing it. He begged for her forgiveness. She felt like he was being genuine so she agreed to move forward in their relationship. She did love him.

They got married in the summer, had a fun honeymoon, and began school together in the Fall. Alecia was happier than she could ever remember. During that first year back at school they were busy with school and work, but they made time for each other and had lots of fun. They both had part-time jobs so they could afford housing and food. They were working together to make life happen.

During the following summer, John got an internship at a prestigious company. They were both very excited for this opportunity. However, a few weeks into his internship, John began to change. He spent more time at his internship and spent very little time with Alecia. She understood he was busy, but when he was home he seemed distant. When she asked him what was wrong, he would say, "I just have work on my mind," or "There's a lot of pressure at work." But things were changing and Alecia felt it. She didn't know how to respond. Her fears of being too needy began to creep up. She started dreaming about her past relationship with Matt. Soon, she was pulling away from John when he would try to be close. Their sexual interaction decreased and John began to complain. Their fights increased and they didn't know how to talk through their problems.

Alecia thought, "If we can just get through this internship, then when school starts again we'll be able to go back to the way things were."

Soon enough their final year of school began, but their fighting pattern didn't stop. Their final year of school was filled with lots of school projects, work, and other social responsibilities. Life had become very hectic and they were still not connecting with each other. Alecia became depressed and anxious. She was having a hard time focusing at school and work.

During nights John would stay up late working on homework and Alecia would go to bed. Their life together had changed. What was once blissful and happy had become lonely and stressful. John was more distant. Alecia too was disconnected. Neither of them knew what to change or how to change it back to the way it was.

At times they would try to work through their difficulties and things would be better for a few days. Then they would revert back to their busy lives and the fighting would resume. John began complaining that they never had sex. Alecia replied back, "You never spend any time with me. Why would I want to have sex when you don't talk with me?" This negative interaction pattern lasted for months until they were both ready to graduate.

As their graduation approached, they had discussed jobs and where to live but hadn't made any final plans. One evening during a difficult conversation, John was upset and exploded in anger at Alecia. He disclosed to her that he had been viewing pornography throughout the entire school year. He proceeded to blame her for it because she had not been sexual with him. He said, "I wouldn't have to view pornography if you would have sex with me." Alecia was deeply hurt and didn't know what to say or how to respond. Finally, when she did speak all she could say was, "All you care about is sex. You don't pay attention to me. All you think about is yourself." He stormed out and she was left crying by herself. He didn't come back that night.

The next morning he came home to a wife that was angry. They didn't talk throughout the day. Finally, Alecia couldn't wait. She said, "Where have you been? Sleeping with some whore? I hope you had fun. Are you going to leave me for her?" John was stunned. "What are you talking about?" He said, "You are going crazy. I went to Steve's and slept on his couch. I didn't cheat on you. You need some help, if you think I would do that." Then his anger got the better part of him and he said, "Maybe I should have." Those words pierced Alecia to the heart. She shut down and went into their bedroom, locked the door, and didn't come out the rest of the day.

The rest of the day John tried to apologize for what he said, but it was too late. Alecia wouldn't let him in. The next morning they had their first meaningful conversation in months. John apologized and Alecia said she was sorry for accusing him of having an affair. They both expressed a desire to make things better between the two of them, but neither knew what to say. They knew they needed help, but they didn't know what to do or where to get help.

Over the next few weeks Alecia had a hard time sleeping. She began having nightmares about John cheating on her. She struggled to eat. She would monitor his time on the computer. She installed a filter on their home computer. He didn't complain but did feel like she she was going overboard.

They also began having sex more often which helped John feel like things were getting better. They had made it through their first big fight with minimal damage.

At least that was what they thought. Alecia didn't talk about the bad dreams, or her fears when he went to work. And she thought she was just being a help by monitoring his computer use.

Over the next few months, their lives changed significantly. They moved to another state where John had gotten a job. Alecia got a part-time teaching job and also became pregnant with their first child. All seemed to be going well. They were not fighting and they were expecting.

In the background what they weren't telling each other was another story. Alecia became even more fearful but hid her fears because she didn't want another fight. John was very busy with his new job and felt a lot of pressure. While he was excited to be a dad, John struggled because Alecia got really sick during her pregnancy and sexual frequency went down again. Once again John turned to pornography to deal with his sexual desires. He felt guilty, but he thought if he told her they would end up fighting again. They were married, but they didn't really know each other.

Once their new baby was born, John was hoping that their sex life would return but instead Alecia experienced a significant bout with postpartum depression. He put more attention on his work. Alecia felt alone and overwhelmed being a first-time mother with very little outside support besides the times John helped.

Alecia's depression and growing anxiety took over. She wasn't sleeping or eating. Her anxiety was overwhelming her. John was working long hours and she felt alone and empty. Her deepest fears, which she didn't discuss, were that John was still viewing pornography or worse having an affair.

John tried to be supportive and helpful with what she was going through, but he didn't know what was really happening. As a result, John assumed she was dealing with typical postpartum depression. Alecia's gynecologist recommended that she begin taking an antidepressant, which she felt ashamed about taking. Fortunately, it helped her and some of her depression and obsessive fears lifted.

The next couple of years were filled with baby and eventually toddler activities. John settled into his job and Alecia went back to part-time work. They had settled into a routine and had informally decided that to not talk about issues was probably best for their relationship.

The next key event of their life happened when John was asked to take a new position at work which would require lots of travel. Alecia was scared of this idea but didn't dare prevent John from moving up to a new position. When they discussed it, Alecia did express some concern, but John assured her the money would be good and they would be able to afford things they hadn't been able to purchase.

The transition required John to be gone two weeks a month. Their arguing again resumed when John was home. Alecia again felt her fears taking over. She asked John about pornography. John got upset and denied his involvement. She also told him she was uncomfortable with him going to lunch and dinner with some of the women from work. He told her he was going out with a group of people and that he wasn't going with the women alone. This did little to comfort Alecia.

Once again they were disconnected and Alecia's nightmares resumed. She went back to the doctor and resumed taking an antidepressant hoping it would help like it did after the baby was born. While it helped some, they still fought when John was home.

During a big fight, Alecia again accused John of cheating on her. He looked at her with a look of guilt and she knew he had indeed cheated on her. She got more angry and began asking who it was and if she was pretty and beautiful. Finally, John said, "I have been having an affair. It's over now so you don't have to worry about it."

Alecia was in shock. She couldn't believe it. She began yelling uncontrollably. "It's over!" she yelled. "You are a lying, cheating bastard! Get out! Leave us alone. I hope she was worth it. We're done!"

John was exasperated. He felt some guilt, but he mostly felt like she was losing it. He was convinced that she was crazy and there was nothing he could do or say to help.

John reached out to a friend that night who let him stay at his home. John reluctantly told his friend what was happening. It was at this point that John received some good advice. His friend said, "You and Alecia are both good people. You ought to try to work things through."

For the first time in a long time, John felt genuinely ashamed of his behavior. He had hurt Alecia, but he didn't know how to make it better. John said, "I think it might be too late. She told me to get out. She is so hurt and angry I can't do or say anything without her yelling and screaming at me." John's friend said, "I know it's going to be hard, but divorce is hard, too. Why don't you try counseling first? Maybe you can get some ideas from a professional."

It was at this point that I met John and Alecia.

Understanding the Depth of the Problem

Day in and day out at my office, I meet couples who share stories similar to that of John and Alecia. Women like Alecia often feel that they are losing their minds or going crazy. When their husbands see their pain, they often feel shame. Instead of staying with their shame, they often get angry and lash out with statements like, "I wouldn't have to act out if you would be more sexual with me." Their way of dealing with their shame often manifests itself in anger. Most husbands struggle knowing what to say because their behaviors created the pain. Men oftentimes don't have a model for how to own their mistakes, and as a result, feel hopeless in how to help make things better. As a result, both women and men feel helpless. They don't know how to fix their problems and consequently begin questioning if they should stay together or divorce. What they do know is that they are in a lot of pain (that's what relationship disconnection does to us) and very little, if anything, has helped them resolve their problems.

So, what's the solution?

The solution begins by understanding the depth of the problem. In order to provide couples like Alecia and John the best help possible, I begin by giving them a battery of assessments in order to truly understand what is happening in their lives. Before I met with Alecia, I sent her electronic assessments that helped me understand her levels of depression, anxiety, and betrayal trauma. In the next chapter you will learn more about the betrayal trauma assessment. I also gave John an assessment that evaluated his sexually compulsive behaviors.

My belief is that it is hard for clinicians like myself to treat individuals if I don't seek to genuinely understand what they are experiencing. In my experience, information provided in assessment is critical to doing good therapy. Let me explain why. The assessment for betrayal trauma allowed me to quickly identify the symptoms Alecia was experiencing. It revealed to me that she was having nightmares, that she was avoiding people and places because they were too triggering for her. She was also feeling angry and upset in ways that were scaring even her. She had been having suicidal thoughts. Her depression and anxiety levels were clinically significant. She was suffering deeply, and I wanted her to know that I knew and cared about what she was going through.

In assessing John, I was able to quickly identify that his sexual behaviors were much more than just an affair. He had been dealing with pornography and other sexual behaviors (e.g. visiting topless bars) for an extended period of time. This was critical to helping John get proper help. Had we just focused on helping them deal with his affair, we would have missed a significant part of his sexual addiction. We would have missed some of the deeper sexual behaviors and those that were triggering his affairs. These actions (e.g. hiding his use of pornography) were a big part of why he was treating Alecia the way he was.

Once I understood the extent of Alecia's trauma, my primary goal was to help her understand that what she was experiencing was actually normal and that she wasn't losing her mind. I explained that trauma is a natural response when we are betrayed; since the first rule of connection and love in relationships is safety, when we no longer feel safe due to our partner's betrayal, our fear and worry grow.

Why do we experience fear? In *Trust: Mastering the Four Essential Trusts,* Iyanla Vanzant explains what happens this way: "Fear is the normal response to the belief that love is not present or that your survival is at stake. The mind conjures up images of being 'out there' on your own." (2)

In order to help Alecia further understand, I shared some of the key findings and areas of concern from her assessment results. My goal was two-fold. First, I wanted to help her feel understood. My message was, "No, you are not going crazy. This is a normal and natural response. There are reasons you are experiencing these difficult emotions." She needed to know that her emotional roller coaster was normal and actually more common than she thought. Second, I wanted to outline the common symptoms of trauma so she would understand that what she was going through really was trauma.

I have found that it is critical to give individuals a way to describe what they are experiencing. Over the years, countless women have come up to me after a presentation on sexual betrayal trauma and said, "You are the first person who has accurately described what I have been experiencing for years. I finally have a language to describe what I have been experiencing."

Before we move on to the sexual betrayal trauma assessment, there is an important question to address. Alecia said to me, "I know that the affair is a huge issue, but why was his secretive use of pornography so triggering to me." She continued, "Why am responding this way to pornography? I don't understand."

Her questions allowed me to share with her what leading marriage therapists are saying about pornography's influence on relationships. Both Drs. John Gottman and Sue Johnson have warned in recent articles and interviews about the negative influence that pornography and other sexual behaviors have on relationships. For example, in 2016, Dr. Gottman wrote *An Open Letter on Porn* in which he states, "Recently, however, research on the effects of pornography use, especially one person frequently viewing pornographic images online, shows that pornography can hurt a couple's relationship."

Dr. Johnson, founder of Emotionally Focused Therapy (EFT), writes, "In the end, Internet porn devastates our capacity for close relationships and good sex. It promotes loneliness and isolation and infuses a person with shame and despair. Porn devotees are left with a broken and fragmented sexuality, in which emotion and the erotic are separate and never integrated."

When I shared these findings with Alecia, she resonated with what she heard. She wasn't needy or overreacting. Pornography in and of itself can hurt relationships. It was at this point that she turned to me and said, "Okay, I need help getting through this. I don't know if my marriage will work out, but I am beginning to understand what you are saying. I wish I had known this years ago."

Chapter Summary

We are born with a natural desire to connect. However, in order to do so we must feel safe and secure in our environment. The core question we ask in all of our relationships is, "Am I safe with you?" If the answer is yes, we bond and connect. If the answer is no, we will naturally hold back.

The story of Alicia and John introduces how sexual betrayal triggers symptoms that match PTSD. Using formal assessments is important to gain a proper understanding of the depth of the trauma and addiction.

In the next chapter, you will be asked to take the same assessment that Alecia took. Over the past ten years, I have identified key results; upon completion of this assessment, you will be given feedback regarding areas you will want to address in your healing based on these findings.

Chapter Two

Assessing Trauma from Sexual Betrayal

The most difficult thing in life is to know yourself.

Thales

When clients set up an appointment to deal with sexual betrayal, I know that when they enter my office they are in a lot of pain. Many are anxious, hoping and praying for some relief from the pain they are suffering. When I ask how I can help, many say something like, "I am sure I am going to go crazy. I can't sleep or eat, and I'm having a hard time thinking about anything besides my husband's sexual behaviors. What is wrong with me? Why do I keep thinking about what he did?"

As mentioned in Chapter One, I respond by looking my client in the eyes and saying, "What you are experiencing is very normal for what your spouse has done. In fact, if you weren't experiencing some of these symptoms, I would be surprised." The response I generally get is, "Really? Others feel like this? I thought there was something seriously wrong with me!" I proceed to share with them what I am going to share with you in this chapter.

Below, I outline the key ways that sexual betrayal trauma manifests itself. You will have the opportunity to take the Trauma Inventory for Partners of Sex Addicts (TIPSA) along with other important assessments. When you complete these assessments, you will be given feedback that will provide valuable insight on the specific areas that you will need to focus on in your healing process. You will also learn how others respond to the questions you answer in the assessment.

Posttraumatic Stress

Professionals who work with couples dealing with infidelity have claimed for years that a common response to betrayal is posttraumatic stress. However, throughout the 1990's, there was very little research to support this claim. In 2006, Barbara Steffens and Robyn Rennie published one of the first studies with real evidence suggesting that disclosure of a husband's compulsive sexual behaviors produced traumatic symptoms that matched most of the symptoms for diagnosing PTSD. Perhaps most importantly, Steffens and Rennie found that almost 70% of their participants reported *most* of the posttraumatic stress symptoms.

This finding supports what I was seeing with my clients when I first wrote the TIPSA. Since 2005, I have been gathering data in an effort to demonstrate the exact ways that discovery of a partner's sexual betrayal influences people.

If you would like to take the *Trauma Inventory for Partner's of Sex Addicts*, you can do so for free at www.discoverandchange.com/tipsa. The rest of this chapter will address each area of the inventory.

Common Symptoms of Sexual Betrayal

In the most recently published Diagnostic and Statistical Manual of Mental Disorders (DSM-5), posttraumatic stress can affect people in five key ways:

1. Life threatening experiences

2. Reliving the events

3. Avoidance

4. Mood and Cognitions

5. Emotional arousal

Below we will explore all five of these areas and the questions we asked to assess them.

Life Threatening Experiences

According to the DSM-5, in order to officially give the diagnosis of PTSD, a person has to report that they were exposed to death, threatened death, actual or threatened serious injury, or actual or threatened sexual violence.

In most cases, the act of sexual betrayal does not feel like it is life-threatening. However, when I began reviewing the results of my research participants, I was surprised at how many reported that they felt unsafe with their partner or felt violated by their partner's behaviors. Nearly 45% of those who completed the assessment reported that they were concerned about contracting a sexually transmitted disease. (See Chapter Eight for more information on these results.) Additionally, over 90% of the participants agreed with the following statement: "I feel violated due to my partner's sexual behaviors." While feeling violated is not the same as feeling one's life is threatened, it does support the idea that they do not feel safe with their spouses anymore.

Discovery can alter the marital relationship in other ways as well. Some individuals become upset and irrational after discovery. We included the following statement to determine how often individuals are physically abused after discovery: "Since learning of my partner's behaviors, he/she has hurt, hit, or threatened me." I did not expect the numbers to be high and was shocked to discover that 40% of research participants agreed with this statement. That means 608 women out of 1527 surveyed had experienced at least occasional violence or threat of violence. An additional 20% stated that physical abuse was happening at least half of the time or more. Though I'd expected before these findings that sexual addiction hurts marriages, I had not known the extent.

These findings clearly demonstrate that a significant amount of women are experiencing some form of life threatening events (e.g. threats, STDs) and, in many cases, physical violence. (To see the results of each of the questions in this section, visit the "Critera A Results" portion of the following website: www.discoverand-change.com/tipsa/assessment.)

Reliving the Events

Do you have nightmares or dream about what your partner did? Or do you find yourself thinking about what he/she did while you are having sex? These are both common outcomes when a partner discovers their partner's hidden sexual behaviors.

When I am talking with clients about reliving events, many respond with a visceral response. They say, "Yes," while shaking their heads and asking me why they can't get the images out of their minds. Why does this happen? One good explanation is that the brain is trying to make sense of what occurred. Our brains are designed to solve problems. However, when the answer is complex, or there isn't a good answer, our brains get stuck. As a result, we end up replaying painful events over and over again, trying to make sense of what happened and to understand the details. This is one reason many women ask the same questions. They ask for details trying to understand what happened. This is the brain's attempt to create a cohesive narrative of their experiences and their partner's betrayal. Unfortunately, many individuals get stuck in the painful memories and, as a result, struggle to move on.

Here are a few examples from our survey regarding reliving events :

Question: I have episodes where I feel like I am reliving the event over and over again.

Responses: Of the 1390 individuals who answered this question, 1094 (79%) reported that at least half the time they find themselves reliving the event over and over again in their mind.

Question: Since discovering my partner's behavior, when I see sexually suggestive images I feel anxious.

Responses: Of the 1387 individuals who answered this question, 974 (70%) reported that at least half the time they feel anxious when they see a sexually suggestive image.

Question: I struggle to think of other things besides what my partner has done.

Responses: Of the 1390 individuals who answered this question, 1054 (76%) reported that at least half of the time they struggle to think about anything besides what their partner has done.

When individuals replay what happened or keep remembering specific memories of what happened, this is a traumatic response. In each of the questions above, the number of individuals who relived what happened, felt anxious when seeing something sexual, or couldn't think of anything else was very high; at least 70% experienced these symptoms half the time. Clearly, after discovery of a partner's sexual betrayal, reliving the event/s is very common.

Avoidance

"What can I do?" Amy asked, "I used to enjoy going shopping, spending time with my friends, and going to church. Now I can hardly leave my house."

Amy is experiencing the symptoms of avoidance. When this happens, an individual's personality begins to change. Previously bubbly and outgoing women begin to avoid environments that trigger memories or difficult emotions. For many, they begin to feel like they are living in their own prison. Many individuals end up cutting off relationships which could have offered support, and they struggle being in public environments (i.e. malls, swimming pools, beaches, gyms). Fortunately, many women learn to work through these issues but resolution rarely happens quickly.

In an effort to explore how pervasive avoidance is after discovering a partner's sexual infidelity, we asked these questions:

Question: I engage in behaviors that distract me (i.e., excessive reading, sleeping, eating, drinking) from thinking about my partner's behavior.

Responses: Of the 1324 respondents who answered this question, 1017 (77%) reported that at least half of the time they engage in distracting behaviors to avoid thinking about what their partner has done.

While some distractions can be helpful, other distractions like excessive drinking, sleeping, or eating can trigger feelings of being out of control in your own life. The key question to ask regarding distractions is, "Are my distractions healthy or not?"

Question: Since learning of my partner's behaviors, I have a hard time participating in things that I previously enjoyed.

Responses: Of the 1319 respondents who answered this question, 1019 (77%) reported that they have a hard time participating in events that they used to enjoy at least half of the time.

The betrayal trauma in this instance makes it difficult to attend events or activities that used to be fun. In my experience, events such as girls' nights out, shopping, going out for the evening, or attending church meetings are all events that many individuals struggle to continue to participate in.

Sex is another key area of avoidance that many individuals ask me about after discovery of sexual infidelity. Upon discovery of sexual behaviors outside of the marriage, many couples' sex lives change significantly. Some people falsely claim that individuals turn to pornography or other outside sexual experiences because they are not "getting enough" sex at home. In my research this is simply not the case.

I asked individuals using pornography about their sexual relationship both before and after pornography use was discovered:

Question: Before pornography became a part of your relationship (or your partner discovered you were involved) how often were you sexually intimate?

Responses:

Answer Choices

Frequency	Percent	Number
Daily	14.90%	97
2-3 times a week	42.24%	275
1 time a week	20.12%	131
Every two weeks	9.98%	65
Once a month	6.45%	42
3-4 times a year	3.84%	25
Once a year	0.92%	6
We stopped having sex	1.54%	10
Total	100%	651

Question: Now that pornography has become a part of your relationship (or your partner discovered you were involved) how often are you sexually intimate?

Answer Choices:

Frequency	Percent	Number
Daily	10.32%	67
2-3 times a week	30.35%	197
1 time a week	21.11%	137
Every two weeks	10.02%	65
Once a month	11.25%	73
3-4 times a year	6.78%	44
Once a year	0.46%	3
We stopped having sex	9.71%	63
Total	100%	649

Considering that the average couple in the United States has sex an average of 2-3 times a week, most individuals using pornography were not sex deprived, as revealed in the findings regarding the first question listed above. Even after the discovery of pornography, most couples still had sex, albeit not as frequently as average. However, couples who stopped having sex altogether jumped from 1.5% up to nearly 10% when one spouse's pornography use began or was discovered.

In contrast, women who discovered their partner's pornography use reported that their sexual interaction after discovery became much lower:

Question: I avoid sexual contact with my partner since discovering his/her behavior.

Responses: Of the 1322 respondents to this question, 841 (64%) claim that they avoid sexual contact with their partner at least half the time or more. It is also important to note that 276 (21%) reported that they stopped having sex all together. It is unknown how long the period of complete avoidance lasted.

Based on these results, it is common after discovery of a spouse's sexual betrayal to isolate, avoid triggering places and/or people, and abstain from sex with their partner. Generally speaking, when you avoid situations that trigger memories or thoughts of what your partner did, you begin to see society very differently. Prior to discovery you probably didn't worry about going to a swimming pool or being in public with your spouse. Now, you may be extremely triggered by even the thought of going to a swimming pool or the thought of entering a mall and seeing how others are dressed. By avoiding people, places, and activities that you used to enjoy, your range of positive emotions will decrease. The end result is that your trauma will likely increase because your whole environment is likely to become threatening.

For how to deal with avoidance behaviors, read on to Chapter Ten.

Mood and Cognitions

In the past few years, professional therapists who specialize in posttraumatic stress have wanted to emphasize the symptoms associated with mood and thinking patterns. To accomplish this, they included the criterion of negative cognitions and mood in the diagnosis of PTSD. There are an infinite number of feelings and self-beliefs that manifest in this area. Examples of these include isolation from others, markedly diminished interest in activities, or a distorted sense of self.

In my clinical work, this is one of the key areas in which I assess my clients. My experience is that many women initially internalize their spouses' behavior as if it were their fault that their partners acted out. This belief can directly come from their spouses blaming them (e.g. "I wouldn't act out if you would give me more sex!") or it can come from the idea that "I must not be enough or he wouldn't do this." When these beliefs are accepted as truth, depression and anxiety increase. This happens because once a person feels that they are not enough, that they are flawed in some way, or that they are a failure, they then believe there is very little they can do to fix it. This triggers a sense of helplessness and hopelessness. None of us do well when we believe we can't fix something because we are sure that we aren't enough.

In this section of the survey, some of the core questions focus on elements of depression, negative self-beliefs, and isolation behaviors. Below you will see some of the questions with the accompanying results:

Question: I feel like my partner acts out because I am not good enough.

Responses: Of the 1284 respondents who answered this question, 1006 (78%) reported internalizing their spouse's behavior and accepting the idea that their spouse is acting out because of them at least half of the time. Nearly one in three (32%) answered that they "always" feel like their spouse acts out because they are not good enough

Due to these results, I spend a lot of time with my clients trying to understand what they have come to believe about themselves as a result of their partner's acting out behaviors. Those who believe that they are not good enough almost always are more depressed and report higher levels of trauma than those who see themselves as good enough. The resolution of this negative self-belief is one of the core issues that needs to be resolved in treating betrayal trauma. For strategies and solutions regarding negative self-beliefs, see Chapter Eleven.

In the next question, we focus on the powerful belief held by a betrayed partner that they are a bad person. This is a strong indicator that trauma is deeply embedded in this person's day to day thinking.

Question: I feel like I am a bad person because of what my partner has done.

Responses: Of the 1282 respondents who answered this question, 521 (41%) believe that at least half the time they feel like they are a bad person because of what their partner has done. Nearly 11% reported feeling that way all of the time. While these numbers are lower than responses to other questions, feeling like you are a bad person all of the time is a clear indicator that extra help and support are needed. When clients always or more often than not believe they are inherently bad, I ask them to help me understand how they came to that conclusion. Making sense of the origin of that self-belief is vital to recovering from betrayal trauma. Therefore, if you in any way believe that you are a bad person because of your spouse's behaviors, please take some time now and write about how you came to that conclusion and what experiences led you to believe you are bad. I explain why this is so important in more detail in Chapter Eleven.

In the next question, I look at the way betrayal influences individuals in mood and thinking patterns in social environments (e.g. with friends, and in other social settings).

Question: When I am in social settings, I don't feel like I belong anymore.

Responses: Of the 1284 individuals who answered this question, 892 (69%) reported that at least half of the time they feel like they don't belong in social settings anymore. This especially manifests itself in religious settings where families are together, when talking with friends, and in situations when individuals are talking about their spouses. When I ask people about this question, I often hear statements like the following: "I just don't fit in anymore. They talk about what they are doing in their family and I don't know what to say. I feel like if I say anything I might just start crying."

When I see this happening in clients, I work to shift their attention toward relationships that they feel are supportive and caring. I am especially concerned about getting them with people who can understand what they are going through without judgment.

When the committee who wrote the DSM-5 added the symptoms outlined above and called it *Mood and Cognition*, it made a lot of sense to me. For years, I have met amazing individuals who have become stuck with negative thoughts and beliefs about themselves as a result of their partner's behaviors. I have come to believe that if these negative thoughts and beliefs are not resolved, trauma won't be healed. I discuss the process of healing such beliefs in Chapter Eleven.

Emotional Arousal and Reactivity

One of the most commonly known behaviors associated with PTSD is heightened emotional arousal. In war veterans, we hear about individuals being overly jumpy and easily startled. Many become hyper-vigilant out of fear of something going wrong. Individuals dealing with betrayal trauma often report having overwhelming emotions upon discovery of their spouse's sexual behaviors. However, when the powerful emotions do not subside after weeks, months, and even years, they begin to have major health problems.

In essence, emotional arousal and reactivity is an internal trigger alerting you that you are not safe. The result is that your body kicks into protection mode and decides whether it should fight, flee, or freeze. Individuals who score high in this category are generally stuck in fight mode. They are constantly looking around for the "tiger" in the room. Eventually, these individuals get worn down and begin to turn on themselves. It is not uncommon for them to have severe depression and even suicidal thoughts.

The questions we use to assess *Emotional Arousal and Reactivity* deal with sleep, anger, hypervigilance, and suicidal thoughts.

<u>Sleep</u>

It is a common problem for individuals to have a hard time getting to sleep due to the common stressors of life. However, when an individual's central nervous system is activated due to betrayal trauma, sleep becomes even more challenging. Over the years I have had many clients tell me that they are hardly sleeping or that they are only getting two to four hours of sleep each night. When this pattern lasts for days or weeks at at time it begins to influence every aspect of their life. Their body begins to weaken, making them more vulnerable to illnesses, mental exhaustion, and physical challenges.

So how is sleep influenced by discovery of betrayal trauma? Here's the question we ask regarding sleep:

<u>Question</u>: Since learning of my partner's behavior I have difficulty falling asleep.

<u>Responses</u>: Of the 1259 respondents who answered this question, 925 (73%) reported that at least half of the time they have difficulty falling asleep. Twenty-one percent say that they always have a hard time falling asleep since discovery.

<u>Anger</u>

What happens when your energy is depleted due to elevated stress? You feel threatened and begin to take actions to protect yourself. While under attack, we naturally fight, flee, or freeze. When sexual betrayal occurs, our minds and bodies often go into fight mode to protect ourselves. Consequently, many individuals report being angrier than they have ever been. Over the years, I have had many clients share with me in embarrassment moments where they hit, slapped, or punched their spouse. I have met individuals who have spent time in jail for their violent outburst after discovery.

Sadly, many people, due to prolonged betrayal in their relationship, get stuck in their anger. As a result, they and their spouse begin to only see the angry person. Over the years I have found that most individuals trapped in anger discover the "real" self when they are taught how to let go of the anger. This is a skill that I discuss in Chapter Twelve.

Exactly how prevalent is anger after discovery? Below is one of the questions we ask regarding anger in the relationship:

Question: After discovering my partner's sexual behaviors, I find that I am increasingly angry in response to my partner.

Response: Of the 1260 respondents who answered this question, 1099 (87%) reported that at least half of the time they respond to their spouse with anger. Nearly 32% reported that they are always angry with their partner.

Clearly, deep emotional pain is triggering this need to fight. Unfortunately, this anger is often used against them by their spouse; I often hear women say, "My husband tells me that when I can control my anger maybe we could get somewhere. When he does this, it only makes me more upset." In the face of this accusation, the partner may then believe that there is something wrong with them because they can't control their anger, which can lead to shame and a consequent belief that there is something inherently "wrong with me." This often becomes a vicious cycle that some couples engage in for months and sometimes years.

Hypervigilance

Hypervigilance is an enhanced state of sensory sensitivity accompanied by an exaggerated intensity of behaviors whose purpose is to detect threats. Hypervigilance is also accompanied by a state of increased anxiety. All this easily causes exhaustion. Other symptoms include abnormally increased arousal, a high responsiveness to stimuli, and a constant scanning of the environment for threats. (1)

The enhanced sensory sensitivity explains why betrayed partners often try to read their partner's emotions. It also explains why they check up on them while at work or while home on a computer. This heightened sense of monitoring often triggers the spouse who betrayed to exclaim, "You are trying to control me!" What they fail to realize is that their lack of fidelity triggered a natural response in their spouse to scan their environment and check for safety. Thus, hypervigilance is a normal reaction and a reasonable defensive maneuver to protect oneself from further harm.

While hypervigilance is a common response, it truly is exhausting and often is one of the key behaviors that is reported to me when individuals talk about the feeling that they are going crazy. Those who are stuck in hypervigilance mode seldom get mental breaks and often have a hard time slowing down their mind to find any peace or calm.

One of the research participants described her experience with hypervigilance this way: "I was super hypervigilant. I was looking for any way to catch him. I couldn't work. I couldn't sleep. My mother/daughter relationship was deteriorating. I wasn't eating. My ego was shattered. And going through my day pretending to be okay was too hard." This type of behavior is frequently how betrayal trauma manifests itself.

In order to assess hypervigilance in betrayed partners, the survey includes the following question:

Question: I closely monitor my partner's behaviors.

Responses: Of the 1256 respondents who answered this question, 1090 (87%) reported that at least half of the time they closely monitor their partner's behaviors. Nearly half (46%) reported that they "always" do this.

With 87% of betrayed partners closely monitoring the behavior of their spouse, there is little doubt that hypervigilance is common after sexual betrayal. Additional symptoms include a powerful need to check up on their partner (e.g. look at phone records, check Internet history), a constant need to read their partner's emotions, a drive to check up on their partner, and a feeling of elevated anxiety.

Suicidal Thoughts

Over my twenty years as a professional counselor, one thing that many betrayed partners reluctantly reveal to me is thoughts about suicide. Many are embarrassed or ashamed to admit that they are having these thoughts, but when I see elevated depression and anxiety scores I have started asking my clients directly if they are having these thoughts. I will often say, "Based on my research, I've discovered that it's common to have suicidal thoughts after discovering sexual betrayal. Is this something that you have felt or experienced?" Quite often, my clients look up at me and say, "Yes. I have had suicidal thoughts."

In most instances they will then say something like, "I have had the thought, but I wouldn't act on it. I can't leave my children." Or they will tell me that even though they have had suicidal thoughts, they wouldn't hurt themselves. What I have come to understand is that most of them are in such deep emotional pain that they want a way to escape it somehow. Most often, the real goal is to escape the trauma rather than end a life. This desperation to escape is understandable given the extreme pain and terror associated with betrayal trauma and subsequent PTSD.

Because many women were willing to open up and discuss these feelings, we include questions about suicidal ideation on our assessment:

Question: I feel suicidal due to this experience with my partner.

Responses: Of the 1254 individuals who answered this question, 371 (30%) reported that at least half of the time they feel suicidal. This number was surprisingly high to me, but when I added individuals who reported that they occasionally feel this way I was surprised to find that another 380 (30%) answer affirmatively. These results indicated that 60% of those surveyed had, at least at one point in time since discovering their partner's sexual betrayal, had suicidal thoughts.

Note: Fortunately, most suicidal thoughts are fleeting thoughts that go away after a short period of time. However, if these thoughts do not go away or you cannot shake them, please reach out for support. Please talk about these thoughts and feelings with a trusted friend or family member. At times like this, you may need to use someone else's brain to help you through this difficult time. Do not be embarrassed or ashamed that you are having these thoughts. My research findings indicate that having suicidal thoughts is common after betrayal, but these feelings can be worked through and there are answers to help heal. If at anytime you feel suicidal, please consider reaching out for extra support by calling the National Suicide Prevention Lifeline at 1-800-273-8255.

Additional Criteria for Diagnosing PTSD

In this chapter we have discussed five criteria for diagnosing PTSD. There are two additional factors that are considered in the diagnosis of PTSD. The first is as follows:

1) Persistence of symptoms (in Criteria B--reliving, C--avoidance, D--negative mood and cognitions, and E--emotional arousal and reactivity) for more than one month.

In order to understand how long respondents have been experiencing the symptoms listed above, we asked the following question: "How long have you been experiencing the symptoms described in this assessment (e.g. recurrent thoughts, feeling anxious, being afraid)?" The participants' answer results are listed below:

Time	Percent	Number
Less than one month	4.84%	60
2-3 months	7.34%	91
4-6 months	9.12%	113
7-12 months	12.19%	151
More than one year but less than two	15.17%	188
More than two years but less than five	28.17%	349

More than five years	23.16%	287
Total	100%	1237

As can be seen above, most respondents reported that they have been experiencing trauma symptoms for well over one year, with the highest percentage having had these symptoms for two or more years. This finding was one of the most concerning for me as a therapist. Our minds and bodies are not designed to deal with these elevated stress symptoms for extended periods of time.

The second additional factor considered in the diagnosis of PTSD is this:

2) Significant symptom-related distress or functional impairment (e.g., social, occupational challenges).

The final step for diagnosing PTSD is that the event influences other areas of life. To address this criteria we ask the following question: "It has become difficult for me to fulfill important roles (that of employee, parent, etc.) since discovering my partner's sexual behaviors."

Responses: Of the 1238 respondents who answered this question, 791 (64%) reported that at least half of the time they have a hard time fulfilling important roles in which they need to perform.

One respondent made a comment about this question. She wrote, "I cannot be there for my children or anyone else, even in life or death situations. I feel paralyzed in my emotional state. Cannot even function at the lowest level of society it seems, let alone have anyone or anything to be dependent upon me."

Understanding And Using Your TIPSA Results

If you haven't taken the trauma assessment yet, you can do so at www.discoverandchange.com/tipsa.

Once you have completed the Trauma Inventory for Partners of Sex Addicts, you will receive your personal results. The assessment findings are designed to help you identify areas in which you need help and should not be used to diagnose PTSD without consulting a professional. You may benefit from taking these results to your doctor to help him or her quickly and accurately understand what you are experiencing.

Your Results: Please take a few minutes now to review your TIPSA results. (If you have yet to take the TIPSA, do so now.) Your scores are summed together for each of the key five categories. In each category there are five possible outcomes:

- Low
- Low-moderate
- Moderate
- Moderate-high
- Elevated

Please remember that the purpose of the results is to help you identify areas in which you are experiencing traumatic symptoms. If you score low or low-moderate, your responses to that particular category indicate that your symptoms are relatively low. If you score in the "moderate" range, that is the category where a majority of those who take the assessment score. A moderate score does not mean you do or do not have trauma, rather it indicates that you are experiencing trauma symptoms. In other words, you are manifesting some of the common symptoms of trauma.

If in one or more of the categories you scored "Moderate-high," your level of trauma symptoms is significantly higher than others who completed the assessment. These findings are probably not too surprising to you since you are living with trauma symptoms day in and day out. While many individuals score in the "Moderate-high" range in one of the categories (e.g. Reliving, Avoidance), if your results indicate that you are "Moderate-high" in more than two categories, it would be helpful for you to seek treatment from someone qualified to treat trauma.

If you scored in the highest level of trauma, "Elevated," this indicates that you scored higher than 90% of those who completed the assessment. If you are experiencing this level of trauma in one or more of the categories, it is especially important for you to seek help from a qualified professional, specifically one who specializes in treating trauma. It is vital to reach out for extra support. In the second section of this book you will be given additional ideas to support your healing and recovery. Later in the book, we will discuss how to find specialists who treat this type of trauma.

Assignment:

Please take a few minutes and review your results. Begin by reviewing each category of your results. In each of the five key categories, how did you score? How many were "Low" or "Low-moderate"? How many were "Moderate"? And how many times did you score "Moderate-high" or "Elevated"?

Next, identify the specific category where your scores were the lowest and highest. By seeing where you scored high and low you will know where to put more of your energy now. Also, it is possible to that your scores can change based on what is happening in your life at any given time.

Assignment:

Please take a few minutes and ponder about your results. Then write down your responses to the following questions. What were the key findings that stuck out to you? In which area do you feel like you need the most support? What is one thing you can do today to get started in your healing journey?

Note: If you have been experiencing trauma symptoms described in the TIP-SA for months or years, it is important to learn how to heal from your trauma. Throughout my career, I have observed that many individuals in trauma wait for years before seeking help. Initially, they were too embarrassed to reach out for support. They felt like they should be able to handle what they were experiencing on their own. Some felt that they just had to deal with their feelings on their own. Others falsely believe that since the addiction problem is their spouse's, they shouldn't need help. I have come to understand that when sexual betrayal occurs, both spouses need help and support, and the sooner after discovery, the better.

Chapter Summary

The TIPSA is a valuable way to measure your level of posttraumatic stress. The five criterion of PTSD are addressed in the TIPSA (through the sample questions listed earlier in this chapter): a) life threatening experiences, b) reliving the event; c) avoidance; d) mood and negative cognitions; and e) emotional arousal. There are several ways to understand and use your TIPSA results.

In the next chapter, we explore three key indicators that explain why some people have higher trauma than others.

Chapter Three

Adding Trauma to Trauma

The past is never dead--it is not even past.

William Faulkner

Elise came to visit me after discovering her husband's latest affair. She was beside herself. In the beginning of their marriage, she had felt something was wrong in their relationship. He would hold back emotionally and then when she talked with him about it, he would tell her that she was making things up.

For years, he had developed friendships with women against her desires. He said that everyone has friends and she didn't need to be concerned. However, throughout the years she would periodically find notes or emails that he had received from some of these women. She knew he was having emotional affairs but did not realize he was lying to her to the extent of concealing physical affairs. The uncertainty and lack of trust was killing her. She exhibited most of the trauma symptoms outlined in Chapter Two.

When she confronted her husband, Curtis, he would minimize the nature of his friendships and only when she got angry enough and threatened to leave would he agree to end his relationships. Over the years, Curtis would argue that she was worrying too much and that she was acting this way because her dad cheated on her mom. When he said things like that, she became confused and questioned herself. Was he right? Her instincts would tell her something wasn't right, but he had a knack for turning things around to the point where she felt maybe she was wrong.

There are some important pieces of Elise's story that show how her trauma began and developed over time. She'd grown up in a home where her father had cheated on her mother. He was also a "closet" drinker who would get angry and upset if the children were too noisy or out of control. Elise grew up fearing her dad. Her mom tried to comfort her and her siblings the best she could, but she was often busy with her own work, household chores, and a husband who was demanding of her time.

When she was just eleven years old, her oldest brother got in trouble with the law which forced a big change in their household. Suddenly dad became more controlling and threatening. He would often yell at their mom and she would take her younger sibling to her room until the emotional storm stopped. Elise, being the second oldest, learned that it was her job to keep her two younger siblings busy while their dad raged at their mother.

Eventually, Elise's mom divorced her dad, but by that time Elise had developed a lot of anger toward her dad and toward her mom for taking so long to divorce him. She knew deep down that her father's affairs and his drinking were to blame for the marriage ending.

By the time Elise was in high school, she had little trust in guys. Fortunately, she developed a strong friendship with her classmate, Savannah, who helped her realize that there was something wrong with her home life. Savannah's parents were kind to each other and their children. They treated Elise with great respect. Elise knew she wanted a family like Savannah's.

Elise ended high school on a good note due to her stable friendship with Savannah and her family. She and Savannah went to college together and developed other meaningful friendships. Elise dated on and off for the first two years of college, but never let anyone get too close. She was often accused of playing hard to get. What everybody missed, including Elise, was the deep impact that her upbringing had on her dating and relationships. Due to her deep connection with Savannah and Savannah's family, she had settled down and emotionally stabilized. However, when it came to new relationships, especially with men, she was very guarded. She kept any potential romantic partners at a distance.

In her third year of college she met Curtis, who found Elise's personality a challenge. She tried to push him away, but the more she tried to distance herself from him the more he pursued her. Finally, she gave in to his charm and persistence. They began dating seriously and she was very happy. Elise still moved very slowly with Curtis, but he said he was okay with that. The only thing she didn't like was how friendly Curtis was with everyone. When they did fight it was usually because Curtis was overly friendly. Curtis would reassure her that if he wanted to be with someone else he would be with them. That made sense to her, so even though she was uncomfortable with his flirting behaviors, she liked how kind he was to her.

Elise and Curtis married after her graduation from college. He was a year ahead of her in school and had been working at a good job with a business firm who sold computer software. His work environment felt like a threat to Elise as he was around other women day in and day out. That environment combined with Elise's knowledge of Curtis' flirtatious tendencies led to the beginning of Elise's uncertainty.

Unresolved Childhood Trauma

By the time Elise and Curtis sought help for their relationship, Curtis had had his affair. They had been married for twelve years. She had become more critical and irritated at him over the years. When he had his affair it confirmed what Elise had felt for years and validated her childhood belief that "all men cheat."

While working with Elise, it became apparent that her relationship with Curtis had triggered many unresolved childhood issues. She was often angry and upset at him. She often accused him of cheating on her and by the time he did have an affair it felt like a forgone conclusion.

As therapists, we often deal with clients' most pressing issues. In Elise's and Curtis's case, it was his affair. I often refer to this as putting out fires. "Is it possible to save our relationship," they asked. I invited them to slow down and evaluate their lives and what they really wanted. They both confirmed that they were committed to saving their relationship, but they were tired and worn out from their fighting.

It is critical to point out that they were both committed to the therapy process. While both needed individual counseling, my focus was with Elise. Curtis was working with another counselor at our agency. In my work with Elise, she wanted to understand what was happening to her. She didn't like being so angry. I invited her to try to understand her anger on a deeper level. I let her know that anger is usually a protective response to a threat, either perceived or real. I asked her about her anger and if she had, prior to marrying Curtis, felt anger like she had with him.

She said, "No."

I pressed that response, asking her to go back in time and review her life to see if she had ever felt anger like she had with her husband. At this point she began to open up. She said, "As a little girl, my dad was always mad at us. He yelled at my mom and I was always scared of him." She told me about her childhood environment and parents' marriage and subsequent divorce. As she discussed these experiences, she began to see how some early life experiences were influencing her now.

As her awareness increased, she realized that she had deeper issues from her childhood that were unresolved. They were preventing her from responding the way she wanted to. She wasn't an angry person nor was she the type of person that couldn't make important decisions in her life. It was these issues that she wanted to focus on in our sessions. While she also felt it was important for her to address the challenges she was experiencing in her marriage, she saw the value of her working on her childhood wounds.

Key Life Events Inventory

Before we explore how Elise's current relationship facilitated deeper trauma, I want to invite you to do an assignment that I give my clients as they explore important events in their lives. I call this the "Key Life Events" assignment. The purpose of this exercise is to identify important events that have significantly influenced your life.

Using Elise's life as an example, she identified one key life event as the day her dad left. She explained that she didn't have contact with her dad now that she was an adult and had seen little of him since he left when she was a teenager. Elise also shared that he never said good-bye; he was so mad at her mom for kicking him out after his last affair that he turned to Elise and her younger siblings and said, "Your mom is kicking me out of your life!" He had then turned and left in a rage. Elise had seen him a few times since that experience years ago, but he never tried to truly reconnect with her or her siblings.

Assignment:

Go to Appendix A and complete the "Key Life-Events Inventory"

Denial, Deception, and Blame

Have you ever heard of gaslighting? The dictionary defines it as "a form of psychological abuse in which a victim is manipulated into doubting his or her own memory, perception, and sanity." (1)(2) Examples may range from denial by an abuser that previous abusive incidents ever occurred to the staging of bizarre events by the abuser with the intention of disorienting the victim.

In 2005, I heard many clients talk about how their spouses would deny acting out and then, only after they were caught, admit they had lied. This form of denial caused me to wonder if it was a contributor to the intense traumatic responses of my clients. As a result, I included two sections in the trauma inventory in addition to the PTSD criteria defined by the DSM-5. These two categories assess how often and to what extent both denial and blame were used by the betraying spouse. Fortunately, this information has helped deepen the understanding of betrayal trauma.

It wasn't until a few years later that I learned the term "gaslighting" and realized this phenomenon describes what I was calling denial and blame. Through my research, I have discovered that gaslighting is very common in sexual betrayal and often increases trauma responses. In addition, assessment results revealed the frequency of the use of denial, deception, and blame as strategies by individuals who are sexually acting out.

Here's a look at how much denial and blame are used in relationships.

Denial

What do you do when your spouse looks you in the eye and denies that he has been sexually acting out and you know he is lying to you? While your natural defenses are to fight, flee, or freeze, often in committed relationships, you instead are forced to question your own reality. Am I going crazy? Am I seeing things? Did it really happen? This type of denial is gaslighting because it makes you question yourself. It also forces you to question whether the person you are married to is who you thought they were. Trust is broken in two ways: both relational trust between you and your partner as well as internal trust between you and your gut.

In the TIPSA, we provide three specific questions related to denial:

- My partner denied his or her involvement in pornographic or sexual behaviors until I caught him/her.

- In our relationship, my partner has been open and honest about his or her struggle with pornography or other sexual behaviors.

- My partner would look at me straight in the face and deny he/she was viewing pornography or sexually acting out.

Let's break down each question to help explain how denial adds to the trauma.

Take the first question: "My partner denied his or her involvement in pornographic or sexual behaviors until I caught him/her." When a spouse denies his/her behavior until they are caught, they reveal their secrets under duress. The disclosure of information is forced under the weight of indisputable evidence and/or unrelenting questions. These types of revelations, called forced disclosures, are especially painful for many reasons. First, forced disclosures trigger the pain of being repeatedly lied to. Second, it makes the offended spouse wonder how long the behavior would have gone on if they hadn't been caught. Third, it opens up an endless amount of other possible indiscretions and the betrayed partner is forced to wonder what else is being hidden from them.

In my results with 1227 participants, 776 (61%) said that their spouse "always" denied their involvement in pornography or other sexual behaviors. Over 82% said that this happened at least half of the time. As I talk with partners, they often tell me that they "hate" the behaviors, but the lying is what is killing them.

When I looked at whether betraying partners were being honest about their struggles, I discovered that 58% of betrayed partners reported that their spouse was "never" open about their struggles with pornography or other sexual behaviors. Only 6% of the people reported that their spouse was always open about their sexual struggles. I believe this question is vital to understanding betrayal trauma, because when we see couples who are healing, we find that honesty is the most critical piece to recovery. If honesty is the most critical piece to recovery, dishonesty may be the most harmful piece of betrayal. Most couples have a rocky foundation as they begin healing because openness has not been a part of the equation.

The final question regarding denial is the most crucial: "My partner would look at me straight in the face and deny he/she was viewing pornography or sexually acting out." The reason this form of lying is so hurtful is that it is through our eyes that we connect on the deepest level. When we are upset at each other we can't look each other in the eyes. Why does this happen? When we feel safe and want to connect, we generally do so with our eyes. When your partner looked you in the eyes and lied to you, your reality became confusing to you. You trusted those eyes and those words while simultaneously receiving the conflicting message (from your own instinct and/or external evidence) that those eyes and words are deceiving. You used to be able to trust those eyes you looked into, now you can't. My clients have told me over the years that this confusion and loss of trust in both other and self is one of the more difficult aspects for them to overcome in their healing process.

How often does this type of direct dishonesty happen within sexual betrayal? According to 1219 people who completed this question, 696 (57%) would "always" be lied to by their betraying partner as they maintained eye contact. If I combine those who reported this occurring "more often than not" with those who reported it as occurring "about half the time," roughly 84% of those who completed this question said their partners did this to them. I personally believe this single behavior is one of the more damaging behaviors to happen in a relationship.

Fortunately, over the years I have worked with many couples who have experienced this challenge and have therefore found specific solutions to help them work toward rebuilding trust. I share these simple yet effective tools in a supplemental video entitled "Seven Steps for Couple Healing and Recovery after Sexual Betrayal." The video is a part of the Treating Trauma from Sexual Betrayal video package series. You can learn more about the video package in the resources section at the back of this book.

Additional Denial Behaviors Used in Relationships

As you go through your assessment, you will find some additional questions in the denial section. My friend and colleague Dr. Sheri Keffer specializes in treating sexual betrayal and helped me develop the following additional questions in order to more fully explore gaslighting behaviors:

- Even when I have evidence regarding my partner's sexual behaviors, he/she still lies to me.

- If my partner disclosed his/her sexual behaviors, he/she would only tell me half the story.

- My partner claimed to have stopped sexually acting out, but later I discovered that he/she hadn't stopped at all.

- My partner tells me I am crazy when I question him/her about a lie he/she has told me.

- In our relationship, my partner lied to cover up money he/she spent while sexually acting out.

Blame

In unhealthy relationships, blame is often used to dismiss misbehaviors. A common behavior is to accuse one's partner for one's own actions. It sounds like, "You made me…" or, "I wouldn't have done what I did if you would have…" When it comes to sexual betrayal, blame is usually placed on a spouse in the following ways: "I cheated because we didn't have enough sex." In blaming one's spouse, the responsibility for behavior shifts to the one who was offended. The betraying partner wants their spouse to take the blame for their behavior.

How common is it for blame to be used with sexual betrayal? Unfortunately, blame, much like denial, is used far too often. In my research, I included five statements regarding blame:

Question: My partner blames me for his/her sexual conduct.

Response: Of the 1225 respondents, 651 (53%) reported that at least half of the time their partner blamed them for why they sexually acted out. Unfortunately, based on research I shared in Chapter Two, many accepted the blame and formed an unhealthy belief that there was something wrong with them or their partner would not have acted out.

Another form of blame is to shift responsibility to one's partner:

Question: "My partner would say that our relationship problems were because of my personal issues."

Response: Of the 1227 respondents, 816 (72%) reported that their spouse used this form of manipulation at least half of the time.

If you recall in Chapter One, while discussing Alecia and John's story, I shared that Alecia was uncomfortable with how much John would flirt and talk with other women. He called them friends. John would often tell Alecia that she was blowing things out of proportion and worrying about things more than she should. This made her question herself and left her wondering, "Am I worrying about things I shouldn't? Am I making this too big of a deal?"

I included the following question to ascertain how often one partner's insecurities are blamed for the other partner's sexual betrayal:

Question: "I have felt something wasn't quite right in my relationship but my partner would tell me it was because of my insecurities."

Response: According to the 1227 participants, 998 (81%) say that at least half of the time they were told in their relationship that their feelings were wrong and were due to their insecurities.

Earlier it was mentioned that some partners will blame their sexual behaviors on lack of sex in their relationship. The following question is included in order to discover how often this occurs:

Question: "My partner told me that if I would be more sexual, he/she would not have to view pornography or act out in other ways."

Response: Of the 1226 participants, 414 (34%) indicated that their spouses had blamed their own sexual misbehavior on them for not being sexual enough.

While blame appears to be very common, I began wondering how often responsibility was taken by offending partners:

Question: "In our relationship, my partner has taken responsibility for his or her sexual behaviors rather than making me feel his or her problems were because of me."

Response: In my clinical experience, I have seen client's take responsibility, but in most cases this usually occurs when the person acting out begins to work on stopping their behaviors and working toward their own healing. Unfortunately, far too many individuals are not taking responsibility. In my findings, I discovered that of the 1225 participants, only 134 (11%) reported their betraying partners taking responsibility for their actions and not shifting the blame onto them.

It has been my experience that when individuals begin taking responsibility, their relationships shift to being more positive and filled with hope. Sadly, this was only happening in 11% of the surveyed cases. If we include those who said this is happening more often than not, that number goes up to 26%, which means that only one in four people are somewhat consistently taking responsibility for their sexual misbehaviors outside of their relationship.

Chapter Summary

We are just beginning to understand some of the behaviors that contribute to elevated trauma responses. As revealed throughout the survey results overall, trauma scores increased significantly the more frequently denial, blame, and gaslighting were used in a relationship.

Additionally, it is my experience through working with betrayed partners that early life experiences can have an additive effect on today's relationships. I've found that the more difficult and traumatic the experiences in childhood, the more likely trust and safety problems will occur in adulthood.

In the next chapter we will discuss what happens when we get stuck in fight, flight, or freeze mode.

Chapter Four

Stuck in Fight, Flight, or Freeze

I couldn't move. I sat there wondering what had happened to my life. It took me months to come out of the fog.

When our minds feel threatened we naturally shift into protection mode. This generally means that we fight, flee, or freeze. This is good news. It means our bodies and minds are doing what they were designed to do: protect us. But what happens when we get stuck in protection mode and can't figure out how to resolve the stress? The answer is that we begin to shut-down physically and emotionally. Our bodies become more susceptible to illnesses and we experience elevated anxiety and depression.

Sadly, this is a common occurrence with clients I meet who are dealing with sexual betrayal. In most instances, they have been feeling the effects of sexual betrayal for years and even decades. As mentioned in Chapter Two, a majority (51%) of individuals surveyed reported that they had been experiencing trauma symptoms for more than two years.

Our bodies are designed to deal with short-term stress, not long-term, unresolved stress. As a result, when we can't find a way to relax, our minds and bodies become overwhelmed which triggers heightened anxiety. When we can't shut down our fears, we deplete our coping skills and end up physically sick and emotionally depleted.

One woman described how she became worn down this way: "It's hard for me to parent when he is gone. I'm so easily agitated, wondering what he is doing and where he is. I become short-tempered with everyone around me."

In this chapter, my hope is to help you understand how you got stuck in fight, flight, and/or freeze mode as well as provide some basic steps you can take to get the ball rolling out of that mindset.

Fight

"I used to avoid fights at all costs. However, over the past few years that's all changed," Jessica told me. "I feel like I am not being myself. I find that I am always irritated and upset with my husband, Brett. I didn't know I could feel so much anger toward anyone! I don't like who I've become, but I don't know how to stop."

Jessica's story illustrates a common experience that many facing sexual betrayal share. They feel like their personality has fundamentally changed. Many report that they were kind and caring, but after discovery of being betrayed they become angry and upset. They don't feel like the same person.

Understanding that anger is a natural defense response, I try to help my clients understand that their anger is their first instinct. They want to avoid being hurt and as a result they respond with anger. This is the way we were designed to respond when we feel threatened. However, it is important to emphasize that being stuck in anger mode for days, weeks, months, or even years at a time is destructive to our minds and bodies. If you are experiencing this, my hope is to help you honor your anger by understanding its original purpose: to protect you. Ultimately, the goal is to shift out of anger and toward a response that helps you feel like they are moving in a positive direction and more like the real you.

When my clients transition out of anger mode, they feel more in control of their emotions and consequently they gain more strength. My clients begin to realize that their anger is not strength. Rather, responding with clarity and purpose to sexual betrayal is much more effective for creating personal and relationship change.

So why do so many people get stuck in anger?

While there are many reasons for anger, some of the more common are as follows:

- A feeling that anger is the only way to be heard
- A temporary, yet false, sense of being in control through anger
- It keeps the offending party away
- Anger can become its own addictive emotion

Let's now look at each of these four reasons for getting stuck in anger and how you can get out of each.

Using Anger to be Heard

Have you ever watched a two-year-old throw a temper tantrum? If so, have you thought through what message they are really trying to convey? It is usually something like, "Obviously, you aren't hearing me, so I better kick and scream..." As adults, we too throw temper tantrums, and much like a two-year-old, our behaviors are rarely understood.

When we use anger in our relationships, our spouse will do one of three things-: fight, flee, or freeze. Yes, when they feel attacked they too resort to their primitive defenses. Usually, when I teach this concept to my clients, they get frustrated. They want their spouse to respond to them by acknowledging their pain. Instead, their spouse usually fights back or flees through emotional disconnection. This usually triggers even more anger in my clients. (Alternately, the betrayed partner will shift into a sense of hopelessness and helplessness. In some ways this is a version of going into "freeze mode.")

When it comes to anger, even if your spouse tries to listen and respond to you, you are creating a pattern that eventually needs to change if you are going to have a healthy relationship. When couples get stuck in the anger-anger dance, or the anger-disconnect dance, or the anger-hopelessness dance, their relationship can't move forward. In fact, it becomes toxic because these patterns harm us emotionally and physically.

Conversely, when individuals learn to process through their anger and communicate with clarity and purpose, their relationships change significantly. When I taught Jessica this concept, initially she was anxious. She said, "I think that I believe the only way he will pay attention to what I am saying is if I am angry or yelling at him."

To this comment I replied, "Let's try an experiment: over the next few days when you are feeling triggered and sense that your anger is rising I want you to pause and accept the emotions underneath the anger. As you analyze your emotions, try to identify what you are really wanting to say to Brett. Once you have identified the core message you are trying to send, share it with Brett." This is what I refer to as "clear" and "purposeful" communication. When people communicate this way they are more likely to express their deeper desires from a calm place. I have also found that they are more likely to affirm their partner and be affirmed themselves.

Initially, she struggled to identify what she was trying to say. However, as she practiced, she got better at realizing what was happening inside of her mind. Often her anger was being triggered by the lack of attention he was giving her. He would come home from work, walk in the door and go to his office to put down his stuff. He would say hi on his way through, but he wouldn't stop and ask about her day or about their kids. This pattern was very triggering for her. She would automatically think to herself, "I bet he was acting out." By the time he came out of his office, she was upset. Usually they would end up getting into a big fight.

Her awareness enabled her to communicate, with clarity and purpose, what she needed from him. She asked him to stop on his way to his office as soon as he got home so they could talk for a few minutes. This simple strategy helped them immensely as they were able to change a key trigger point for her. In most cases, our anger usually goes down when we feel our most basic needs are being met. In this case, Jessica realized that asking Brett to talk with her as soon as he got home reduced her fear significantly.

Over time, Jessica and Brett developed better communication skills. Jessica still fought through days where her anger was strong, but she focused on her commitment to communicate with clarity and purpose. At times she had to distance herself from Brett because he was not following through on keeping his recovery commitments. Instead of yelling at him or getting angry, she would simply say, "I would like to be close to you [here she is using clarity by expressing a desire to connect and simultaneously sending Brett the affirming message that he is worth connecting with], but when you aren't keeping your commitments, I can't be close to you [here she identifies the purpose of her communication]."

The greatest benefit Jessica found from practicing with these tools was a sense of being in control of her own emotions. She truly disliked being angry, because it was preventing her from being the "real" her.

Here's a principle that I have found to be true over the years: When we can regulate our emotions, we feel more strength and control over our lives and it is easier to experience happiness. This was true for Jessica.

Sense of Being in Control

Some individuals have experienced such deep wounds in their lives that they have consequently vowed to never let anyone hurt them again. As a result, they try to control all aspects of the environment around them. When they feel overwhelmed, due to chaos or uncertainty, they tend to demand that others around them change. If they can't control the outcome, they may completely disengage or become angry. In other words, their desire for safety triggers them into monitoring or limiting others' behaviors so that they feel less threatened. Unfortunately, their need for being in control tends to push others away from them. Others usually call them controlling. Unfortunately, what most people aren't seeing is the fear that drives their need for being in control.

Here's an example of how this could play out. Jenae, a mother of three teenage boys, wouldn't let her boys watch any movie with questionable scenes, even if the movie was rated PG. Her need to protect her sons from becoming "like their dad" pushed her to implement this strict standard. She would often tell them that if they watched bad shows they would end up becoming like Jared, their father. Due to his sexually acting out behavior, Jared felt like he didn't have the right to defend himself. Her mandate put him in a difficult situation because he wanted to support Janae, but he felt like she was being too restrictive with their sons.

In this case, Janae's desire to protect her boys backfired because their friends were talking about shows that they weren't allowed to watch. Eventually, they began resenting her and would sneak behind their parents' backs and go to the shows anyway. Janae's fear and her inability to see through her hurt, pain, and hidden anger triggered her to take control of a situation that pushed her boys away, promoted secret-keeping, and limited their ability to take responsibility for their own actions.

In addition, when she threatened the boys that they would "become like their dad," they felt her anger and felt like they were being punished for what their dad did. They ended up resenting both parents. They were mad at their dad for hurting their mom and they were mad at her for being so controlling.

When I experience individuals who have a strong need to be "in control" of their environments, the first step is to understand their desires. In most cases, their fear of something going wrong is so high that they overreact. Helping them see the consequences of maintaining strict control can be a slow process because to give up control feels like they are giving in or giving up. They can't predict that outcome; letting go of control leads to unknown territory. Their need to manage their world is a defense mechanism they have created to protect themselves and their loved ones and lessening or abandoning that coping mechanism can be very scary. Sadly, this approach does not work well in human relationships. We all want to make our own choices and when others limit our choices, we tend to push back.

In Janae's case, it took time for her to realize what was happening. She was losing control of her boys. They had stopped listening to her and instead were turning to Jared to support them. She learned through her own therapy that her need for control didn't begin until Jared had betrayed her trust. As she explored her need for control, she realized that Jared's behavior had created a belief in her that "all men cheat." This belief originated when her dad left her mom for another woman. She wanted to teach her boys to avoid all sexual behaviors that would make them be like her dad and Jared. This powerful awareness enabled her to deal with her beliefs about men and helped her begin to resolve her need to control others' behaviors. Her healing took time because she had to redefine how she saw men, including her boys. Fortunately, she wanted nothing more than to connect with her boys; she just hadn't ever allowed that to happen because they represented a gender that would hurt her.

Assignment:

Question: On a scale of 0 (not at all) and 10 (all the time), how often do you try to control the environment around you? Please don't judge your answer. Instead, identify how your actions are being received by the people around you. If your scores are high, how does being in control influence you day in and day out?

Anger Keeps the Offending Party and (Unfortunately) Others Away Too

Someone once said that some dogs bark so loud that they keep people away. This may be a technique individuals in trauma use to prevent others from coming close to them. The belief, although it may not be known in the conscious mind, is that if I get angry enough, I know that he won't want to come close to me. Some individuals live in their anger because it protects them from having to be close to others.

It is nearly impossible to connect on a deep level with someone who is angry. Dr. Stephen Porges explains why this happens: "As long as people (and animals) feel threatened, they cannot meaningfully engage with members of their tribe and will resort to more primitive and solipsistic fight-or-flight behaviors (mobilization mediated by the sympathetic nervous system) to ensure survival." (1) While the fight response (anger) is a normal biological response, when individuals get stuck in it they often struggle to transition from angry, protect-mode to friendship and connection with others. Their protective anger toward their spouse crosses over into other relationships and prevents them from developing close connections with anyone.

In my research on sexual betrayal, a high percentage of participants reported that they had struggled to trust people who used to be close to them after discovery. What I have observed is that as trauma increases, individuals feel less overall trust. They become confused and don't know who they can trust. This in turn triggers a constant state of stress and a perceived need to constantly be on guard. As a result, the body begins to break down and get worn out. Next, the worn-down body is extra sensitive to perceived threats. Finally, out of self-protection, they are prone to either fight (anger) or flee (shut down) responses. Dr. Porges describes why this happens: "People with impaired social engagement systems are prone to misinterpret safety as a threat and objective danger as safety. Their visceral feedback system fails to protect them, or prevents them from engaging in the fullness of what life has to offer." (2)

When I see this happening to my clients, I realize that my first role is to help them build trust with me. In far too many cases, highly traumatized clients do not trust anyone. They often feel like everyone will hurt them and as a preventative measure they don't let others close to them. In order to reintroduce trust into their lives, they need to start to experience it, however slowly and cautiously, in the therapy office.

Recovering the ability to trust takes time. It begins by establishing a foundation to build upon. In therapy, after therapeutic trust is experienced and solidified, we usually begin by identifying at least one person who has been safe in the client's life. It may be a grandparent, aunt, friend, leader, co-worker, neighbor, or teacher. If there truly isn't a single person, I have them identify at least one possible person with whom they *might* be able to start building trust.

Over the years, I have given this assignment to clients who can't identify anyone as being safe to them. In situations like this, I begin with me. Do you trust me? This is an honest question. Most say, "I think so." To this I respond, "I don't expect you to completely trust me, especially given what you've been through. Over time I invite you to let me know if I do something that breaks your trust. I will also ask you to tell me when you feel like you are trusting me." By talking about trust, we begin to identify the characteristics of people with whom we can trust. This is the starting point.

In Chapter Ten, we will discuss more in-depth strategies for how to build a trusting network of people to aid in your healing. In the end, the goal is to help you establish meaningful relationships and to help you build a team to support you through the recovery process.

Assignment:

If you find that anger is there to protect you, I invite you to pause for a moment and consider whether you are able to detect with whom you are safe and with whom you do not feel safe. Make a list of people who you absolutely trust. Why do you trust these individuals?

Anger can be Addictive

Have you ever felt like anger has taken over your mind? When this happens consistently over weeks or months, your body adjusts and creates more chemicals to match the survival demand. The constancy of the anger changes our set point. When we don't feel intense emotions like anger, we actually feel like something is wrong. Dr. Joe Dispenza states in his book *Breaking the Habit of Being Yourself* that "the body becomes addicted to guilt or any emotion in the same way that it would get addicted to drugs." (1) That is, because our bodies produce powerful chemicals when we experience an emotion like anger, we can get addicted to having these mind-altering chemicals in our brains and bodies. He believes that when we don't have these chemicals running through us, we go through withdrawals.

If anger can be addictive, the healing process then requires not only a shift in thoughts, but also an altering of the body's need for the chemicals associated with addiction. For example, when anger is triggered, our bodies prepare us for a fight. It sends out adrenaline and nor-epinephrine to prepare us for what is perceived as a threat. We are then flooded with chemicals until we somehow determine that we are safe and away from the threat.

When individuals get stuck in fear and feel continuously unsafe, their bodies continuously produce fight chemicals. When this happens, the body struggles to relax. Sleep becomes difficult and exhaustion can set in. Eating and digestion become a problem which can trigger irritable bowel syndrome, ulcers, or other stomach problems. The mind races, activating heightened anxiety.

One of the research participants described her experience this way: "When I learned of my partner's acting out, the stress, anxiety, and general upset followed me around at work. I lost my appetite and sometimes I wouldn't eat for days. I could easily not eat for a week because the anxiety and feelings were so intense."

After experiencing this type of trauma, the body wears down and shifts from anger into needing a break. At this point, you may attempt to escape and enter flight mode.

Flight

It is natural to want to flee or escape when we realize that we aren't safe or when we know that we can't win by fighting. The methods individuals use to flee after discovering sexual betrayal are very diverse. One common way people flee is through ending their relationship. However, this is usually not the first response after discovering sexual betrayal. Most couples try to stay together after the initial disclosure, but that doesn't necessarily mean that they resolve their problems. They just don't divorce.

It is actually quite common for couples to spend years together trying, with limited support, to resolve their problems. This phenomenon is supported in my research; most of those who completed the assessment were still married and had known about their partner's pornography use or sexual betrayal for at least two years or longer. As a result, many were using a variety of strategies to cope with the lack of trust in their relationship.

Here's a look at some of the most common ways that people use the "flight" strategy to cope with sexual betrayal:

- Excessive sleeping, usually with sleep aids

- Binge eating or starving oneself

- Excessive drinking

- Spending an inordinate amount of time on social media sites (such as Facebook, Pinterest, etc.)

- Watching television

These coping strategies usually provide temporary relief, but they don't solve the underlying suffering and pain. In fact, in many situations, these distractions unhelpfully trigger feelings of guilt. One woman described her experience of fleeing from life: "I became emotionally detached from family and friends. Weeks would go by without me going out. Household chores became an exceedingly huge burden."

Unfortunately, far too many individuals don't know how to respond to betrayal trauma and they end up escaping from life with coping strategies that do not resolve their problems. In Chapter Twelve, we will review specific solutions to help you avoid staying in "flight" mode.

Freezing

Have you ever been in a situation where you wanted to say something and didn't? Or perhaps you wanted to get out of a difficult situation and couldn't? What do we call this when it happens? In extreme cases, we refer to it as "freezing up." The act of freezing usually occurs when fear immobilizes you to the point that you can't respond even if you want to. The idea of freezing in the past has been linked to fainting. In the most extreme cases, the body faints or shuts down. This paralysis, under some life-threatening experiences, can actually save your life; if you are being attacked by a bear, playing dead has been found to be an effective and recommended strategy.

Professional therapists now believe that freezing up can manifest itself in other ways besides fainting (e.g. Not being able to talk or respond to protect oneself). A term I have often heard clients use to refer to their inability to act is "numb" or "numbing out." They describe themselves as simply being numb to everything around them. They report that they can't respond to life events even if they want to.

I have observed that freezing (or the act of not acting) is very common with sexual betrayal trauma. In a cyclical way the inability to act is traumatizing and the fear based trauma then prevents individuals from taking action. This lack of action seems to be part of the freezing response.

However, when we freeze in relationships, our lack of response is often seen as not caring or, in worst case scenarios, as consent. This is why many rape victims are unable to defend themselves in a court of law. If they freeze-up when a date is being sexually aggressive and are unable to say "no," and the case is brought before a judge, the defendant's attorney will often use the lack of response as consent. Unfortunately, what is missed in cases like this is that when individuals feel threatened to the point that they freeze, they can't say anything. They may sense a threat and fear that if they say anything that things will go from bad to worse. As a result, they feel betrayed by the other person and betrayed by the self due to their lack of ability to respond in such a difficult moment.

Researchers Peter Levine and Pat Ogden have both found that when individuals freeze up and are unable to move to defend and protect themselves, their level of trauma increases. Thus, when you can't or don't stand up for yourself when your partner betrays you, there is a high likelihood that your trauma level will increase. Examples of this include feeling obligated to have sex with your partner out of fear of being abandoned if you don't and wanting to physically leave the home but you can't because you are afraid to leave your children alone with your spouse.

The freeze survival response can also be activated when individuals feel helpless, as if no matter what they do, they can't change the outcome. When betrayal happens over and over again in relationships, a feeling of helplessness often sets in. Thoughts like, "No matter what I do, it doesn't really matter," begin to dominate. When talking with clients I often hear them say things like, "It doesn't really matter what I do or say, my spouse is going to act out anyway."

In an effort to study the extent that betrayed partners feel helpless to create change in their relationships, I included the following in the TIPSA:

Question: "I feel like my partner will never stop sexually acting out."

Response: Of the 1529 respondents, 1302 (85%) reported that they felt this way at least half of the time. This sense of helplessness is another layer of the traumatic response prominent in those who are sexually betrayed.

As humans, we want to be able to influence outcomes, but when we can't, we either give up (flight), get angry (fight), or become apathetic or hopeless (freeze). Though they are all three natural survival instincts, none of these responses promote the long term healing of trauma or rebuilding of a relationship.

Chapter Summary

If you are experiencing sexual betrayal you probably relate with many of the symptoms described above. Fortunately, these symptoms can be resolved and you can return your mind and body to a more calm and relaxed state. While it may not feel like it right now, I invite you to continue reading to learn how others before you have resolved their trauma.

In the next chapter we discuss the steps that are necessary for healing to begin.

Part Two

Starting the Healing Process

Chapter Five

Discovery: The Painful Beginning

If we can really understand the problem, the answer will come out of it, because the answer is not separate from the problem.

Jiddu Krishnamurti

In order to truly understand sexual betrayal, it is important to understand the history of each relationship. While every relationship is different, there are some common behaviors that many people I have interviewed report. For example, most individuals report that they felt something was wrong in their relationship long before they knew the truth. I asked one woman to reflect on her experience after discovery and then share what advice she would give to herself if she could go back to that day. She stated, "I would have told myself that I wasn't crazy. That my gut was right. Things had never been right."

While there are some cases in which individuals were completely surprised when they discovered their partners' sexual betrayal, most report that their thoughts, feelings, or instincts had detected something but they couldn't quite put their finger on what was wrong. Once the secrets are revealed, many inconsistencies and certain thoughts and feelings that didn't make sense before start making much more sense.

Many people call the day that they discovered their partner's sexual behaviors their Discovery Day or D-Day. This day can be one of the most painful days imaginable. One woman said this about her experience: "My first D-Day: I was alone. I went downstairs and curled up on a couch. I felt like a huge part of me had died. I waited there nearly fainting from shock and agony until my husband came home. I felt paralyzed. I felt like I had been shot in the chest and stomach: true and unbelievable physical pain, nausea, racing heart. I didn't know what to think. I experienced confusion... bewilderment. After the second disclosure I said to myself,

'Okay, our marriage is over. You have made your choice.' I thought I would throw up. My heart went crazy. Again the unbelievable physical pain in my torso. Rage, and unbearable grief… I wanted to rip his arms off, hurt him somehow, have him arrested, something! It was unspeakably awful."

Most of my clients tell me that D-Day was one of the most difficult days of their life. Sadly, as the description above suggests, many people report multiple D-Days in their marriages. As is discussed below, understanding both your physical and emotional response to that day will be an important part of your healing process. Understanding how the disclosure happened is very important from a professional standpoint. Therapists who understand the value of disclosures know that the way a disclosure happens can significantly influence the discovering partner's trauma level and ultimately the outcome of the relationship.

I have found that as I work with couples, it is very important to understand how their discovery happened. Did the betrayed spouse discover on their own? Or did the betraying spouse choose to confess? Or did someone else share the secret? My clients have helped me understand that not all disclosures are the same. However, there are two common ways that most disclosures happen: forced disclosure or self-disclosure.

A Forced Disclosure

Most disclosures are what we refer to as "forced disclosures." A forced disclosure happens when the betrayed person discovers their partner has been lying or cheating on them. This can happen by catching them, being told by another person, or when the betraying spouse is forced to disclose their sexual behavior. However it occurs, forced disclosures are not initiated by the betraying partner.

Here's a painful example of a forced disclosure:

"I found out about my husbands addiction on July 3rd. I always had my suspicions but it had finally been confirmed and there was no lie that could get him out of it. My husband had told me a few days earlier that he was going to take someone from work down to the airport. He is the kind of man that would give service to others constantly so this was normal and I had no reason to think anything was wrong. I texted him most of the morning about buying a present for a wedding we were going to, and asked him to get some pajamas for our youngest child. He left at 1:00p.m. for the three hour drive to the airport. I received a phone call that night from the police station at about 6:30 p.m. asking me if I would come in so they could ask me some questions. I had just had my high school class ten year reunion a few days earlier, so I thought someone was playing a prank. When I got to the police station, the officer put me in a room and told me that our conversation would be recorded. I started freaking out and wondering what this was about. He asked me if I knew where my husband was and I told him that he was driving someone from work to the airport but I didn't know who it was. The officer then told me that my husband had been arrested in a sting operation for sexual predators. I just sat there and couldn't believe what he had said. This couldn't be my husband; this was not the man that I knew and had been married to for the past ten years."

A forced disclosure like this is especially difficult to deal with because it includes painful memories associated with police, lies, deception, and long-term legal issues. In a forced disclosure, usually neither party has a choice about whether the information is revealed or not. Over the years I have heard countless forced discovery stories. The most common include:

- Discovery of pornography on a spouse's phone or laptop

- Chat discussions that are sexual between one's spouse and another person

- A note, phone call, picture, or other piece of evidence of sexual betrayal

- Being caught in the act (e.g. viewing pornography)

Forced disclosures often lead the betrayed spouse to question if the betraying spouse would have ever disclosed their behavior had they not been caught. This unknown question is always hard to answer, but when the betraying spouse owns their behaviors and prepares an effective disclosure, as described later in this chapter, the healing process can begin in full. I have also found that the opposite is true. When betraying partners behaviors are discovered and they refuse to discuss any of their behaviors, the healing process cannot begin.

Self-Disclosure

Self-disclosure happens when a spouse intentionally reports their sexual betrayal without being forced to disclose what they have done. Self-disclosure doesn't lessen the blow of what happened, but if it is done right, it can help both partners begin the long healing process on a stronger foothold.

It is important to understand that self-disclosure is not simply telling one's spouse about sexual betrayal. There are significantly different ways self-disclosure can be done. Consider the following two examples:

John attended a men's retreat where he learned about the importance of being honest with his wife. Previous to attending the retreat he had been viewing pornography and every once in awhile, while he was out of town, he would get a "massage" that usually ended with sexual release.

After attending the motivating weekend retreat, he went home and told his wife that they needed to talk. He was very anxious to tell her but he had committed to his group that he would tell his wife. She was excited to hear about his weekend experience. He proceeded to tell her that he had been struggling with pornography on and off throughout most of their marriage. Before she could respond or ask any questions he said, "Just let me finish before you respond." He continued, "When I go out of town there have been a few times I have gotten a sexual massage." Finally, he had told her the truth. He felt relieved that he had kept his commitment.

He was not prepared, however, for her intense response.

His wife, Amber, was caught completely off guard. She felt like many women I talk to when they hear for the first time what their spouse has been doing. Amber said, "I immediately felt so sick to my stomach that I wanted to puke. I cried and cried. I screamed and yelled at him. I lashed out. I was so angry at him for keeping this from me. Why didn't he trust me enough to tell me the truth? Why did he lie to me?" She continued, "Question after question filled my mind. Over the next few hours and days, the more I thought about it, the more angry I felt. How could I have been stupid enough to not know?"

While John's desire was good, his approach and preparation was not sufficient. He wasn't ready for the questions she was asking him. He had thought that if he just told her the truth, they could work through things. He wasn't prepared for the countless questions about the type of pornography he was viewing, when he was viewing it, if he was viewing it when the kids were home, if he was thinking about pornography while they were having sex, if he preferred porn stars' bodies over hers. On and on the questions came. He thought she would be upset, but he wasn't prepared to discuss all of her questions. He was so overwhelmed by what she was asking him that he nearly shut-down. He didn't know how to respond, so he stammered through, giving her the best answers he could.

About the time he thought her questioning was finally over, she began asking questions about his sexual experiences at the massage parlors. By this time, he was worn out and said, "I'm not going to talk about this anymore." She interpreted that statement to be, "I will never talk about this with you." She exploded, "You come home from this 'wonderful' weekend while I sacrifice watching the kids and taking care of things here and then you tell me all of this stuff you have done and then you won't talk about it! Who do you think you are? Get out!"

By the time they sat down with a trained sexual-addiction therapist, their marriage was on the brink of divorce. John had thought he was doing the right thing being honest with her, but now he was confused and questioned whether he should have said anything at all. He told their therapist that he only wanted to be honest with Amber and her response was way over the top. He continued by saying, "I'm getting frustrated because she's so upset I can't even talk with her. She won't give me a chance to explain."

Amber, on the other hand, felt overwhelmed with what John had told her. She was frustrated that he wouldn't just tell her all of the details. She felt like he was withholding information and was unwilling to honestly answer her questions. He thought he had told her everything. They both were very confused and looking for help.

In contrast to John and Amber's self-disclosure story, Kurt and Stacey had a very different experience with disclosure. They had been going through some difficult times. They had been trying to have children but couldn't. Stacey became depressed because she longed to be a mother. Each month when she began menstruating, she lost hope and felt like they would never have children. Kurt wanted children too, and kept himself preoccupied with his work.

Kurt was busy at his job, but he was also struggling with Stacey's depression. When she went into her depressive state, she was unavailable to even have conversations. He would come home not knowing what kind of day she had had. Soon he was spending more time at work and less time at home. He wasn't always working at work; some evenings he would stay late and view pornography before he went home.

One evening while Kurt was working late he had a coworker ask him how he was doing. They had developed a friendship so Kurt opened up and shared a little of what was happening at home. It was the first time he had told anybody. His friend said, "Why don't you talk with a therapist? I have been seeing someone who has really helped me." Kurt had never thought about counseling before. Kurt, curious, asked what counseling was like. His friend said, "I don't talk a lot about this, but I have struggled with pornography for many years and my counselor has been helping me deal with that problem."

Kurt was startled at his friend's openness. Even surprising himself, Kurt said, "Pornography? I have had challenges with pornography, too. I've been afraid to tell Stacey because it might push her over the edge." The next week Kurt met with his friend's counselor. Kurt told Stacey he was going because he wanted ideas on how to deal with her depression. Stacey thought it was a good idea. When Kurt met with the therapist, he was honest and they explored his history with pornography and his relationship with Stacey. Since Kurt had hidden his use of pornography from Stacey, the therapist began helping him understand the importance of being honest with her, but told him he needed to prepare before he did. This made him uneasy because he feared that Stacey wouldn't be able to handle it. The therapist then suggested that Kurt encourage Stacey to seek support from a counselor as well.

Stacey was open to the idea and set up an appointment to see a different therapist in the same office so that her and Kurt's therapists could collaborate. Over the next few weeks, Kurt wanted to tell Stacey about what he was learning. He wanted to blurt out what he was learning about pornography and what it was doing to him, but his therapist told him he needed to prepare before disclosing. He was confused. He thought he should just tell her.

Then the therapist asked a few questions:

• How will she respond when you tell her you have been viewing pornography at work?

• What type of questions will she have for you?

• How will you respond if she wants to know your full history with pornography?

• How will you respond when she asks if you have been doing other inappropriate sexual behaviors besides pornography?

• How will you respond when she asks what type of pornography you have been viewing?

Kurt had never thought about those questions. He was especially worried about telling Stacey his history of involvement because she had asked him before they got married about his use of pornography and he had said, "I have seen it a few times, but it's not a big deal now." He knew this would be hard on her now that he was reflecting on the lies he had told her over the years to cover up his use of pornography.

Before therapy, he hadn't known how much pornography was influencing his life. After a few sessions, he realized how frequently he had lied to Stacey. He thought he had just been hurting himself, but now he was seeing how his lies were hurting his wife, too. He wanted to tell her and he wanted to apologize. Through this process, John's therapist had been collaborating with Stacey's. What John didn't know was that one of the things that was triggering Stacey's depression was a fear that he was using pornography and wasn't telling her.

Through collaboration, their therapists began preparing John and Stacy for a joint meeting. Stacey told Kurt about her fears of him viewing pornography and he replied that he wanted to answer her questions and would be willing to answer anything she wanted to know. Stacey worked with her therapist to prepare. Stacey was anxious, but her therapist did a good job helping her realize that Kurt was doing a thorough self-inventory so he would be prepared to talk with her openly and honestly.

Stacey and Kurt's therapists set up a joint appointment for them to meet together to discuss the full disclosure. This process took two therapy sessions which occurred over one month because Kurt had realized that he had left out some behavior that he had not disclosed to Stacey. Stacey also had a few questions about his use of pornography early in their relationship that she had been wanting to ask him, so she gave her questions to Kurt so he could work on answering them with his counselor.

When Kurt and Stacey met with their therapists, they were anxious, but Kurt had prepared well. His heart was in the right place. His disclosure was still extremely hard on Stacey, but, as 96% of couples who participate in formal disclosures report, they were happy they did the disclosure. (1, 2) Unfortunately, many couples don't have the opportunity to experience this type of self-disclosure.

The disclosure process outlined above is not complex but it does require an honest self-evaluation and patience by both partners during the preparation process. Often when couples prepare for a full disclosure they need to have an agreement in place that they will avoiding discussing the details until they are fully prepared. This helps them avoid having difficult conversations too soon.

There are some additional factors for couples to consider as they prepare for disclosure. First, disclosures are usually most effectively done with professional guidance, but if this is not an option, some general guidelines for disclosure are helpful. I have included these ideas and resources in Appendix C. Second, disclosure is most effective when the offending person has committed to stopping their behavior and has been sober for a period of time. Third, both partners benefit when they have support from caring people around them (e.g. a sponsor, accountability team, or trusted friend). Fourth, when the offending party is being proactive in this process, it helps the betrayed partner feel more hopeful. Many betrayed spouses have told me that when their spouse chose to work on the disclosure and take accountability, it was a turning point in their relationship. Although it was very painful to hear the truth, it gave them hope.

This experience was a game-changer for John and Stacey. Stacey said, "I finally knew what was happening. I had felt something wasn't right; now I know and have a chance to make a decision about our relationship. Knowing the truth can make all the difference in the world." While the idea of disclosure is not easy, the betrayed spouse deserves to know the truth so that they can make an informed decision regarding their relationship.

A Comparison of Disclosures

Unfortunately, most disclosures are done poorly. While John's intentions were good, neither he nor Amber were adequately prepared. In contrast, Kurt and Stacey had both been prepared and were receiving support. Other observable differences in their disclosure include the following:

- John wasn't prepared to tell the whole truth. He hadn't thought through his whole sexual history. Instead, he was talking about his current involvement in pornography and his few visits to massage parlors. Amber wanted to understand his full history. She wanted to understand how much he had been lying to her. Kurt, on the other hand, took the time to prepare and explore his history. In his search, he found experiences that had contributed to his problems with Stacey.

- John was not prepared for Amber's intense emotions and could not support her. Kurt and Stacey both had emotional support as they went through their disclosure.

- Kurt took his time and thought about specific times he had lied and was prepared to own his mistakes and admit how he had lied. John was looking to tell what he thought was the truth, but hadn't yet discovered how much he had lied over the years. This resulted in a staggered disclosure, meaning that Amber continued to get more information in bits and pieces as John slowly remembered more.

- Amber was blindsided, while Stacey knew that Kurt was working with a professional who understood how to help.

Many first attempts at disclosure fall short of being effective due to lack of preparation. Others don't work because they are filled with half-truths. Sometimes this happens intentionally and other times it is due to a lack of understanding of how to do an effective disclosure.

In John's case, he wanted to disclose his past to Amber, but he thought he would just need to tell her what had been happened and that would be enough. He wasn't prepared to tell the whole story. When this happens healing cannot begin because additional information about what happened will be revealed. These talks usually surround how sexual secrets were maintained. Due to additional discoveries, betrayed partners feel like they don't know the whole story and feel like they are being lied to. This usually increases their trauma since the full truth was not revealed in the initial disclosure. This is one reason why well-prepared full disclosures are so helpful.

As I have interviewed and counseled with many individuals regarding their disclosure process, I have found that many couples who have tried to do a disclosure on their own end up doing it over again. Why does this happen? The betraying spouse often has lots of questions and they usually want to know more details about what happened.

What to do if Disclosure Has Been Done Poorly

If your discovery left you with more questions than answers, or if you feel like you didn't get the full story, it may be best for you and your spouse to prepare to do another disclosure with professional help. If your spouse resists this idea because they like you have already discussed their sexual misdeeds and they want to move on, your challenge will be to communicate why this is important to you.

The following may be of help to both you and your partner when you discuss why a well-prepared disclosure would be helpful to you and your relationship.

In his book *The Science of Trust*, Dr. John Gottman shares a story of a 1927 psychologist, Bluma Zeigarnik, who first studied something her professor, Gestalt psychologist, Kurt Lewin, noticed. Professor Lewin found that a waiter had better recollections of still unpaid orders in contrast to paid orders. After the completion of the task, when everyone had paid, he was unable to remember any more details of the orders. (3)

The implication is that once something we are working on is completed, we are less likely to remember the details. Dr. Gottman believes that this principle works in couples relationships. Here's what he wrote about this concept: "Negative events in couple relationships are inevitable. The way relationships fail is through something called the 'Zeigarnik effect.' If a couple's negative events are not fully processed (by attunement), then they are remembered and rehearsed repeatedly, turned over and over in each person's mind. Trust begins to erode." (4)

Because the issue often feels unresolved, it can be difficult to move on in the aftermath of a sexual betrayal revelation. There are often more unanswered questions and until painful memories are fully processed, healing will be limited.

If we apply the Zeigarnik effect to betrayal trauma, we see that most couples get stuck because the negative events are not fully processed. The attunement process that Dr. Gottman references begins when the offending party becomes completely open in disclosure. Researchers who have studied the disclosure process extensively have found that betrayed spouses report the following benefits after disclosure:

- Obtaining clarity about the events of the relationship

- Validation that they are not crazy

- Hope for the future of the relationship

- Finally having the information necessary to decide about one's future (5)

This brings up another important point about disclosure. Disclosures are most effective when both spouses are committed to repairing the relationship. If one or both of you are not committed, disclosure will be less effective. There are circumstances where the information provided in the full disclosure becomes a deal breaker. When this happens, the disclosure is still beneficial because the information provided helped the betrayed spouse make a decision with all of the information rather than some or none of the information.

Preparing for a Full Disclosure

If your spouse is willing to do another disclosure, consider talking about and implementing as many of these suggestions as you can:

1. Seek help from a Certified Sexual Addiction Therapist (CSAT)

2. Review the resources found in Appendix C.

3. Think through what questions you need answered. By preparing these questions, you are working to resolve things that haven't added up in your mind. Your spouse needs to prepare to answer these questions. Be careful to avoid asking questions that would provide information that you do not need, (e.g. types of sex positions) or that require comparisons (e.g. "Did you like sex better with her?"). When individuals ask for these types of details, they often come back to haunt the relationship. It has been my experience that too much detail paints images and impressions that linger in the mind of the betrayed long after disclosure. I often tell my clients, "You may want to get a ground level view of what happened, but in some situations the 5000 foot view of what happened may be better."

4. One of the purposes of doing a disclosure is to help you decide, once you have all of the information, if you want to continue your relationship. Therefore, you want to be emotionally prepared to hear the details. It helps to have professional guidance and emotional support as you go through this process.

5. Don't rush or force a quick disclosure. Good preparation on both sides generally leads to the best outcomes.

Note: Disclosures are designed to help both individuals heal. Only with truth can important decisions be made regarding the relationship. Many couples report that disclosure helped them establish new patterns and resolve other relationship problems. However, disclosures are for couples who are attempting to try to repair their marriage. If you are going through a divorce, a disclosure is not advised.

Understanding First Responses to Discovery

I have listened to countless people share their experiences with discovery. I have found that most individuals and couples are not prepared for the shock of discovery. In the final part of this chapter we will explore how discovery triggers intense traumatic responses. While nobody would ever want to relive D-Day, there is valuable information available by exploring the first thoughts, emotions, and memories that occurred at the time of discovery.

In an effort to help individuals identify their first response and then observe how they have changed since discovery, .I gave participants from one of my online classes an assignment to identify their story. The assignment was titled, "Share Your Story" (See Appendix B). Here are a few of the questions and answers that I received.

Question: The day you discovered your partner's behaviors, what happened and how did you respond?

Response #1:

I was instantly so sick to my stomach that I wanted throw up. Eventually, all I could do was cry. Then I got very angry at him for keeping this from me. Why didn't he trust me? Why did he lie to me? Why? Why? Then I thought about how stupid I was for not knowing. Then I had so many questions, but the more I thought about it, the more angry I felt.

This explains why he acted the way he did for our whole married life. Pieces of this shattered mirror started to fit into places where it was once fractured beyond repair. I thought to myself, 'Wow! So that is why he looked at me the way he did on our wedding night dressed in beautiful lingerie.' I told him on our wedding night when I came out, 'Well, we have waited a long time. Would you like to play?' He replied, 'No. I'd rather watch Rain Man.' The movie! Yeah, so pretty much our whole marriage I was rejected by him. I was once thin, beautiful, and sexy. Now I am a fat, ugly, overweight woman. Physically I wanted to die at first. Then I wanted to slap him across the face.

Observations:

First, notice how many physical symptoms she experienced in discovery. Recognize statements such as, "I was so sick to my stomach," and "I wanted to throw-up." Second, observe her emotional responses: "I cried and cried," and "I was very angry at him." And third, look at how she turned it on herself: "Why didn't he trust me?" and "How could I have been so stupid not to know?"

The second paragraph in her response reveals one of her deepest wounds. Her husband was abusive on their first night together. In this case, you can see that he rejected her playfulness. You can see how and why her trauma is so deep. Her husband's behaviors demonstrate that he was not ready for marriage and it showed in how he treated her.

Response #2:

The first discovery made me feel physically sick. I felt dirty and had to take a shower. While in the shower, I found some comfort by prayer and I was able to get to a calm state of mind. I then confronted my husband. He seemed only remorseful that he was caught and promised not to do it again. The second time, I didn't believe him when he said he wouldn't do it again and demanded that he see our religious leader and a therapist. I also let him know that I would never feel comfortable having a baby with that kind of influence present in my home.

When I caught him the third time, I felt sick again, but I felt more hurt than anything. I felt completely betrayed and deceived. I started researching if I was able to get a divorce based on the grounds of pornography use. I was in a zombie-like state for several days as I processed what was going on. I spent hundreds of hours doing research and ordered lots of books. It was through this education that I felt like I gained an understanding of what I was up against.

Observations

In this second response we again see physical symptoms manifesting themselves right after discovery. I have found that feeling dirty and sick are common physical responses after discovery. Another common response is becoming "zombie-like." Women have shared with me that they walked around dazed for days and weeks at a time. Most are in a state of shock.

We also see in the second response that this person turned her attention to things she could control. She began studying and learning about what she was up against. This is very normal. In fact, it's what you are doing as you read this book. You are getting information so you can heal.

Below, some women who have been through betrayal trauma assess their initial responses on discovery day. I have found that by thinking through these questions, many see their progress but also realize that there are issues that they still may need to resolve.

Question: Knowing what you do now, is there anything you wish you would have said or done differently that day?

Response #1:

Yes I would have demanded to know everything, instead of finding bits and pieces and trying to draw a picture and fill in the missing pieces to a huge ugly puzzle.

Observations:

This feedback is one of the key reasons we emphasize preparing for a formal disclosure. It is also important to note that in demanding to know everything in the beginning, her husband most likely would not have been willing or ready to give her all of the information. This is one reason we have to slow down the disclosure process. By slowing down and identifying issues to include in disclosure, such as sexual history and patterns of lying and deceit, this person wouldn't have experienced a staggered disclosure. Disclosure doesn't take away the pain of what happened, but it does allow full truth to come and then, and only then, can healing occur. I often say that when the spouse who has betrayed their partner discloses small amounts at a time, it is the equivalent to vomiting in every room in the house and asking your spouse to clean it up again and again.

Response #2:

When I made the first discovery, I wish I would have known it was an addiction. With this knowledge I would have begun my own recovery and encouraged my husband to do the same. For years I felt crazy and allowed my husband to make me feel unrighteous for not feeling comfortable having children with him. I would have trusted my instincts more and not blamed myself for my husband's unhappiness. This would have saved us a lot of pain and heartache and we might have children by now.

Observations:

This response brings up a very important point. She wishes she had known it was an addiction. Unfortunately, many people who disclose their sexual behaviors are not asked the right questions to determine if sexual addiction is present. As a result, the focus is on the current behavior and does not address whether this behavior is a manifestation of deeper sexual compulsivity. This is a good reason for a thorough evaluation to be completed for both spouses.

Note: In our clinic, we use some of the best assessments available to identify betrayal trauma symptoms and sexual addiction. See Appendix D to learn how Addo Recovery uses assessments to identify trauma levels in the betrayed as well as level of sexual addiction or compulsivity in the betraying spouse.

Chapter Summary

As we begin discussing the steps toward healing, the initial focus is on understanding the differences between disclosure processes. Unfortunately, far too many disclosures (forced or self-disclosure) are done in ways that increase the trauma. While all disclosures are extremely painful and difficult to endure, when they are done right, they can act as the beginning steps toward long-term healing and relationship recovery.

See Appendix C for more information on effective disclosures.

In the next chapter, we will focus on how to successfully establish safety in your life so that you can truly begin the healing process.

Chapter Six

The Secret to Healing:
It Starts with Safety

To keep oneself safe does not mean to bury oneself.

Marcus Anneaus Seneca

Imagine that you are getting ready to walk into a room filled with people you do not know. What is happening in your mind and body? If you are like most people, you are feeling some stress. Your heart rate increases, and you are suddenly feeling a little anxious. You don't know what to expect when you walk through those doors.

Now imagine that you walk into that room. As you look around, you scan to your right and left and you don't see anyone you know. You are in a room full of people and recognize no one. What happens next? According to Dr. Stephen Porges, the first thing you do is so natural that you won't even think about it. In his research, Dr. Porges has found that your primal instinct is to determine if you are safe or not. This is all done in your subconscious mind. As you walk around, you try to determine if you should override your natural tendency to protect yourself (i.e. quickly leave) or if you are safe enough to socially engage.

When you are faced with situations like this, it doesn't take long to decide if you should stay and mingle for a while or if you should leave. In most scenarios like this, it is usually just a matter of seconds before you will decide how to respond. Most of the time, you will choose to override your natural fears and stay. By doing so, you give yourself a little more time to determine what to do next.

By staying a little longer, you are taking a risk, but you also give yourself a chance to meet others. As you walk around, you see someone that you know, someone you didn't see when you first entered the room. Now your mind relaxes a little more and you walk toward them. Your body begins to relax as well. Over the next few minutes, you start to integrate yourself into this new environment.

So exactly how do we make this decision about whether or not we are safe? According to Dr. Porges, our nervous system gathers the clues we need to determine whether a person is safe, dangerous, or life-threatening. He writes that "new technologies, such as functional magnetic resonance imaging (FMRI), have identified specific neural structures that are involved in detecting risk. Specific areas of the brain detect and evaluate features, such as body and face movements and vocalizations, that contribute to an impression of safety or trustworthiness."

Isn't it amazing how our bodies work? Through our sensory network, we have a built-in alarm system. "Researchers have identified an area in the cortex that becomes activated when we see familiar faces and hear familiar voices. This process of identifying familiar and trustworthy people and evaluating the intentions of others based on 'biological movements' of face and limbs seems to be located in the temporal lobe of the cortex. If neuroception identifies a person as safe, then a neural circuit actively inhibits areas of the brain that organize the defensive strategies of fight, flight, and freeze." (1)

The purpose of our alarm system is to warn us. It is very important to understand that our first priority in any and every environment is to determine if we are safe or not and only when we determine we are safe, can we socially bond with others. This concept applies to all of our relationships and plays an important role in understanding betrayal trauma.

From Bond Building to Protection Mode

If your relationship developed like most, then in the early phase you spent hours talking and enjoying each others' company. You felt safe enough to let your guard down. You found that it was okay to be open and share personal things with each other. You began sharing some parts of you that you had never shared with anyone else before. You felt accepted and validated; you felt safe.

Stephanie and Justin reported that they got along great while they were dating and throughout most of their engagement. Their first real problem came up just a few weeks before they got married. Out of curiosity and because some of her friends had husbands who were involved in pornography, Stephanie asked Justin about his use of pornography. Initially, he was hesitant and a little anxious, but he started opening up. He told her that he had viewed it, but he initially led her to believe that it was a thing of the past. She wasn't satisfied, so she asked him more in-depth questions: When were you first exposed to pornography? When in your life were you viewing it the most? How frequent was your viewing when it was the worst? Have you viewed pornography while we've been dating? When was the last time you intentionally viewed pornography?

While he appeared to be anxious answering these questions, he was honest and shared the following: "I first saw it when I was ten. I viewed it throughout my teen years and I viewed it the most between eighth and tenth grade. I viewed it daily then. Then my parents caught me and I tried stopping for a while. That lasted for a few months. However, I still found ways to access it and watched it every few weeks throughout high school. I stopped for a while before my graduation; then I went to college and it escalated again. The last time I viewed it was two months ago when you left town with your family."

While Justin was honest, Stephanie was upset that he hadn't told her before they were engaged. She was also upset that he had viewed it while they were dating. Justin reassured her that he was done viewing pornography. Stephanie wasn't sure what to think. She asked to take a break for a few days before she decided if she still wanted to marry him.

Over the next few days, Stephanie looked at both sides of their relationship. Their relationship had been so much fun and Justin was one of the first guys that had really listened to her. After thinking through things, Stephanie decided to move forward with their relationship. After all, Justin promised her he was done with pornography.

After their wedding, they had a great few months together. They both reported that they felt good about their relationship. They were having a good time. They had been married about six months when Justin began acting a little strange around her. They had been busy, so Stephanie blamed his changed behavior toward her on stress. However, when Justin's strange new behavior continued, Stephanie started to feel like he was holding back. She asked him if anything was wrong. "No, what makes you think something is wrong?" he replied. Stephanie said, "Just a feeling. You seem a little distant lately." Justin replied, "I think we have just been busy."

Things were better after that for a few weeks, but Stephanie still felt something was not right. She didn't know what it was. Then one day while he was in the shower, she felt like she should check his phone. She did and discovered that he had been using his phone to access pornographic websites. He had been lying to her. When he got out of the shower, she confronted him. He then disclosed to her that he had been viewing pornography again and had been doing so for the past few months.

Stephanie's intuition was right that something had changed. She didn't know exactly what until she felt the impression to check his phone. Dr. Porges describes how this process works: "Most people are able to gauge danger and love by means of their 'gut feelings,' which generally accurately detect the relative danger or safety of their situation."(2)

It has been my experience that most individuals dealing with sexual betrayal are able to detect something is wrong, but they can't put their finger on the problem. Once they have full disclosure, they realize that their instincts were correct.

Justin was surprised by Stephanie's perception. What was she picking up? According to Dr. Porges, "slight changes in the biological movements that we see can shift a neuroception from 'safe' to 'dangerous.' When this shift occurs, the neural systems associated with prosocial behavior are disrupted, and the neural systems associated with defensive strategies are triggered." In other words, Stephanie had seen ever so slight changes in Justin's behaviors. When I asked her about this change she identified behaviors such as his unwillingness to look her in the eye, his emotional distance when she tried to connect, and his physical distance, unless he wanted sex.

Based on Stephanie's discovery, she naturally moved out of safe mode and into protection mode. Justin had promised prior to marriage that he would never view pornography again and now they were married and he was viewing pornography, and he'd been lying to her about it. Over the next few weeks, their marriage was filled with arguments. Justin tried to assure her that he would not return back to pornography again, but he had promised that before.

It was at this point that Stephanie made one of the biggest decisions of her life. She said, "If you want to save our marriage, I need you to go to counseling with me and by yourself. I am not going to live with pornography in our lives."

Justin, realizing that she was serious, agreed to go. It was soon after that I met them for the first time.

I began by doing an evaluation of Stephanie's level of trauma as well as gathering information on Justin's pornography use and other sexual behaviors (see more in Chapter Two about this process). I also asked them about their current commitment levels and desire to heal their relationship: "On a scale between zero (not committed at all) and ten (very committed), how committed are you to making your relationship better?"

Stephanie turned to Justin and said, "Why don't you answer first?" He responded, "I am a ten. I really want to make things better." Stephanie looked at him and said, "Do you really? Your actions haven't been showing it." In response Justin said, "I know I have been lying to you, but I am willing to do anything. Just give me a chance." She responded, "If you are a ten, then show it."

I turned to her and asked about her commitment level. She said, "I don't know... maybe a six or seven. I do want it to work, but I won't live with lies and him using pornography. I just won't live my life that way."

Due to Stephanie's commitment to improve the marriage and Justin's level of commitment to change, I knew that their relationship had a good chance to make it. However, I also knew that they both had work to do. What I shared with them is important for all couples to understand as they attempt to rebuild trust in their relationships after discovering sexual betrayal.

Healing: It Really Does Begin with Safety

After discovery, many couples spin their wheels for months and years because they don't know how to resolve their problems. The partner dealing with sexual addiction often feels helpless. Meanwhile, their partner is feeling similar emotions because they have come to believe their spouse will never change. These mindsets perpetuate their problems because neither knows what to do or understands how to do anything different. They are stuck.

When I meet couples who are feeling this way, I like to share with them the research findings of Dr. Carol Dweck. In her wonderful book, *Mindset,* she shares the concept of having a fixed mindset versus a growth mindset. Dr. Dweck has discovered that individuals who have a fixed mindset struggle to find options when they encounter challenges. They believe that they are not smart enough or good enough to change their circumstances. They might say, "This is just the way I am. I will always be an addict." In contrast, individuals who have a growth mindset believe that if they do not know the answer to a problem, they can always find an answer if they work hard enough. They say things like, "I don't know how I am going to solve this problem, but I will find a solution."

Once my clients understand this concept, I then encourage them to develop a growth mindset for their healing and recovery. I let them know that countless other people have been or are going through what they are going through and that together we can help them find solutions.

Finally, to give them additional tools, I share with them the three principles listed below. As an offending partner applies the growth mindset and changes behaviors, their actions help create a feeling of safety because they are actively working on their healing. Or, as Stephanie put it, they are "showing" their partners that they want to change themselves and heal the marriage. The following actions need to be taken in the early stage of marital recovery:

Principle #1: No Secrets

If you want to develop healthy relationships, you cannot keep secrets.

Simply said, secrets destroy safety. This is one of the key reasons we emphasize to couples the value of participating in a formal disclosure, having an accountability team, and finding a sponsor. Simply put, addiction grows in silence. Adopting a "no secrets" policy in one's relationships lessens the likelihood of relapse and promotes the rebuilding of trust.

The same principle holds true to individuals who are dealing with sexual betrayal. Many betrayed partners, women especially, are afraid to talk about their spouses' behaviors because they don't want to be judged. As a result, many wait months and years before they tell anyone. The consequence of keeping this secret is that they often begin to lose their knack for confiding in others and find it difficult to establish and use supportive relationships.

I am not advocating that you purchase a billboard on a major interstate to "out" your spouse. Instead, I am suggesting that it is critical to share what you are experiencing with someone that you trust or with someone with whom you can develop a trusting relationship.

Principle #2: Take Responsibility for Your Own Actions

Safety increases in the relationship when individuals take responsibility for their own choices.

Over the years, one of the common traits used by individuals hiding their sexual behaviors is to blame their spouse for their actions. If healing is going to start, blaming your partner for your actions needs to end. Stephanie took responsibility for her choice regarding the marriage when she said to Justin, "I won't be in a relationship where pornography is present." This approach gave Justin the choice to make the changes requested or end the marriage. Justin also showed ownership at this moment by expressing willingness and desire to change his own behaviors; had he chosen to shift responsibility to Stephanie and blame her for his pornography use, their relationship would have been over.

In order for healing to occur, each individual within a marriage needs to be accountable for his or her actions.

Principle #3: Find an Accountability Team

Safety usually increases in the relationship when accountability increases. When individuals begin working their recovery they often realize that they need more support. As they begin reaching out for support they come to understand that they are not alone in their battle. In a presentation that I gave at the Utah Coalition Against Pornography conference in 2016, I explained with the help of a friend in recovery how accountability changes the entire dynamics of the healing process. You can find the link to watch that presentation in the resources section. It may be especially helpful for your spouse to watch to understand how accountability can significantly improve the likelihood of a successful recovery.

Many spouses of sex addicts have shared with me that they do not want to be their spouse's sponsor. They prefer that their spouse find someone else to whom they can be accountable. When an accountability team is in place and utilized, trust begins to build because they see their spouse engaging in their own recovery. They also feel like they are not the only one who is carrying the burden.

When the three principles above are not upheld in relationships, trust cannot develop and safety in the relationship is further impaired. In such situations, I strongly suggest that the betrayed spouse seek safety in other meaningful and healthy relationships. In some situations, safety in the relationship is not an option due to the depth of deception and multitude of lies that have occurred over the years. Therefore, finding outside support is critical because your spouse cannot provide the support you need to heal.

After discovering sexual betrayal I emphasize to my clients that they would benefit by doing one or more of the following:

- Attend a 12-step support group (See resources section for where you can find a 12-step group in your areas.)

- Find a sponsor who understands addiction and betrayal trauma (usually 12-step groups can help you find a sponsor).

- Talk with a religious leader (if available and if they are supportive).

- Talk with a trusted friend (an example of how you can do this can be found in Chapter Ten).

- Seek support in your family.

- Talk with a professional counselor.

In my work with couples, I try to emphasize that if they are practicing the three principles above, their relationship is heading in the right direction. When the principles are not upheld, safety is rarely an option.

Fortunately for Stephanie, she had enough awareness to take a stand early in her relationship with Justin. Additionally, Justin was committed to healing himself and the marriage. When I explained to him the principles behind safety and why Stephanie wouldn't feel safe with him until he took action, he realized that he couldn't expect her to simply trust him right away. That was not an option due to his secrets and lies. I told him it was a possibility again, but he would have to be patient and follow the three principles outlined above.

While many of the people I work with want help, they often do not know where to begin. One of my primary goals is to create an environment where my clients feel safe enough to share their deepest challenges with me. I know that if my work is going to be successful, my clients have to have complete trust in me. As trust is established between the client and me, I then shift the process to helping them develop trust and safety with others. I often emphasize to them that creating safety in the relationship is most likely not an option in the beginning of their healing process. Instead, our goal is to identify individuals already in their lives with whom they can build a trusting relationship. This outside support is designed to help stabilize each individual regardless of whether the relationship works out or not.

If you struggle to feel safe with anyone, it is critical that we start at the most basic level. If you are reading this book and cannot think of anyone to open up to, consider joining a group or program specific to betrayal trauma and addiction. This will help you become more comfortable with talking about sexual betrayal in general as well as your specific experiences. Safety can be experienced through group participation and you are likely to develop friendships that can help you put into practice the three principles above. Working with an individual therapist can be another step in the right direction toward building safety. Right now, you may not know a person who is safe to you. That is okay. Please consider each of the bullet points listed above.

Establishing Safety in Your Relationship

When couples come to my office for help with sexual betrayal, I try to emphasize the importance of being patient with the process. It takes time to understand the extent of the problem, create a solid healing and recovery game plan, and to implement the plan. In addition to sexual betrayal, many couples also have to learn how to effectively problem solve, resolve conflict, and learn how to connect on a deeper level all while they are dealing with trauma and addiction recovery. These are no simple tasks.

Regarding this process, Dr. Gottman writes that "once the forces leading to betrayal are understood and reversed in the relationship, trust must be rebuilt by: 1) replacing conflict avoidance through constructive conflict management, 2) creating trust through attunement, and 3) building intimate trust through personal sex." (3)

By personal sex, Dr. Gottman is referring to meaningful connected sex in contrast to what he refers to as impersonal sex (e.g. pornography).

The final section of this chapter will help you understand how key elements in your relationship patterns can either help resolve the forces behind betrayal or prevent healing.

Solution #1 for Reestablishing Safety: Eliminate Toxicity

Safety in relationships comes from creating a healthy environment. In contrast, it is impossible to feel safe when certain conditions like criticism, denial, and blame are present in your relationship. In Appendix E is a short quiz to assess your relationship for toxicity levels. In the quiz you will find some of the common behaviors that help and hurt relationships. Take the time to complete the quiz now.

So, how did you score?

If you are like many women and men I talk to, you may be feeling a little guilt and frustration right now. Guilt usually comes from seeing that you are doing more of the unhealthy things and not as much of the healthy things as you thought you were. Frustration comes from seeing that your relationship is toxic and not what you want it to be.

The purpose of the quiz is not to make you feel guilty or frustrated, but rather to help you understand what is really happening in your relationship. We can't change what we can't see. If you find that you are being toxic in your relationship, my guess is that it is due to your hurt and pain. It has been my experience that when I help clients give language to their anger and resentment, they usually find that they feel inadequate, unloved, or unimportant. Their anger is masking their deeper hurts.

Furthermore, when you understand your anger is preventing you from being the real you, it becomes a challenge to return to your true self. Most of the people I have worked with respond well to this concept because they know in their heart of hearts that they are genuinely kind and loving, but betrayal trauma has brought out the worst in them.

If you are in a relationship with someone who is toxic, it is easy to lose yourself in the day-to-day battle. You will need to stay focused on being the real you while establishing and maintaining emotional and physical boundaries. (See Chapter Eight for more information on boundaries.) In addition, you will want to learn how to communicate your expectations in your relationship. Toxicity doesn't usually stop on its own; identifying and explaining what you will no longer accept are important steps to take.

Perhaps understanding exactly how toxic your relationship is or isn't is a good place to start. As you evaluate your relationship, look at the level of tension and level of attunement that is happening now. Identify areas that need to change and if possible discuss them with your spouse. If you want to reduce the level of toxic behaviors in your relationship, focus on reducing the tension behaviors and increasing the attunement behaviors as found in Appendix E.

If you and your spouse can't discuss the Relationship Tension Scale and the Relationship Attunement Scale as found in Appendix E, you will likely need professional support to help change the patterns.

Solution #2 for Reestablishing Safety: Be Proactive in Healing and Recovery

I have observed that couples who do the best in recovery usually do so when both parties are engaged in their own individual healing processes. I often hear resentment from the betrayed when I mention this. They say, "Why do I have to go to therapy or attend groups? I wasn't the one who cheated." Unfortunately, your spouse's behaviors have changed your life. They have brought up thoughts and emotions that have changed you.

Mary was worn out from the lies Tom had been telling her. She had been dealing with his betrayal for years. He had often tried to shift their problems onto her by saying she was distant and cold. Finally, as a last-ditch effort she told him that she was done. She wasn't sure she was ready to end their marriage, but she was done dealing with his lying, blaming, and cheating on her. This was the first time she had shown this much strength. It actually caught Tom off-guard.

She told him, "If you don't go get help, I am done with our marriage." He suggested marriage counseling. To this she replied, "Are you kidding me? You got us into this! Go figure out your own stuff. Then maybe we can talk about marriage counseling."

Tom wanted to save his marriage, so he set up an appointment with a therapist. In the beginning, he wasn't really sure what to expect in counseling. In fact, he later reported that he was just going to counseling to "check off a box." However, things changed quite quickly when he was asked to attend an educational group to learn about sexual addiction. Within a few sessions, he realized he had a problem.

As he listened to others discuss their sexual acting out, he began to see how his own behaviors had gotten out of control. He was especially touched when one man stood up and read a letter he had written to his addict self. In the letter, this man described how addiction was hurting his relationships. Tom began to understand Mary's pain, but he didn't know how to make it better. He started talking with his counselor about how he had lied to and deceived Mary throughout their marriage. He wanted to earn her trust again, but he didn't know how to do it on his own, and she wasn't yet interested in seeking counseling.

He began preparing a disclosure letter for Mary. His therapist called and invited Mary to come for a couple of sessions. The therapist indicated that he would like to meet with her first to make sure she had adequate support before their disclosure. Since she had seen some change in Tom's behaviors, she had become curious about what he was experiencing in therapy. She agreed to meet with Tom's therapist.

When she met the therapist, he asked her about what she was experiencing with Tom and if she was seeing changes. They talked about how Tom was treating her. Then, the therapist did something that surprised her: he asked how she was doing, stating, "I'm concerned about you. You've been dealing with his behaviors for a long time. How is this influencing you? Are you able to sleep, eat, and focus? Do you have dreams about what Tom has done?"

She thought, "How does he know that I haven't been sleeping or eating well? Why did he ask me about dreaming about what Tom has done?" After a few seconds she responded, "No I haven't been sleeping or eating. My mind is racing. And yes I have had a few bad dreams." For so long she had tried to ignore and distance herself from Tom's behaviors. She was embarrassed by what he had done and felt ashamed that she hadn't taken a stand earlier.

Now, in the therapist's office, she realized she too needed help. Over the next few weeks, Mary did receive help and Tom completed his disclosure. This case illustrates two common scenarios. First, many people do not realize the changes that are necessary. Tom, had he not participated in the group, would likely have continued to blame Mary for their problems and not see how his actions were hurting her. Mary, on the other hand, had hidden anger and felt shame for what Tom was doing. She was running from her problems.

When individuals like Mary and Tom become proactive in their recovery, it usually changes the dynamics of their relationship. Change becomes more evident and confidence begins to grow in the person seeking help. If their spouse is also engaged in recovery (e.g. 12-step groups, sponsorship, psychoeducation, therapy, etc.), there is usually a mutual feeling of hope and commitment.

Solution #3 for Reestablishing Safety: Be Honest and Truthful

Over the years, I have heard many betrayed spouses say a version of the following: "I hate what he has done, but I cannot live with his lies." When working with couples to rebuild safety in their relationships, we begin by focusing on eliminating secrets and lies. It is imperative that honesty and truth be established if the relationship is going to be repaired.

I often have to talk with both men and women about it. The betraying spouse has usually been minimizing their actions or straight-out lying about what they have done. However, their spouse too has been holding back. They have been afraid to open up and share their deepest hurts with their spouse because they felt it would either cause their partner to relapse or that their feelings would not be validated.

In working with a couple, when I am confident that both partners are fully committed to and engaged in their individual and couple recovery, I encourage the betrayed spouse to share their hurt and anger with their partner in a letter. This is the betrayed spouse's form of disclosure. Below is Mary's letter to Tom:

Dear Tom,

For the longest time I have wanted to tell you how deeply you have hurt me. I have felt like you didn't love me, that there was something wrong with me. Early in our relationship, I was sure that you didn't find me attractive enough. Then after having our first child, I knew I wasn't attractive enough. I felt fat and ugly. Then, when I asked you not to stay up late at night and you still did, I felt like I was not important enough to you. That's when I first caught you chatting with other women on the Internet.

That was it. I had proof. I wasn't enough for you. If we hadn't had our son, I would have been done. I told myself that I would stop trying to make things better. I became cold and distant from you. You may have been trying then, but I was too angry at you. I began hating it when you wanted to have sex. I couldn't stand when you tried touching me. I thought all you wanted me for was sex. My anger grew and grew. I found power in my anger. I knew you wanted me to be nice, but, in my mind, you didn't deserve it.

You have betrayed my trust. I don't know how to trust you again. I don't know if I want to at this point. As I write this, there must be some part of me that wants to try because I do want to love you. I do want to be married to you, but I can't live with secrets and lies anymore. Are you in? Do you want our marriage? Are you willing to commit to me? Please think through these questions and give them serious consideration. I don't want to be doing this again in a year or two.

Whether we choose to stay married or not, I am committed to work through

(cont.)

---

my anger. I am not sure how I will do this yet, but I do not like who I am when I feel so angry. I am going to become the real me again. I hope you choose to join me. It's time for change.

Love,

Mary

This type of letter is very valuable for couples as it helps them establish a new baseline of where their relationship stands. This letter helps Tom clearly understand where Mary is regarding their marriage. Her letter is well thought-out and shows her honest feelings, thoughts, and insights as listed below:

- She admits that after discovery, she wasn't sure she wanted their marriage.

- She owns her anger and commits to work through it.

- She identifies when she pulled back in the relationship and why it happened.

- She discusses some of the things that pushed her away from him (e.g. sexual advances).

- She is vulnerable in telling him that she wants their marriage to work out

One of the key actions that helps couples successfully heal and recover is talking through difficult issues. It is in difficult, heart-felt discussions that couples discover whether they can work through their challenges or not. While holding back from honest and truthful feelings is common, when we speak our "truths," it allows better and more-informed decisions to be made.

The questions below have shown to be helpful for couples to consider before they discuss if they are going to try and work through sexual betrayal. Think carefully through each question, using journaling if needed, before you respond.

Questions for the Betrayed Spouse:

- How committed am I to this relationship on a scale of 0 (not at all) to 10 (completely)?

- What do I need to hear from my spouse if I am going to try?

- What do I need to see from my spouse if I am going to try?

- What key issues do I need to address on my end (i.e. distancing myself, letting him close again, anger, etc.) if this marriage is going to make it?

- Do I want this relationship to work? Score betwee

Questions for the Spouse who Betrayed

- How committed am I to this relationship on a scaic ⌣.
  (completely)?

- How committed am I to stopping my behavior? Score between 0 and 10.

- Am I willing to do everything I can (e.g. seek professional help, go to a 12-step group, get a sponsor, etc.) to stop betraying and hurting my spouse? Score between 0 and 10.

- What do I need to change in order to heal and recover?

- What does my spouse need from me in order to heal?

- What do I need to hear from my spouse if I am going to try?

- What do I need to see from my spouse if I am going to try?

As individuals answer these questions with openness and honesty, they will begin to see what is needed for them to move forward. While discussing the answers to these questions with your partner may be very hard, it is only through these honest and difficult conversations that couples begin moving forward in healing.

Chapter Summary

Establishing personal and relationship safety is an important first step in the long-term healing and recovery process. In fact, if an individual does not feel safe (both emotionally and physically), healing is not an option. Safety is often dependent upon the creation of an environment where honesty and truth are present.

When sexual betrayal occurs, the spouse who was hurt naturally shifts to protection mode. One key strategy to avoiding long-term trauma is to establish trusting relationships with others. When individuals have someone who is "safe" to them, they usually can work through their trauma in a more efficient and effective way.

Honesty, ownership, and accountability are critical principles needed in order for couples to rebuild safety and therefore trust in their relationships. Addressing specific difficult questions as a couple aids the effort to bring honesty and truth to the healing process.

In the next chapter, we will focus on helping you take the necessary action to move forward if you feel that you are stuck.

Chapter Seven

Getting Unstuck: Learn to Take Action

One starts an action simply because one must do something.

T.S. Eliot

Dr. John Leach, an expert on survival psychology, observes how humans respond to crisis. He has studied how humans respond in crisis situations and used his findings to train people around the world, increasing their chances of survival in the most difficult of circumstances. In his studies, Dr. Leach has found that people naturally divide into three groups in an emergency. The first group are the survivors; about 10% of us are prepared to think clearly through a crisis. Those who fit into this group are able to remain relatively calm and rational under pressure as well as make sharp and focused decisions. Dr. Leach's findings suggest that most of us, up to 90%, simply haven't learned how to be this way. However he does believe we can all learn how to be calm and rational while in high stress.

Of the 90% who are unprepared for crisis, the second and third groups emerge. The second group, according to Leach, freezes. He estimates that roughly 80% of us do so during a crisis. We get stuck and initially do not know how to respond. "Under tremendous pressure, most of us will feel lethargic and numb. We'll sweat. We'll feel sick. Our hearts may race. And we'll experience 'perceptual narrowing' or so-called tunnel vision… In short, most of us will turn into statues in the first moments of crisis." (1) Dr. Leach refers to this as cognitive paralysis, which results in complete inaction. This group is by far the largest of the three; therefore, freezing is too common an occurrence to be ignored.

Because the bulk of us tend to freeze up rather than run away or fight, it's inaccurate to simplify our instinctual options as only "fight or flight." As a result of

Dr. Leach's and others' work, the case has been presented for the classic "fight or flight" response to be renamed the "fight, flight or freeze" response (2). In terms of trauma recovery, Dr. Leach's work reveals that it is usually possible for someone who freezes to learn how to recover quickly and figure out what steps need to be taken next in order to protect themselves. This means that most of us can recover from our trauma responses.

The third group, the final 10%, create more problems during their crisis. In an emergency, they tend to complicate matters. If they were drowning, they would pull down the person who was trying to save them. Their brains get flooded and they lose control.

There is great parallel between Dr. Leach's crisis work and individuals dealing with betrayal. If we apply the 10-80-10 breakdown to sexual betrayal, the discovery of which certainly qualifies as a crisis, one in ten people know how to respond in a rational, collected manner to the revelation of their partner's infidelity. They are able to analyze the situation and determine what actions they need to take. These individuals are able to slow down their minds, analyze what is happening, and identify how to respond.

The majority of people initially freeze up. They are in shock and don't know how to respond. Once their shock wears off, their frozen state of mind shifts to the common fight or flee responses. However, when their fight or flee response doesn't solve their problems, they may again return to freeze mode. They learned that yelling and screaming didn't change what their spouse had done, and fleeing the situation didn't heal the trauma.

The final 10% of individuals dealing with betrayal lose control of themselves. Some end up in jail for abusing their spouse. Others have a retaliation affair which complicates their life even further. Still others end up turning to an addiction as they try to cope. In the end, what was already bad has gotten worse.

If Dr. Leach's theory holds true with individuals dealing with sexual betrayal, the focus of professional therapists and their clients should be to help the 80% of individuals who feel stuck or frozen as well as the 10% who make matters worse. It is important to teach those who are stuck or have lost control how to respond as quickly and effectively as possible.

Based on my research, many individuals have been stuck for more than two years and some people for five years or more. More than 50% of those who completed the TIPSA reported that they had been dealing with PTSD symptoms for more than two years.

It may seem unclear why people in trauma after sexual betrayal don't just move on and end their relationships. This assumes that the trauma will deactivate after the relationship is over. However, ending the relationship alone does not put an end to the pain, as found through one man's description of his experience trying to move on after infidelity: "I suspected something was going on a year ago, but my ex-partner (I have now left her) always denied she was betraying me, to the point of accusing me of having a mental health problem and trust issues due to my last partner cheating on me. Each time I found some evidence and sought explanation, it was met with aggression, tears, breaking things, and finally hitting me for the 'false accusations' and to get me to stop accusing her and end the conversation. Since realizing the truth, after a year of lies and these repeated awful scenes, I struggle to think about anything else. I'm trying to get on with my life, but this discovery has rocked my world."

This man's experience gives us insight into the deep emotional pain associated with sexual betrayal and the challenge of trying to move on. He wants to stop thinking about the past and move forward, but the emotional memories still linger in his mind. Why do we get stuck with the traumatic memories constantly on our minds?

Why We Get Stuck

According to Dr. Leach, "analysis of disaster incidents show that survival behavior follows a pattern reflected in the following psychodynamic sequence: pre-impact, impact, recovery, rescue, and post-trauma." (3) In the pre-impact phase, many individuals can feel that something is wrong in their relationship, but they generally don't know what the problem is. Others, however, are completely caught off-guard by what their spouse has been doing. In my research, roughly 48% of individuals reported that they always felt safe with their partner prior to discovery and another 31% more often than not felt safe with their partner. (See "Criteria A Results" at the following website for the full report of this section's research findings: www. discoverandchange.com/tipsa/assessment.)

During the other survival behavior sequences (impact, recovery, rescue, and post-trauma), Leach emphasizes that victims will commonly show cognitive paralysis, stereotypical behaviour, perseveration, hyperactivity, and hypoactivity. All of these are common behaviors that we see in traumatized individuals.

While there are potentially many reasons for getting stuck in a frozen state, four common explanations are explored below.

Reason #1: Stuck in Paralysis

Being stuck in a frozen state can be caused by a long-term paralysis. While in most situations paralysis is a short-term experience, in relationships where there are consistent acts of betrayal, the trauma hits again and again. This creates a consistent feeling of helplessness. When I asked research participants if they "feel like my partner will never stop sexually acting out," an astonishing 75% reported that more often than not they feel this is true. Their inability to act is generally the outcome of not knowing what action to take in order to protect themselves. They get stuck in the question of whether or not they should leave the relationship.

This pattern creates cognitive paralysis because the decision to stay or go is complex. Everything from finances to children to lost hopes and dreams can trigger feelings of being overwhelmed. If the decision is to stay when the sexual behavior does not stop and has not been resolved, paralyzing behaviors can last for weeks, months, or even years. One woman described her response to betrayal this way: "When I first found out about his affairs and hooking up with random partners, I closed myself in my bedroom for 5 years. During that time I was going through the motions of caring for my 3 kids but I have no recollection or memories of that period. I remember crying incessantly." Though this seems like an extreme case of paralysis, it is likely more common than we realize.

Reason #2: Stuck in Old Patterns

In some cases, individuals who are trying to do their best to create change end up acting in ways that maintain the same unhealthy patterns they are trying to avoid. In essence, they are trying to create change, but everything they try doesn't work, so old patterns are reverted to. When individuals and couples get stuck in unhealthy patterns they usually experience perseveration, the inability to change goals, tasks, or activities. (4) As a result, old unhealthy patterns are maintained and new healthy patterns are not created.

Here's an example of a common pattern I have observed:

The individual struggling with addiction becomes stressed. His stress makes his spouse nervous, because she has seen this pattern before and knows it can lead to a relapse. She begins to ask passive questions like, "Are you doing okay?" Knowing she is referring to his addictive behavior, he responds defensively because he hasn't acted out, at least yet. They get into an argument about her not trusting him. As a result, he feels like she doesn't understand him, and he chooses to act out, blaming her in his mind. Next, she senses he has acted out and confronts him. He admits it. She gets upset and pulls away for a few days. The addict promises to change and they reconcile for a period of time. The cycle repeats itself.

It is not uncommon for couples to go through this sequence countless times before they discover how to break out of their cycle. Here's how one woman described these cycles in her relationship:

"It's difficult because it's still ongoing. Just when I think we have this figured out....boom....something else happens. Just when I feel like I'm learning to heal and trust and let my guard down and be open and vulnerable....it happens again. It's been 3 years since the last incident....and then it just happened again. I'm married to a sex addict. Who tries really hard. Who loves me like a fairy tale.......and then out of the blue something goes wrong....stress...life...finances....a bad fight...and here we go again."

It is a very common mistake to think that time of sobriety equals recovery. However, in cases like the one above, some underlying issues remain unresolved despite the absence of acting out. Her husband does well for years at a time and may even think he has conquered his demon, but still ends up relapsing. In this case, as she describes his relapse after three years of sobriety, she experienced it as seemingly "out of the blue." However, in each of the previous examples she provides, it is revealed that stress, financial trouble, or relationship problems trigger a relapse. More likely than not, emotional issues rooted in his background exist that haven't been processed. If indeed his relapses are stress-related, even after three years of sobriety, he needs to learn how to effectively reach out to others for support during difficult times.

Reason #3: Old Patterns Die Hard

Another key reason for getting and staying stuck is a lack of understanding that change takes time and consistent effort. There is a common consensus among professional therapists that addictive habits can take three to five years to overcome. This is the time required to effectively rewire the brain. The rewiring process in the brain occurs when new habits replace unhealthy older patterns. Recent research regarding alcoholism and relapse support this claim. After five years of abstinence, a recovering alcoholic has approximately the same chances of lifetime relapse as a randomly selected member of the general US population. (5)

I believe that the same can be said of deep, emotional trauma triggered by sexual betrayal. Change requires consistent effort over time, and unfortunately, many people do not realize this. As a result, they begin down the pathway to healing, but become unfocused when stress and problems occur and turn to old habits to cope. Getting and staying unstuck is a process and not an event.

<u>Reason #4: Your Environment Prevents Change</u>

After years of trying to change her relationship, my client was worn out. She said she was at her wit's end. Her husband kept relapsing with pornography. She wasn't sure if pornography was a good enough reason to file for divorce, but she was done with her marriage. She had had enough.

However, as usual, each time she explored leaving her husband, she kept coming back to what life would be like without him. She worried about him and how their kids would respond. In the end, it wasn't bad enough to leave, but it wasn't what she wanted either.

In situations like this, confusion swirls around for years with nothing really changing. The environment of the relationship is neither good enough to be happy nor bad enough to leave. The answer seems impossible and confusion becomes a steady state.

The Beginning Steps to Create Lasting Change

The process to create meaningful change begins with small steps. In his book *The Power of Habit*, Charles Duhigg shares a story about Lisa, a woman whose life was turned upside down when her husband came home and told her he had fallen in love with another woman and he was leaving her. Over the next few months her life fell apart.

She drank often and one night ended up at the "other" woman's apartment threatening to burn the place down. She was depressed, ate for comfort, and felt completely out of control. Her life was going nowhere. Then, on a whim, she found herself in Egypt. In her car ride to to the Pyramid of Sphynx she found herself thinking, "I have to change something. I need a goal." She decided in that moment that she would hike across the desert she was looking at. After making the commitment to herself, she decided that if she was going to hike across the desert, she would have to quit smoking.

Over the next year, she transformed her life. She quit smoking, began running, got a better job, paid off debt, and eleven months later was traveling across that desert. She had completely changed her life.

Lisa's story is powerfully motivating in and of itself, but her experience is also scientifically helpful: researchers at the National Institute of Health were monitoring her physiology which allowed them to detect changes in her brain. "One set of neurological patterns, or old habits, had been overridden by new patterns. They could still see the neural activity of her old behaviors, but those impulses were crowded out by new urges. As Lisa's habits changed, so had her brain." (6)

Here are some of the key steps to help you create lasting change as you recover from sexual betrayal:

1. *Accept that there is a problem.*

Upon first discovery, it is common to try and ignore that there is a problem. So an important first step to create change is to accept the truth that a problem does exist. You won't change something if you do not believe it is a problem.

2. *Seek knowledge.*

Most couples get stuck trying to resolve problems using the same methods over and over again. This is perseveration in action. By gathering new information and learning how others have healed, you can discover your own path to healing. In addition, by seeking knowledge, you will be able to identify the best treatment methods available for healing.

3. *Prepare to take action.*

In order to make positive changes in your life, you will need to prepare. Some years ago the head of the Industrial Engineering Department of Yale University said, "If I had only one hour to solve a problem, I would spend up to two-thirds of that hour in attempting to define what the problem is." (7) When you commit to making a change in your life, it is important to understand the problem.

One way you can do this is to ask yourself the following questions:

1) Do I know if my spouse is a sex addict or not? Or have I been focusing on his/her sexual betrayal alone?

2) How have I been responding to my spouse's sexual betrayal?

3) Why have I been responding the way I have?

4) If I could change one behavior that would help me heal, what would it be?

5) What do I need to do to prepare to make lasting changes in my life?

I have found that by thinking through questions like these, you will gain much more insight into your life and the changes that you need to make. (For more questions to ask yourself as you prepare to take action, see Appendix F).

In Lisa's case she made a goal and, over the next year, made the preparations necessary to return to Egypt. She found a better job and paid off debt in order to be financially prepared for the trip. By quitting smoking and picking up running, she prepared her body for the physical challenges of the hike. The preparation stage is very important as it helps us identify the problem and discover new habits.

In later chapters, you will be asked to evaluate personal habits that are slowing your progress. You will also be asked to identify self-beliefs that keep you stuck. As you learn how habits and beliefs are holding you back, you will be better prepared to take action to resolve them.

4. Take action.

Once you are prepared and have learned how to make the right changes, the next step is acting on that preparation and knowledge. A few years ago, I interviewed world-renowned neuroscientist, Dr. Joseph LeDoux. (You can listen to this interview under LeDoux at www.discoverandchange.com/tipsa/audio. I had read Ben Sherwood's book, *The Survivors Club*, where he discussed Dr. LeDoux's response to how Americans responded after 9-11. In the book, Dr. LeDoux describes how we sat on our couches, hour after hour, rewatching those planes fly into the twin towers. Witnessing this tragedy over and over without knowing how to respond led most of us to feel angry and scared. We wanted to stop those planes; we wanted to help the people in need. But in most cases we could do very little to change the outcome.

In my interview, I asked Dr. LeDoux about 9-11 and he stated, "The challenge we faced at that time was that we were stuck not knowing how to respond. So we sat and watched in horror." This is often referred to as learned helplessness. In other words, we became paralyzed. What he said next has stuck with me ever since: "If we are going to move forward after a crisis, we need to get up off our couches, turn off the television, and begin moving forward. By doing this, we are taking back control of our lives."

It is in taking action that we develop a belief that we can change an outcome. In his research, Dr. LeDoux found that when we take action we create entirely new neuropathways in our brains. That is, by taking action when we are stressed or in a crisis, we rewire our brains. In essence, we prove to ourselves through both our behavior and our neurology that we are not stuck and we do have options.

Since that interview many years ago, I have contemplated how transitioning from paralysis into action occurs when inaction has been the norm. I have found that the answer is not to take just any action. Some actions are clearly not as helpful as others. The goal is to take meaningful actions that will help reach the goal; in betrayal trauma, the goal is healing and recovery.

According to Dr. Leach, the goal in any trauma is to get our brains "back online" as quickly as possible. The initial shock of discovery will naturally trigger powerful emotions like elevated anxiety and possibly a hijacked brain. These are the natural fight or flight responses. A good first step in knowing how to respond is to simply understand whether you are in fight, flight, or freeze. Self-awareness can be used to slow down the natural survival responses and create space for clarity as well as purposeful decision making.

The importance of returning to normal cognitive functioning cannot be over-stated. It allows you to reason quickly and accurately. As you become attuned to your own mind, you will begin to see how to respond to your situation with more confidence. My hope is that as you read through the next few chapters, you will gain insight into how you can prepare and take action to create the changes neces-sary for your well-being.

Chapter Summary

This chapter began with Dr. Leech's research on how people respond during a crisis. Three specific approaches were described. In the first group these individu-als remain calm and collected in a crisis. The second and largest group 80% freeze up and experience cognitive paralysis. The third group simply make matters worse. According to Dr. Leech skills can be developed to improve our ability to respond during a crisis.

Because of paralysis, old patterns, the difficulty of breaking old habits, and en-vironmental influences, it can be easy to get stuck. For those who get stuck in an unhelpful trauma response, most likely freezing, there are basic steps to be taken to get unstuck. These include accepting there is a problem, seeking knowledge, preparing to change, and taking action.

In the next five chapters, each of the ways PTSD manifests itself after sexual betrayal will be addressed. The TIPSA provides solid evidence that sexual betray-al triggers symptoms of PTSD. Armed with this knowledge, it is critical that we identify the best solutions for each of the symptoms and create a treatment plan. In essence, knowing how trauma is manifesting itself allows us to help you prepare for what you are most likely to experience (i.e. intense worrying, negative self-be-liefs, rage, etc.). Much like Dr. Leach's crisis survivors, you will learn how to train yourself to respond to sexual betrayal. By doing so, my hope is that you will feel prepared to tackle whatever challenges you may face. I know this is possible as I have witnessed many betrayed spouses begin to take action and experience genuine healing in their lives.

Part Three

Treating Posttraumatic Stress

Chapter Eight

Sexual Betrayal and Sexual Trauma: How Boundaries, Support, and Taking Action Can Help You Heal

Boundaries are not something you "set on" another person. Boundaries are about yourself.

- Henry Cloud and John Townsend

As a therapist, I often hear stories that break my heart. These stories usually include an absence of safety in a marriage due to both sexual betrayal and sexual trauma. There is no safety and often intense fear and terror are present. In situations like these, physical safety in threatened and sexual abuse often occurs.

Two years ago, I received the following email from a woman:

"You are addressing many important issues regarding sexual betrayal in your work, but I wonder if you are aware of the extent of sexual violations that are occurring in married relationships. Some women are being raped by their husbands while others are having to visit emergency rooms because of the painful sexual acts their spouses insisted they perform. Finally, there are others who are forced to ask their medical doctor to test them for STDs because their spouse has been sleeping with prostitutes. I know this is difficult to address, but will you please address these challenges in your presentations so there is more awareness? Many of us women feel like we are alone with these issues."

The issues she outlines in her email address many of the behaviors that fall under Criteria A for PTSD diagnosis in the DSM-5: "The person was exposed to death, threatened death, actual or threatened serious injury, or *actual or threatened sexual violence* (emphasis added)." (1) In the treatment of sexual betrayal and sexual trauma in relationships, Criteria A applies in two ways. The first and most frequently observed is threat to life due to the transmission of sexually transmitted diseases. The second way clinicians see Criteria A present is through partner to partner sexual violence or threat of violence.

If PTSD cannot be diagnosed in relation to sexual betrayal, it is usually because Criteria A is not present. However, each of the other criteria for PTSD (Criteria B: Intrusive thoughts; Criteria C: Avoidance of stimuli; Criteria D: Negative alterations in cognitions and mood; and Criteria E: Alterations in arousal and reactivity) are usually very high when sexual betrayal trauma has occurred. In subsequent chapters, I will identify how each of the other criterion for these trauma symptoms manifest as a result of sexual betrayal, and I will offer specific treatment solutions. This chapter focuses on the symptoms associated with sexual violence or threat of violence that fits Criteria A of PTSD diagnosis.

In the assessment described in Chapter Two, the following questions are provided in relation to Criteria A:

1. Since learning of my partner's behaviors, he/she has hurt, hit, or threatened me.

2. My partner has hurt me while acting out his/her sexual fantasies.

3. My partner threatens to hurt me in some way if I do not comply with his/her sexual fantasies.

4. Due to my partner's sexual behaviors, I have become concerned that I might contract a sexually transmitted disease.

5. I feel violated due to my partner's sexual behaviors.

6. Since learning of my partner's behaviors, I am afraid of my partner.

7. My partner forces me to have sex with him/her.

8. My partner pressures me to perform sexually in ways that are uncomfortable to me (i.e. forced painful sex, being watched while having sex with others, anal sex, sexual domination, being filmed, etc.).

9. I have been physically harmed through sex acts with my partner.

Each of these questions deal directly with Criteria A and are specific to sexual trauma within the relationship. Until I gathered research in this area, I was unsure about the frequency of these behaviors in relationships. After reviewing the data, however, it is clear sexual trauma in relationships that involve sexual betrayal is common. As mentioned in Chapter Two, fear of getting an STD is the most commonly reported concern. Below are the findings from this specific question:

Question: Due to my partner's sexual behaviors, I have become concerned that I might contract a sexually transmitted disease.

Results:

Never	22.66%
Occasionally / Rarely	32.15%
About half the time	14.33%
More often than not	13.82%
Always	17.04%

These findings suggest that, of those who answer this question, roughly 77%, or all of those who chose an option besides "Never," worry about getting a sexually transmitted disease. As I reviewed these results, I looked at how their spouses betrayed them. Participants were able to check multiple boxes. Roughly 51% had experienced multiple affairs in their marriages and 40% reported spouses who had brief sexual encounters with strangers. These sexual behaviors outside of a committed relationship clearly make one vulnerable to contracting a sexually transmitted disease. The betraying partner's behaviors match their spouse's fears.

Another survey question that looks specifically at Criteria A addresses sexual trauma in the relationship through the use of threats:

Question: My partner threatens to hurt me in some way if I do not comply with his/her sexual fantasies.

Results:

Never	86.59%
Occasionally / Rarely	8.20%
About half the time	2.52%
More often than not	2.20%
Always	1.49%

This question addressed sexual trauma in the relationship related to threats. As seen above, this happens much less frequently in relationships than the perceived risk of STDs. However, it does appear that in about 13% of the cases, a partner has threatened to hurt their spouse if they didn't perform their desired fantasy. Due to an increase in both violent pornography and mainstream media that glorifies sexual violence (e.g. *Fifty Shades of Grey*), it may be more culturally acceptable that fantasies become acted out. Let me be clear: experiencing threat of physical harm due to not participating in a fantasy crosses the line and is considered psychological abuse.

If you would like to assess your relationship for the potential of abuse, the *Intimate Justice Scale* by Dr. Brian Jory may offer additional insight. For more information on this scale, please visit the resources section at the end of the book.

Responding to Sexual Trauma in Your Relationship

If you have experienced one or more of the behaviors listed above in your relationship, my research shows that you are also likely to experience other PTSD symptoms such as 1) reliving the experience; 2) avoiding situations, people or places that remind you of what happened, 3) negative cognitions and mood; and 4) intense emotional arousal.

Any combination of PTSD symptoms signal a level of relational safety lost. The first step in your healing is to establish safety for yourself. Specifically, any further experiencing of the sexual traumas described above must be prevented. If you have been dealing with these behaviors for years, you are likely emotionally exhausted and perhaps feel helpless in your ability to create change in your relationship. The rest of this chapter provides critical steps for taking action to protect yourself and potentially see significant changes in your relationship.

It has been my observation that individuals who experience sexual trauma in their relationships are more prone to feel stuck or frozen. Usually, the intensity of sexual trauma in their relationship triggers feelings of helplessness. Therefore, we will first address ideas on how to resolve the sense of helplessness (a frozen state of mind) by learning how to search inside yourself for answers. Second, we focus on helping you create healthy boundaries. And third, we conclude by discussing ideas for how you can find support outside of your relationship and why that step is vital to the healing process.

#1: When You are Frozen and Can't Respond, Look Inside to Protect Yourself.

As mentioned above, if you scored high on the questions in this particular section and have therefore experienced sexual trauma within your relationship, you are most likely more prone to be frozen. This usually happens to individuals who believe that nothing they do will change what their spouse does. This belief can dominate for years, leading to inaction, until finally the sexually traumatizing behaviors can no longer be tolerated. At this point you may have thought to yourself, "Why have I taken so long to take a stand?" When my clients ask me this question, they often follow that question up with, "What is wrong with me? Why have I put up with my spouse's behaviors?" I often respond to these questions by saying something like, "I have been pondering that question for years. I too wonder what it is that keeps individuals just like you from taking a strong stand." Then I reassure them that they are not alone and I share with them why I think this happens as described below.

In watching individuals respond to sexual betrayal, we know that in the beginning they naturally turn to fight, flight, or freeze. However, I have wondered why some people are more likely to stay stuck in fight, flight, or freeze mode while others transition out of these states of mind and move on. I have also wondered why one person becomes stuck in fight mode while another stays stuck in flight or freeze. My conclusion is that we all develop unique coping methods to deal with trauma.

For example, some people use anger because that is how they learned to cope with the stress of trauma. They may have found that their anger is a helpful defense mechanism that prevents their spouse from getting close to them or attempting to get close to them. Their anger is used to keep their spouse at a distance.

In contrast, individuals in flight mode have learned this strategy helps them avoid the pain of difficult situations. Or perhaps they find that by emotionally distancing themselves from their spouse, their partner gives them more attention by chasing after them. By fleeing, they have found an effective way of getting the connection they crave.

I have found that individuals stuck in freeze mode are complex. They are not fighting or fleeing, they are not making decisions or moving in any direction. They are more prone to depression and anxiety. This type of behavior was identified by Dr. Martin Seligman and his colleague Steven Maier in 1967 when they studied how dogs responded to being shocked. The purpose of their study was to understand more about depression, but they also discovered much about what happens when helplessness is present. (2)

"Group 1 dogs were simply put in the harnesses for a period of time and later released. Dogs in Group 2 were given electric shocks at random times, which the dog could end by pressing a lever. Each dog in Group 3 was paired with a Group 2 dog; whenever a Group 2 dog got a shock, its paired dog in Group 3 got a shock of the same intensity and duration, but its lever did not stop the shock. To a dog in Group 3, it seemed that the shock ended at random, because it was his paired dog in Group 2 that was causing it to stop. Thus, for Group 3 dogs, the shock was "inescapable."

"In Part 2 of the experiment, the same three groups of dogs were tested in a shuttle-box apparatus. All the dogs could escape shocks on one side of the box by jumping over a low partition to the other side. The dogs in Groups 1 and 2 quickly learned this task and escaped the shock. Most of the Group 3 dogs, which had previously learned that nothing they did had any effect on shocks, simply lay down passively and whined when they were shocked." (3)

This is a dramatic example of the regression of adjustment responses that typifies learned helplessness. Since Dr. Seligman and Maier's initial discovery regarding learned helplessness, countless other studies have been conducted to better understand how and why this occurs. It is now believed that "learned helplessness is behavior typical of a human or non-human animal that has endured repeated painful or otherwise aversive stimuli which it was unable to escape or avoid. After such experience, the organism often fails to learn escape or avoidance in new situations where such behavior would be effective. In other words, the organism learned that it is helpless in aversive situations, that it has lost control, and so it gives up trying. Such an organism is said to have acquired learned helplessness." (4)(5)

A common manifestation of learned helplessness is immobility. According to Dr. Levine, when fear is coupled with immobility, the lack of ability to move or protect oneself creates deeper trauma. In his book *In an Unspoken Voice*, he shares the findings of an important study: "In a carefully thought-out and well-controlled experiment, the authors (Gordon Gallup and Jack Maser) demonstrated that if an animal is both frightened and restrained, the period during which it remains immobilized (after the restraint is removed) is dramatically increased. There is a nearly perfect linear correlation between the level of fear an animal experiences when it is restrained and the duration of immobility." (6)

While we humans may respond somewhat differently than other animals, Dr. Levine outlines what fear and the inability to act does to us: "While traumatized humans don't actually remain physically paralyzed, they do get lost in a kind of anxious fog, a chronic partial shutdown, dissociation, lingering depression, and numbness. Many are able to earn a living and/or raise a family in a kind of 'functional freeze' that severely limits their enjoyment of life." (7)

As cited in Chapter Four, 85% of surveyed betrayed partners feel, at least half the time, that their partner will never stop acting out; this includes the 40% that always feel like their partner will never stop acting out. That is, nearly half of those surveyed live with the constant belief that they will be further traumatized by their partner's sexual betrayal. If an individual always believes that their spouse will never stop hurting them *and* they are still in the relationship, they are likely emotionally paralyzed and in an anxious fog as described by Dr. Levine above.

If you feel like you are frozen and cannot respond to what your spouse has done, there is hope. Overcoming learned helplessness is possible and can free you to take necessary action to protect yourself. You don't have to feel frozen any longer.

You may be surprised to learn that getting unstuck requires you to turn inside of yourself. Let me explain why this is helpful.

Your Body, Your Beliefs, and Why You've Been Stuck

Throughout this chapter I have shared some of the writings of Dr. Levine, the author of many books and the founder of the Somatic Experience. Through his work, it is clear that individuals trapped in trauma are more likely to heal by attuning to their body sensations. In the book *In an Unspoken Voice*, Dr. Levine shares a powerful example of how he had to do this himself after being hit by a car in an intersection. He shared the process of how he attuned to his body sensations. As he explored his physical experience of responding to being hit by a car he used the following statements, "My body continues to shake and tremble. It is alternately icy cold and feverishly hot. A burning red fury erupts from deep within my belly," and, "I consciously direct myself to go inward. I begin to take stock of my body sensations. This active focusing draws my attention to an intense, and uncomfortable, buzzing throughout my body." (8)

As he attended to these and other inner sensations, he found himself feeling a tension in his left arm. Regarding this he writes, "I let this sensation come into the foreground of my consciousness and track the arm's tension as it builds and builds. Gradually, I recognize that the arm wants to flex up and move up. As this inner impulse toward movement develops, the back of my hand also wants to rotate. Ever so slightly, I sense it moving toward the left side of my face--as though to protect it against a blow. Suddenly, there passes before my eyes a fleeting image of the window of a beige car, and once again--as in a flashbulb snapshot--vacant eyes stare from behind the spiderweb of the shattered window." (9) By carefully tracking and paying attention to what his body was wanting him to do, he realized that his body wanted him to go through the physical motions of protecting himself as though he were in the accident. By going through these motions, he ultimately was able to resolve his trauma.

You can learn to do the same by discovering how certain thoughts, feelings, and emotions are keeping you paralyzed emotionally and/or physically. For example, if you responded that you have felt violated by your spouse's sexual betrayal, the next question I would ask you would be, "Where do you feel this violation in your body?" By attuning to the physical sensation, you may realize that the feeling of being violated is stored in your stomach. As you continue to search inside like Dr. Levine, you discover that you feel upset when you think about what your spouse did. Next, you find yourself getting tense and uptight. Soon, you feel angry at your spouse. However, as you track the anger in your body, you realize that your instinct is to turn it back inside and shut it down. You discover you have internalized the message, perhaps from friends and family or religion and society, that anger is never okay. This has caused your anger to stay stored in your body rather than being healthily expressed. Through further guided exploration of your body sensations, you also learn this message has been reinforced since you were very young. It expands to mean that anger itself is bad and anyone who feels angry is also bad. Paying attention to your physical sensations has helped you discover a belief about anger: I am bad if I am angry.

So how does this belief contribute to keeping you stuck?

When you want to talk with your spouse about something difficult and you start to get angry, the belief that you are bad because you are angry is activated. As a result, you become more tense, which triggers your fear that you are doing something wrong. You quickly shut down your feeling of anger and stop any conversation that could cause conflict. This pattern then becomes the norm for you and anytime you feel internal tension, you shut down because of that internalized belief that it is not okay to experience the emotion of anger. Instead of being able to accept it is normal to experience anger, you believe you are a bad person. You aren't allowed to be angry, yet your natural instinct is to feel anger at times. Anger isn't acceptable and yet it continues to happen, which activates the belief that you are a bad person, which leads to more tension and promotes more anger. You become trapped in a hopeless cycle.

In his work, Dr. Levine has found that as individuals learn to listen to their bodies they begin to understand what physical sensations are teaching them. In this approach, the sensations are not good or bad, rather they are simply sensations designed to help them respond to life.

Let's look at an example of how this works. Imagine that you are able to express your hurt and angry. It is okay to feel anger. Now that it is okay to talk openly, you want to discuss boundaries with your spouse. In the past, the physical feeling associated with fear of becoming angry would shut you down. With your new awareness, instead of being worried about the physical feeling of being upset, you realize anger is there and accept it without judgment. The physical feeling associated with anger no longer prevents you from having this important discussion. Ironically, by allowing yourself to feel the anger, you are less likely to become angry in your conversation.

When I see clients who are frozen, I realize that they will benefit by understanding what their physical sensations are trying to teach them. Sometimes trying to take action like creating boundaries before they have this awareness can be counterproductive. Instead of creating boundaries, they shut down because of the conflict those discussions create with their spouse. Once clients attune to self, they usually discover the underlying beliefs that are guiding their actions (e.g. anger means I am bad). This awareness helps them realize how their physical sensations and feelings have kept them trapped and often creates an internal motivation that drives them to take action.

The steps listed below, from Dr. Levine's book *In An Unspoken Voice,* are designed to help clients respond to physical sensations associated with their trauma.

Step #1: Establish an Environment Where You Can be Calm and Relaxed

If you feel frozen, the first step is to find and create a calm relaxing place even if that place is just in your mind. Effective treatment approaches like Eye Movement Desensitization and Reprocessing therapy (EMDR) and The Somatic Experience both strongly recommend establishing a place of refuge. This is a place where your mind can go to feel safe at anytime. Some people imagine being in the mountains or on a beach. (Note: I have created a short audio exercise to help you find your safe/calm place: www.discoverandchange.com/tipsa/audio).

Additionally, the support and comfort of a safe, trusted person is very helpful. "Such soothing support in the midst of chaos is a *critical* element that trauma therapists must provide for their unsettled and troubled clients." (10) He suggests that the therapist and client first develop a relationship built upon trust before attempting to resolve intense trauma. If you do not have a therapist yet, finding someone who can offer soothing support is a good starting point; they may not know how to help you process through the trauma but they will be able to listen.

Step #2: Support Initial Exploration and Acceptance of Sensation

In the next phase, the challenge is to learn to listen to your inner promptings and feelings. What are these sensations telling you? For a long time, you may have felt something was wrong in your relationship, but you didn't know what. Now you know something is wrong and your instincts were right. But as you think these thoughts, you find yourself upset. You look inside and wonder, "Why is this upsetting me? And where am I feeling it in my body?" As you go inside, you feel yourself becoming tense as you think to yourself, "Why didn't I act sooner?" As you attune to your body, you feel the internal tension rising just because you thought that question. As you explore your sensations, you find that you are mad at yourself for not acting on what you felt a long time ago.

Fortunately, by this point in your healing you have learned to have compassion for yourself, so you comfort yourself by thinking, "Self judgment won't help; in fact, if I'm being kind to myself, I did have inklings that something was wrong. Those were the inner sensations that were telling me something wasn't right. My instincts were intact and correct." As you go through this process, you explore your thoughts, emotions, and physical sensations. Often the sensations will help you identify the thoughts (e.g. "I'm mad at myself for not acting sooner.") and emotions (e.g. anger).

Your task is to learn how to access, tolerate, and utilize your own inner sensations. As you do this, your awareness will increase and your ability to deal with difficult emotions will improve. This is a gradual process that takes time and practice. As you get better at it, you will find that your body sensations offer valuable insight into how you can best respond.

If you have felt frozen, your body can offer ideas on how to actively cope with your trauma. The goal is to learn how to listen to your mind *and* your body. As you heal, you will need to notice more intently what your body is trying to tell you. You will begin to notice shifts in your heart rate, your body posture, and your breathing. By using your senses, you can gain greater insight into what steps you need to take next. Valuable tools for learning how to do this are described in later chapters, where the scientific benefits of using yoga and mindfulness in your healing are discussed.

Step #3: Establish Pendulation and Containment, The Innate Power of Rhythm

While you may not have heard the word pendulation before, the concept will feel familiar. "Pendulation is about the innate organismic rhythm of contraction and expansion. It is, in other words, about getting unstuck by knowing (sensing from the inside), perhaps for the first time, that no matter how horrible one is feeling, those feelings *can and will change.*" (11)

Over the years I have heard many stories from women who in their trauma have entered their closets and cried and cried while they rocked back and forth in an effort to find comfort. Why would this help them? According to Dr. Levine, "one surprisingly effective strategy in dealing with difficult sensations involves helping a person find an "opposite" sensation: one located in a particular area of the body, in a particular posture, or in a small movement, or one that is associated with the person's feeling less frozen." (12) While listening to these women tell their stories of how they rocked until they felt comfort, I realized that they were attempting to self-soothe in their time of need. They were looking to be comforted, and by rocking and crying, they somehow transitioned out of their frozen states.

The process of pendulation is most effectively done when you can contain the trauma. In other words, if you can not contain it, it means that the trauma is overwhelming you. When this happens, it is best to go back to a safe place in your mind. When you are able to explore the pain and then contain it if it becomes too painful, you are pendulating between emotions (pain and safety).

Usually, when you have experienced sexual trauma in your relationship, the painful memories can easily overwhelm your mind. Therefore, being able to contain the pain while processing through it is critical for healing. For this reason, when it comes to dealing with highly traumatizing memories, it is not advisable to explore the depth of your trauma by yourself. When you begin processing your trauma, whether it is from your current relationship or from earlier life experiences, there are important guidelines to follow:

1. Never delve into trauma without first creating a safe, calm place in your mind. It is critical that you first establish a calm place, a place of refuge for your mind to return to when it has gone into the painful experiences of the past. It is best to practice going to a calm place so that you can access that place mentally anytime you need to. Most people tend to find their safe place by thinking about the sounds, feelings, and sights of a beach, mountain, or other beautiful place. (See Appendix G for additional suggestions on how to create a powerful calm place for yourself.)

2. Understand that pendulation is a process of going from a relatively calm place, to a stressful place (the memories or images associated with trauma) and then back to a calm memory or image. If you cannot create a place of mental safety, it is best to wait until you develop the ability to intentionally calm your mind.

3. While processing through trauma, it is best to have someone who can be

by your side to comfort or guide you as you process in and out of your traumatic memories. When individuals are working through trauma, they often need a calming reassurance that things will be okay. A therapist or other mental health professional trained in the treatment of trauma is most helpful.

As you increase your skill and learn to attend to your physical sensations, you will become more comfortable dealing with your own thoughts and emotions. As this happens, you will naturally want to protect yourself from further harm, first through the creation of appropriate boundaries.

#2: Create Healthy Boundaries

In *Mending a Shattered Heart*, a book edited by Stefanie Carnes, Cara W. Tripodi writes, "Boundaries are critical to your recovery from your partner's sexual addiction. You will find that they will become a cornerstone for lifelong change and help to redefine the direction of your life and your relationship to the sex addict." (13)

Regarding the importance of boundaries, Anne Wallace writes in *Setting Psychological Boundaries*, "As we draw invisible boundary lines, we are not building walls to keep the enemy out. On the contrary, we keep our lines intact to preserve our relationships! Once we clearly define our boundaries, we begin to communicate openly and directly. And we establish guidelines for what we expect of others, and what we should give them in return. But if we grow up in homes that don't function well in terms of communication or understanding or enter into destructive marriages, boundaries are not respected and we become confused, vulnerable, and insecure. We don't attempt to defend our rights because we don't realize we have any." (14)

When boundaries break down in relationships, common outcomes include physical, emotional, sexual, psychological, and spiritual abuse. The boundary violations of threatening a spouse with harm if they do not perform a sexual act or forcing one's spouse to have sex are extremely traumatizing. Healing from these types of trauma requires identifying and establishing clear boundaries.

Unfortunately, many of my clients have felt lost, unsafe, and unstable in their relationships because of boundary violations. They have lost their identities and at times question whether they should establish boundaries or not. They are afraid of being abandoned or rejected. Some are afraid of being further hurt. Still others have tried to establish boundaries, but have not been able to maintain their boundaries and feel like failures.

In some situations, implementing boundaries creates an increased risk of abuse. In such situations, it is extremely important to have a safety plan in place to protect yourself and any children involved. If you find that you are not safe, please consider visiting The National Domestic Violence Hotline website (www.hotline.org) and working closely with a therapist who specializes in trauma.

While creating boundaries is not easy, it is truly essential for abusive relationships. It has been my experience that individuals who have experienced sexual trauma in their relationships often wonder if they are doing the right thing by seeking help. To them, I often share the importance of doing *something*. As explored in Chapter Seven and exemplified in the scenario below, research shows us that the deepest form of trauma occurs when we are both stuck *and* do not take action.

Imagine that we had two guinea pigs and tried an experiment with them. With the first guinea pig, we held it and played with it. As we played with it, placed it on its back and let go, it naturally turns over and moves away. With the second guinea pig, we didn't play with it but instead chased it, creating fear. Then as it was trying to escape we grabbed it and placed it on its back. When it was turning over to get back on its legs, we grabbed it again and placed it on its back again. Suppose we did this over and over again. What differences would we see between the first and second guinea pig?

The first guinea pig would most likely not be afraid if we placed it on its back again. However, according to research, the second guinea pig would likely stay on its back much longer. Why does this happen? According to Dr. Levine, "When an animal is purposefully frightened before being captured and/or is repeatedly placed on its back it is more likely to remain paralyzed for longer periods of time. When a fear-induced process is repeated numerous times, the animal remains immobile for a significantly longer period." (15)

So what happens when you feel fear but do not feel like escape or movement is possible? You become much like the second guinea pig, wanting to move but unable to respond. When your natural instinct is to get away or escape, but the person you are afraid of is your spouse, a problem is created. Most likely your internal self is confused. You want to connect and feel safe, but cannot deny the reality of disconnection and fear.

This response is especially common when your spouse continues acting out or when you attempt to help in some way but changes do not occur. You find yourself feeling like no matter what you do, things will not change. According to Dr. Levine, when we are under stress or feeling anxious, our natural instinct is to protect or defend ourselves. He believes that if we cannot act on this instinct or find a way to respond, we are much more likely to become stuck in trauma. When we are not able to move, or if we feel trapped, the chance of us experiencing trauma increases significantly. (16)

There is a good chance that if you have been experiencing sexual trauma and you haven't been able to take action or create lasting change, you are likely stuck in trauma. Change begins with establishing boundaries. By creating boundaries, you are taking necessary action to reclaim your identity. "In recognizing and respecting our boundaries, we affirm ourselves, our rights in all our relationships, and the rights of others. When we fail to defend ourselves, when we fail to stand up for ourselves under attack, we lose some treasured part of ourselves: our integrity, belief in ourselves, the real 'I' at the core of the inner self, and each time this is a little death. And when we fail to respect the rights of others, we inflict losses, large and small, that may shake the core of the lives of all we touch." (17)

By creating healthy boundaries, your sense of self worth begins to increase because you are being proactive in your healing, respecting yourself, and respecting others. Therefore, one of the most important early steps to your healing is establishing boundaries.

Different Types of Boundaries

As a therapist dealing with sexual addiction and betrayal trauma, I am often asked about boundaries. The questions range from, "How do I create boundaries?" to "What is a good boundary if my spouse has…" Over the years my understanding of boundaries has changed due to continually changing circumstances. For example, when I first began working with individuals dealing with pornography and sexual addiction, there weren't smart phones with dating apps or websites that promote having affairs. Today there are countless opportunities for people to act out. This means that when partners create boundaries, they have to be clear about their expectations and consider addressing the use of technology so there is no misinterpretation.

When creating boundaries, it is important to understand that there are different types of boundaries. You may need to set different boundaries for different purposes. Below are the four types to consider:

Deal Breakers

Most people don't begin a relationship expecting that they will need to consider what they will and won't accept from their partner. As a result, most people have not thought through what they would do if their spouse cheats on them, pays a prostitute for sex, or visits a topless bar. Therefore, when sexual betrayal occurs, they are usually left scrambling with no idea of how to respond. They thought certain things were simply understood and are unprepared to act after the betrayal.

In an effort to help you take more control of your life, it is important to think through this process in order to feel prepared if something like this happens again. The first boundary you will want to consider with sexual betrayal is what we refer to as "deal breakers." A deal breaker is something that you absolutely will not tolerate in your relationship and if it does occur, you will take action by terminating the relationship. Remember you cannot change the past, but you can be clear about your expectations for the future.

One way to do this is to spend some time thinking about what you will and will not accept in your relationship. It is important that you really think through your deal breakers. For example, while most people may think to themselves, "I will never tolerate infidelity in my relationship," a majority of relationships do not initially end when infidelity occurs. Most people say they would leave right away, yet most people initially stay. It is important to give serious thought to your deal breaker boundaries so you can do what you say you will do (e.g. leave if there is another affair, etc.).

Do you have an idea of what your deal breakers may be? If not, here are a few. Please remember that other people's deal breakers do not have to be your own. It is vital that you look inside of yourself and identify what *you* absolutely can and cannot live with.

Examples of potential deal breakers:

- I won't accept you having another affair. If you cheat on me again, I will end our marriage.

- If you choose to contact or visit a prostitute, I will file for divorce.

- If you choose to meet a random person you do not know for a sexual encounter, I will file for divorce.

- If you try to force me to have sex with you, I will end our marriage.

When trust is completely eroded through sexual betrayal or sexual trauma, the way to create change is through protecting yourself. This will require that you do hard things. Identifying your deal breakers is an important, if difficult, first step.

Note: If you are in a physically abusive relationship where you fear for your overall safety and well-being, please seek outside support to help you establish a plan of action. In some situations, there are times when it is best to keep your deal breakers to yourself and not share them with your spouse for safety reasons. If your spouse does the deal breaker, the next step is to enact your safety plan (e.g. staying with a family member, calling the police, going to a shelter, etc.).

<u>Physical Boundaries</u>

When sexual betrayal occurs in a relationship, it is common for the betrayed spouse to loathe being close to their spouse. When their spouse enters the room, their stomach turns over. They feel stress in various locations throughout their body. Usually, they simply want as much physical distance from their spouse as they can get. These intense negative feelings may be fleeting or they may last for an extended period of time.

When you feel a strong desire to avoid being around your spouse, it is important to pay close attention to what your body is telling you. In all likelihood, you want space away from him because his presence triggers intense negative emotions (e.g. anger, rage, disgust, etc.). These are fight emotions. So instead of fighting, your body is asking you to flee, get away as fast as you can!

Boundaries are paramount to physical and emotional safety. Imagine that you are in a jungle with tigers. You are by yourself and have nothing to defend yourself with. Your natural instinct is to be as quiet as you can as you listen for threatening movements. As you go about trying to find food, you are cautious and on high alert. This type of environment offers no boundaries and your mind and body are constantly hypervigilant and hyperaware. No breaks from scanning your surroundings with all five senses. Eventually, this becomes exhausting and you wear down.

The purpose of physical boundaries is to put up a wall to protect yourself from the tigers. By so doing, you are giving yourself a chance to relax and rest. You are also able to do other things like enjoy a meal, talk with friends, or get sleep at night. You can begin thinking about other things beside your safety. Your creative juices can start flowing again.

If being around your spouse feels like being in a jungle teeming with tigers, creating physical boundaries will be a valuable step for you in the healing process. By establishing concrete physical boundaries, you are providing yourself an environment where you can focus on healing your mind and body.

Here are a few examples of physical boundaries:

- If you continue to view pornography, I will ask you to sleep downstairs for a week.

- If you try touching or fondling me, I will ask you sleep on the couch.

- If you come into the bathroom while I am showering, I will ask you to give me physical space for the rest of the day.

- If you touch me when we are in bed, I feel uncomfortable. If you choose to try and touch me, I will ask you to sleep somewhere else.

When physical boundaries are established, two things need to be present. The first is physical space. You will see in the examples above that the request provides physical distance between partners (e.g. sleeping in different rooms). The second is a time limit on the consequence (e.g. one week sleeping downstairs, or physical space for the rest of the day). Boundaries are more effective if they include specific space and time requests.

Emotional Boundaries

As I have observed couples in the aftermath of sexual trauma, I have discovered significant emotional turmoil in their relationships. Usually, both partners struggle to regulate their emotions. As a result, conflict and tension abound. As the emotional climate becomes tense, couples engage in a harmful dance. Usually, there is blaming, denying, anger, and fighting. As mentioned in Chapter Three, denial, deception, and blame are common.

The purpose of setting emotional boundaries is to reduce conflict and avoid engaging in conversations that involve crazy making behaviors (e.g. deception and gaslighting). Common emotional boundary violations include 1) continually hiding behaviors and denying them (crazy making), 2) minimizing one's actions, 3) badgering the partner, and 4) what I call "Eeyore" behaviors, which include playing the victim and verbally shaming one's self. When these behaviors are used in relationships, the betrayed spouse feels like they are in an emotional war zone. It is hard to heal when the emotional climate is so unstable.

When individuals use any one of these techniques to get what they want, their spouse generally feels resentful. For example, one client described it this way: "I would tell my spouse I didn't want to have sex. He would say, 'Okay,' and I would think he understood. Then a few minutes later I would walk by him and he would say, 'Are you sure?' I would say, 'No. I already told you I don't want to.' Then he would give me the silent treatment for hours. He would walk around all sad and melancholy. Eventually, he would wear me down and I would give in because it was the only thing that got him to stop. I end up resenting myself each time I give in."

Emotional boundaries are set because unhealthy behaviors are brought out into the light. Any form of minimizing behavior is openly discussed. Any denial has a consequence. Badgering is not allowed. And when Eeyore comes out, he won't be attended to.

By establishing emotional boundaries, it is easier for you to reduce the number of unhealthy dance moves you make in your relationship.

Here are some examples of emotional boundaries:

- When you deny your behaviors and lie to me, even about non-sexual matters, it breaks my trust and makes me question whether I can trust anything you are saying. As a result, if you hide behaviors from me I will not trust you and won't want to be close to you. I will ask you to not expect me to be close to you when you violate this boundary. I will need my space for a day or two.

- When you are mopey, I feel like you are trying to manipulate me into giving into what you want. When you do this, I don't want to be close to you. So please understand when you are mopey, I am not going to give in. My boundary will be to call you on it each time I see you this way and then let you decide if you want to talk to me about what you are feeling.

- When you badger me for sex, I am going to ask you to go sleep somewhere else in the house. I can't relax and sleep well when I feel like you are hovering over me. I need to feel safe in my own bed.

Sexual Boundaries

Pia Mellody and her colleagues writ the following in *Facing Love Addiction*, write the following regarding boundaries: "I have the right to control distance and touch with you, and you have the same right to do so with me." (18) This applies to distance and touch in both sexual and non-sexual ways. Boundaries are important in general, and the ability to create personal physical safety is vital for all people; in relationships where sexual trauma has occurred, a sexual boundary is especially critical.

Many people in relationships rationalize that because they are married, they "have to" engage in sexual behaviors with their spouse, as if it were a duty they signed up for on their wedding day. Others believe it is their right to have sex with their spouse no matter what. These beliefs are myths and operating from them often leads to boundary violation and the destruction of safety, both emotional and physical. Under no condition should any individual be or feel forced to have sex against their will.

There is no more vulnerable position than that of engaging in sexual intercourse. We are sexual beings and our bodies are designed to experience that vulnerability and enjoy the sexual experience. However, if sexual boundaries have been violated, fear can override the system and sex may become painful and emotionally difficult. "This active inhibition of motor activity [relaxing during intercourse] optimally occurs in humans, not in a state of terror or fear but in a state defined by safety and trust of the mate. If trust and safety do not characterize the period of copulation, intercourse may be painful and produce tissue damage." (19)

The importance of safety during sexual relations may be best explained in the book *Ina May's Guide to Childbirth* in which Ina May Gaskins outlines the Sphincter Law. According to Gaskins:

1. Excretory, cervical, and vaginal sphincters function best in an atmosphere of intimacy and privacy; for example, a bathroom with a locking door or a bedroom where interruption is unlikely or impossible.

2. These sphincters cannot be opened at will and do not respond well to commands (such as "Push!" or "Relax!").

3. When a person's sphincter is in the process of opening, it may suddenly close down if that person becomes upset, frightened, humiliated, or self-conscious. Why? High levels of adrenaline in the bloodstream do not favor (sometimes, they actually prevent) the opening of the sphincter.

4. The state of relaxation of the mouth and jaw is directly correlated to the ability of the cervix, the vagina, and the anus to open to full capacity. (20)

These four core ideas make it clear that safety is the foundation of true sexual intimacy in relationships. We naturally open up when we feel safe and we close down both physically and emotionally when we don't. If we attempt to override this protective response, usually painful experiences occur.

Over the past few years, I have taught many classes regarding betrayal trauma. One of the most common questions revolves around sex; most women asking the question express their frustrations with sex. Many wonder whether it is okay for them to establish sexual boundaries. As aforementioned, if they have grown up in homes where boundaries have been violated, there is a good chance that the very idea of establishing boundaries feels strange. This sense of uncertainty often transfers into their relationship and they end up being sexual when they don't actually want to. This can trigger feelings of self-doubt as well as a belief that they are unable to protect themselves. When this occurs in relationships, I often hear clients say, "I feel like a prostitute when we have sex," or, "I hate myself for giving in and having sex when he pressures me." These feelings will keep a person feeling stuck, and without upholding sexual boundaries, this inability to move forward will likely remain.

If you have questions about establishing sexual boundaries in marriage, it is a good idea to start asking yourself questions. For example, you might ask yourself something like, "What is happening inside of me when we are being sexual?" Or,

"What happens in our relationship if I ask that we don't have sex for a while?" Or, "Do I want to establish a sexual boundary?" When I ask clients to think through these questions, they often come up with other questions. As an example, one client said, "I thought having sex after his affair would make things better, but when it didn't improve our relationship, I wanted to set boundaries. Then I wondered if that would just make matters worse. I guess I'm just confused." It has been my experience that when individuals establish strong boundaries with clear expectations and still communicate a desire for connection, positive outcomes are possible.

Here's an example of what that might sound like, "I thought after your affair that being sexual with you would help you choose me, but after a while I realized that it didn't matter if we were having sex or not. As a result, I would like to ask that we stop having sex until you are clear that you want to choose me and our relationship. I have enjoyed our sex life and I still love you, but right now I don't feel safe being that vulnerable with you. I hope you will honor my request until you can fully commit to me in your actions."

As I talk with clients, I try to emphasize that boundaries are not for control, they are for safety. It is important to remember that you always have rights in your relationships and you need never be forced to do something you do not want to do. When I communicate the value of establishing safety, clients often ask me what types of boundaries are normal.

Here are examples of some common sexual boundaries:

- I want you to stop touching me in a sexual way without my permission. It feels degrading to me and I feel like an object. If you continue to touch me in sexual ways without my consent, I will not be able to rebuild my trust in you. The consequence of that will be that we won't be able to heal our marriage. I would like things to work out, but I won't accept that behavior any more.

- If you have a sexual affair with anyone again, I will file for divorce and end our relationship.

- If you can't respect my desire to not be sexual with you in the ways you want, I will not feel comfortable having sex with you at all. I feel uncomfortable with your fantasy sex. If you choose to push me to act in ways I don't want to, I will not be able to trust you. I want to trust you again someday, but right now any form of pushing me will put a distance between us.

Notice that, in these examples, the established boundaries come with explanations and are not just the behavior they are asking their spouse to stop, but also the end consequences. There are clear and specific statements such as, "I will not be able to trust you," and, "I would like things to work out." There are specific reasons for why the behavior is being asked to end ("I feel like an object," and, "I feel uncomfortable."), and both the behavioral consequences (e.g. the marriage will end) and emotional consequences (e.g. trust will be lost) are clearly outlined. There is also hope and vulnerability: "I want to trust you again some day," and, "I would like things to work out."

I have found this type of clear and open communication is most effective. The explanations add clarity to why the boundary is being established, what happens if the boundary is violated, and the spouse's desired goal in setting the boundary.

Finally, a commonly held but not commonly discussed difficulty behind establishing sexual boundaries is the sex drive of betrayed spouses themselves. Many women have told me, "It isn't fair. He goes and looks at porn and masturbates and then can't perform or have sex with me. He is turning to pornography instead of me." After hearing this from enough women I began wondering how often this really happens in relationships. So in my blog on Psychology Today, I asked readers whose partners were involved in pornography about their sex life and use of pornography in their relationship. Since posting that blog, over 4000 people have responded. The question I posed regarding pornography and sex in their relationship was:

Which statement best describes your sexual relationship before pornography became a part of your relationship.

<u>Responses</u>

I was satisfied with our relationship.	58.84%	n = 1653
My partner wanted sex more than I did.	18.21%	n = 539
I wanted sex more than my partner did.	25.95%	n = 768

As I looked at the results above, I was caught off-guard when I saw that almost 26% reported that they wanted sex more than their partner did. It was also surprising that nearly 60% were satisfied with their sexual relationship before they discovered their partner's use of pornography. For so long, many proponents of pornography have argued that individuals turn to pornography because they are not getting enough sex. And yet, in my research, I discovered that nearly 83% felt good about their relationship or wanted more sexual relations with their partner.

Even more revealing was what happened when I asked those viewing pornography what their sex life was like before the discovery of pornography in their relationship. They reported the following:

I was satisfied with our relationship.	46.22%	n = 306
My partner wanted sex more than I did.	12.69%	n = 84
I wanted sex more than my partner did.	41.09%	n = 272

While 41% reported that they wanted sex more than their partner, a surprising 46% were satisfied with sex in their relationship. If we combine those who were satisfied with those whose spouse wanted more sex we discover that in nearly 60% of the cases, individuals cannot claim they are turning to pornography because of a bad sex life.

In an effort to dispel the myth that people turn to pornography because of their lack of sex, I often discuss these findings at conferences. The more I talk about it, the more I find people want to talk about pornography and how it influences their sex life. It is a hot topic. After my presentations, I have many people come up and ask me about establishing sexual boundaries if their spouse is acting out. I am often asked questions like, "If I hold a boundary and we stop being sexual, will he just keep acting out?" and, "Will it be my fault?" What is often not said but felt is the question, "What about my own sexual needs?"

Seldom do we discuss the sex drive of the betrayed spouse. Primarily because it is assumed that their trauma prevents them from wanting to have sex. What is missed in this perception is that even with trauma, individuals still have a sex drive. They may not trust their partner, but in many instances, they still long for this type of human connection.

So what's the answer? I wish there were an easy response, but there isn't. When my clients or others ask me questions regarding boundaries and their sexual relationship, I usually end up by asking them a few more questions. My hope is that by answering my questions they will be able to increase their personal understanding of their relationship and identify how to respond. The following questions seem to be effective in helping clarify sexuality and boundaries in their relationships:

1. How will your relationship change if you are or are not sexual?

2. What would abstinence for 30, 60, or 90 days do to you and your relationship?

3. Would establishing sexual boundaries help you heal? If so, what specific boundaries do you feel you need to establish?

4. Would your spouse criticize you if you established a boundary?

5.   How would you feel about yourself if you created sexual boundaries?

By answering these questions my clients often gain a better understanding about themselves and their relationship.

#3: Find Support Outside of Your Relationship

One of the biggest challenges you may be facing is knowing where to find meaningful support. While talking with a betrayed spouse, I often find that they have not told many people what is happening in their relationship because they are trying to protect their spouse. In many cases, they are also embarrassed by what their spouse has done and are afraid of how their family and friends might respond. They have begun to believe that they are different from the people around them in their everyday lives. Sadly, they have begun to lose trust in others. They start to wonder if they can trust even their closest family and friends. This isolation is excruciating, but the pain and suffering can be lessened by giving it a voice.

After observing this process in many betrayed spouses, it became clear that it was a common trauma response. Therefore, I included the following question in the TIPSA: "After what my partner has done, I feel like it is hard to trust anyone." Over 52% indicated that they "always" felt that way. Combined with those who felt this way "at least half the time," an astounding 90% of those surveyed found it difficult to trust at most times.

This information provided me solid evidence that when trust in a spouse and people in general is lost, individuals become more isolated and lonely. They have temporarily lost the ability to detect whether they are safe in any given situation. Dr. Porges refers to this as faulty neuroception: "From a theoretical perspective, faulty neuroception — that is, an inability to detect accurately whether the environment is safe or another person is trustworthy — might lie at the root of several psychiatric disorders." (21)

While sexual trauma is always difficult, learning to reconnect with others is one of the most important and helpful steps you can take as you begin the healing process. My research made it clear that keeping sexual trauma to yourself will likely create feelings of self-doubt, make you question your overall safety, and trigger fear around trusting everyone around you.

In interviewing individuals who experienced sexual trauma in their relationship, I have found that shame is one of their biggest fears; they fear that others will judge them for not taking action earlier and wonder how others will see them if they disclose what is happening in their marriages. Shame and embarrassment often prevent these individuals from seeking necessary support.

Learning how to trust again is a slow process that takes time. Fortunately, there are things that can be done to facilitate the healing process, as illustrated in Janine's story below:

Janine had experienced years of a painful marriage. She introduced herself to me after one of my presentations on betrayal trauma, saying, "You are the first person who seems to understand what I have been going through." As I came to know Janine, she shared her story. Her husband had been unfaithful to her many times throughout their marriage. He had often blamed her for his actions by saying, "If you would have sex with me more often I wouldn't have to turn elsewhere." She responded by being more sexual with him, but his behaviour didn't change.

After years of playing his games, the pain of betrayal and isolation became overwhelming for Janine. She felt as if she was slowly dying inside. She had hidden her turmoil from others, and, although those close to her knew something was wrong, she never opened up and talked with anyone. Finally, when things were the worst for her, she spoke to an old friend who had reached out to her. Janine reluctantly shared what was happening in her marriage. It was her friend that encouraged her to attend my workshop.

Over the next few months, she realized how deeply she was lost. She hadn't noticed how little she trusted others. She had lost her playful and fun self. As I heard her story, I discovered that she had been dealing with her husband's sexual betrayal for more than twenty years. It is hard to imagine carrying that type of pain by herself for twenty years, but Janine had done it. Fortunately, the more she talked, the more she found she wanted to talk. Through her voice, Janine's pain and suffering were finally coming out.

We helped her build a support team around her. She continued talking with her old friend. She came to professional counseling and began attending a group similar to S-Anon (a 12-step recovery program for those who have been affected by someone else's sexual behavior). While it was difficult for her to participate in group, she found valuable support there. In particular, one woman's story really resonated with her. Over the next few weeks and months, Janine developed a meaningful friendship with this group member. She began creating clear boundaries with her husband. In this case, he responded as she gained strength. He started therapy and began his long recovery process.

Not all cases turn out this way. I have seen instances when the betrayed spouse gains strength and decides they cannot continue in the relationship. I have also seen cases where the betraying spouse responds poorly to the creation of boundaries and the marriage ends.

The key changes in Janine's life were: a) a friend who she confided in; b) getting more information by registering for a seminar; c) attending therapy; d) participating in a recovery group, and e) creating a close connection with another member of her group, who became her sponsor and supported her tremendously.

If you are struggling with finding helpful social support, I encourage you to complete the following exercise:

Imagine that you could say anything to a friend about what you're experiencing in your marriage. As you think about what you would say, write it down. What would you want to say? What would be the hardest thing or most embarrassing thing for you to share with them? What would you hold back and never reveal? As you write this letter, you are beginning to give a voice to your pain.

Once you have completed this letter, find someone you trust to share it with. This may take time and that is okay. Since your trust in others is likely low, it is okay to spend time identifying whom you might want to trust with your story. Sometimes a good starting place is a therapist who understands betrayal trauma, specifically someone with one or both of the following credentials:

1. Certified Sexual Addiction Therapists (CSATs) attend an extra 120 hours of training and are required to complete another 30 hours of supervision. This extensive training prepares them to deal with some of the most difficult cases surrounding sexual addiction and betrayal trauma.

2. The Association of Partners of Sex Addicts Trauma Specialists (APSATS) specialize in working with sexual betrayal. This organization trains and certifies Certified Clinical Partner Specialists (CCPS) and Certified Partner Coaches (CPC) who subscribe to a developing treatment model that acknowledges and responds to the traumatic stress found in partners affected by sex addiction.

If you have been holding your pain in, please consider reaching out for support. It will not be easy; it can empower you to create the changes necessary for healing. Remember that it is inaction that keeps us in trauma and by taking action you can begin the process of moving out of trauma.

Chapter Summary

Sexual trauma within a relationship (such as fear of contracting an STD, threats regarding sexual behavior, or threatening sexual behavior) meets the diagnostic requirements described in Criteria A of PTSD diagnosis in the DSM-5. In order to heal from such trauma and become unstuck, action must be taken. Becoming familiar with your own physical sensations can help you look inward and ascertain your emotional needs; once those needs are known, it is easier to identify which specific actions need to be taken. It then feels possible to take action and become unstuck. One of the most important actions to take early in recovery is the establishment of boundaries. Physical, emotional, and sexual boundaries need to be placed in order to recreate safety for yourself. Because boundary setting and holding can be difficult, establishing and utilizing a support network is vital.

In the next chapter, we discuss how to respond when your mind gets stuck and it feels impossible to think about anything besides what your spouse has done.

Chapter Nine

Healing Painful Memories

Ultimately, healing is an inside job.

Mark Wolynn

A few years ago, I interviewed neuroscientist Dr. Joseph LeDoux and asked him about some of his recent research findings. (1) He had just published a paper outlining his research that illustrated the possibility that we may be able to erase memories. While he doesn't advocate memory erasing as a treatment model, he does believe it is possible.

It is likely that you, as the reader of a book about sexual betrayal, would love to erase some of the memories that run continuously through your mind. If you are like most, you relive what your spouse has done over and over in your head. The memories come both day and night. They come when you are with your friends or family. They come when you are trying to pay attention to others. Often, these memories will simply not stop wreaking havoc. One woman described it this way: "D-day was 8 years ago, and we divorced last year, but I still can't wrap my brain around what he did, how he treated me, how he still treats me...Six years after d-day I started planning my divorce because I couldn't take it anymore, but he's still in my head everyday...him and the pain he caused. I struggle to let go."

One of the primary symptoms of PTSD is recurrent, involuntary, and intrusive memories as described in Criteria B under PTSD diagnosis in the DSM-5. In the trauma assessment from Chapter Two, you were asked questions related to intrusive memories.

There are nine total questions in that category; they address the key intrusive symptoms outlined in the DSM-5:

1. Since discovering my partner's behaviors, I can't look at him without

thinking about them. ✓

2. I have strong memories that remind me of my partner's participation in sexually inappropriate behaviors.

3. I have disturbing dreams that remind me of my partner's sexual problems.

4. When my partner tries to get close to me or we are sexually intimate, I cannot help but question whether my partner is thinking about me or things he/she has done.

5. I have episodes where I feel like I am reliving the event over and over again.

6. I have a hard time with media because so many things remind me of what my partner has done.

7. I have a hard time being in public places with my partner because I have become highly sensitive to what my partner is looking at.

8. Since discovering my partner's behavior, when I see sexually suggestive images, I feel anxious.

9. If I am exposed to things that remind me of what my partner has done, I suddenly become physically ill (i.e., nausea, headaches, anxiety).

Note: To see the results from more than 1400 research participants regarding the questions above, please visit www.discoverandchange.com/tipsa/assessment and view the "Criteria B Results."

When you can't get obsessive thoughts out of your mind, you eventually wear down. It becomes hard to think about anything else besides what your spouse has done. What used to be creative thinking and enjoyable memories have morphed into unwelcome intrusive thoughts.

When Courtney came to my office, she was visibly upset. She hadn't been sleeping or eating well for months. She was struggling to stay focused at work because she wondered what her husband, Adam, was doing at his job. Six months earlier she had discovered that he had been having an emotional affair with a co-worker. He still worked with this person and Courtney constantly worried about him. Two weeks before Courtney came to my office, her husband finally disclosed that he had done more than just have an emotional affair. He had been having a sexual affair for the past six months.

Every evening for months she would ask Adam about his day and inquire if he had talked with the other woman. She would often ask for more information about what had happened with his co-worker. By the end of the evening, they hadn't talked about much else and they were both upset. Since his recent disclosure, Courtney had even started dreaming about Adam and the other woman. She couldn't get away from her own thoughts.

By the time she came to my office, she had been dealing with her obsessive and intrusive thoughts for months, but the past two weeks had been especially difficult. After discovering the emotional affair, they had sought help for their marriage, but that hadn't helped her stop obsessing. They were trying to work through some marital difficulties, but she still had a lot of questions. Was this the first time this had occurred? Had he engaged in other sexual behaviors outside of their relationship? She had felt something was wrong in their marriage for years, but she couldn't figure out what. When she first discovered his emotional affair, she began wondering if there was even more to the story.

She began asking him about his past behaviors in their marriage. He denied that there was more, but she felt he was holding back. After months of asking and during the big disclosure two weeks earlier, he admitted that he had been viewing pornography throughout most of their ten years of marriage. He also confessed that he had been to a few topless bars and had once hired a prostitute. She was devastated. The initial shock had not worn off when I first met her.

I helped Courtney understand that in the beginning phase of discovery, it is very common to have intrusive memories come both day and night. They will come when you are trying to focus on other things or when you are talking to someone else. They will invade nearly every part of your thoughts. I emphasized that this is normal in the immediate aftermath of discovery.

"How do I get rid of these thoughts?" she wanted to know.

My response to her and to all who ask this question is below.

Steps to Reducing Intrusive Thoughts

Step #1: Obsessive thoughts will come; this is a normal response to the abnormal situation you've found yourself in. The challenge is learning to actively respond to these thoughts rather than become overwhelmed by them.

In *White Bears and Other Unwanted Thoughts,* Daniel Wagner suggests that when we have thoughts that we do not want, we usually attempt to suppress these thoughts by saying things to ourselves like, "Don't think about that," or, "Stop thinking that." He has found that when we tell ourselves not to think of something, we actually bring more attention to the thing we don't want to think about. In other words, if you tell your mind not to do something, it usually will. As an example, try to not think about a white bear in your living room. According to Wagner, if I left you alone for five minutes, you would think about a white bear in your living room five to seven times in that short period of time. We focus on what we try to suppress; the effort to suppress not only doesn't work, it is counterproductive.

Instead, Wagner believes that our best strategy to deal with our unwanted thoughts is to distract ourselves with healthy behaviors and thoughts. By distracting ourselves, we shift our attention somewhere else and essentially take control of how we are going to think. While suppression is the most common response, it is far more effective to acknowledge the intrusive thoughts and then shift our attention to other matters. For some individuals, this is a great starting point. However, many of my clients say to me that it doesn't matter how they distract themselves, nothing seems to work. Keep in mind this is only the first step.

Step #2: Openly Acknowledge the Unwanted Thought

When I taught Courtney about acknowledging the obsessive thoughts rather than suppressing them, she asked, "Are you telling me to think more about these freaking thoughts? The last thing I want to do is focus on them." "Let me clarify," I responded. "You're going to have the thoughts whether you want them or not. All I'm asking you to do is acknowledge them. For example, you might imagine that the thought is a twig and when it comes you simply say, 'Hi, thought. I acknowledge you are here. Now I am going to imagine you floating down a river and around a bend and out of sight.'" The challenge, I told Courtney, is to not avoid the thought, because it is going to come. That cannot be changed. What can be changed is how she responds to it. This simple exercise allows for the thought to come, be acknowledged, and let float down and away from your mind.

Courtney protested, "Knowing my mind, it will keep coming back."

I replied, "It might, and that's normal. It wants to come back because it wants you to solve the problem. You see, your mind is a problem solver, and it cannot figure this problem out. As a result, it keeps analyzing, thinking about it, wondering what if, and asking why?" I explained to her that our minds get stuck in any memories that are not resolved. When your mind cannot integrate a memory, it continues to focus on it until it finds a solution.

"So, what is the solution?" Courtney asked.

The solution is to create real change, as outlined below.

Step #3: Identify Five Whys

The next step to slowing down your racing mind actually comes from Taiichi Ohno, pioneer of the Toyota Production System in the 1950's. Here's what Toyota

Motor Corporation wrote about the process created by Ohno: "We come across problems in all sorts of situations in life, but, according to Taiichi Ohno, 'Having no problems is the biggest problem of all.' Ohno saw a problem not as a negative, but, in fact, as a kaizen (continuous improvement) opportunity in disguise. Whenever one cropped up, he encouraged his staff to explore problems first-hand until the root causes were found. "Observe the production floor without preconceptions," he would advise. "Ask 'why' five times about every matter." (2)

I have found this technique to be one of the most helpful for my clients when they don't understand their own actions. This is the process I use when clients are stuck in obsessive emotional patterns. Here's how it worked with Courtney:

I began by asking her to identify her most common intrusive thoughts by writing them on a piece of paper. I gave her one minute to write them down. Within a minute she had a list of seven thoughts. Next, I asked her to choose the top three that were most intrusive. Once she identified the three most frequent, I asked her to identify the one most intrusive thought.

She thought for a minute and said, "If there is one thought that keeps running through my mind the most, it is when I imagine him with her eating lunch together at a local restaurant. That restaurant is one that we used to enjoy together. I can't think of that restaurant anymore without feeling nauseous. The image of him and her sitting down talking and laughing together keeps playing in my mind."

Usually, this exercise helps my clients identify not only the most frequent thoughts, but also the most painful or disturbing. In this case, Courtney's facial expression and quivering voice made it clear that she was in a lot of pain as she recalled that thought. I told Courtney that each time that image played in her mind, her body would naturally release anxiety- or fear-based hormones in her body.

She asked, "Is that why I feel flushed and easily upset when I just think about it?" I let her know her physiological and emotional response makes perfect sense given what she's been through and shared the following information with her:

"Some of the hormones involved during the state of fight-or-flight include epinephrine, which regulates heart rate and metabolism as well as dilates blood vessels and air passages, and norepinephrine, which increases heart rate, blood flow to skeletal muscles, and the release of glucose from energy stores. (3)

After a situation which incites fear (or anxiety) occurs, the amygdala and hippocampus record the event through synaptic plasticity. The stimulation to the hippocampus will cause the individual to remember many details surrounding the situation. Plasticity and memory formation in the amygdala are generated by activation of the neurons in the region. Experimental data supports the notion that synaptic plasticity of the neurons leading to the lateral amygdala occurs with fear conditioning. In some cases, this forms permanent fear responses such as posttraumatic stress disorder (PTSD) or a phobia. (4,5,6, 7)

"Okay," Courtney said, "If I understand this right you are saying that my brain is reliving this because of fear and when I experience things that remind me of what happened, my body releases stress hormones again and that is why I am reliving this." I replied, "Now our next step is to help you make sense of the specific thoughts and in the next exercise I will help you do this."

I then guided Courtney through identifying Five Whys regarding the specific image of her husband eating with another woman. "Okay. We have identified one of your most painful and intrusive memories. Let's ask your mind why that memory is so painful."

Why #1

She thought for a while and said, "I think what makes what he did so painful is that he took a place that had such special meaning to me and shared it with another woman."

"Okay," I replied, "Let's try to identify why that is so important to your mind."

Why #2:

She thought for another few seconds and said, "We have had our problems throughout the years, but having an emotional affair with someone makes me question if he has ever been committed to me."

"Good. Now let's look at what it means to your mind if he wasn't ever committed to you."

Why #3:

"Hmm." She said out loud. It was almost as if she was doing this process on her own. She said, "If he is not committed to me, how could I have missed it? Is there something wrong with me?"

"Now you are getting it. If you missed it and there is something wrong with you, why does that matter to your mind?"

Why #4:

This time it took a little longer. She thought for a while and said, "If I couldn't see what he was doing, there must be something wrong with me. I must be stupid to not have seen it."

"Okay. You have hit a belief that comes from his emotional affair. Maybe the core pain has to do with feeling stupid for not seeing it. Let's ask one more why to see if this is it."

Why #5:

Her initial response was, "I think that's it. How stupid could I be?" But then she thought for a minute and said, "I am not sure that's the only thing about what he did that bothers me. I thought we had something special and now I feel like I really didn't matter to him. I'm just not important. It wasn't just his emotional affair. He had sex with a prostitute. He has been lying our whole marriage. I really am just not that important to him."

At that point she had hit her core pain, and she began crying.

By following this simple process, we slowed down her mind so that she could identify the root of her pain. When individuals gain insight into their core beliefs ("I'm stupid," and, "I'm not important."), the issues that need to be addressed in therapy become clear. In Chapter Eleven, I will discuss another strategy that can be used to identify negative self-beliefs. One of the most effective tools in recovery from trauma is the therapeutic processing of painful beliefs. It has been my experience that when key core beliefs are worked through, traumatic responses such as intrusive thoughts are significantly reduced.

After working through her whys, Courtney slowly stopped crying, looked up, and said, "I didn't realize I believed that about myself. I had never thought about those things. Now what do I do?"

I said to her, "You have done a lot of work today. I want to help you process through those painful beliefs in our next session. In the meantime, journal each day between now and our next session. At least one time each day follow the process outlined above by identifying the Five Whys for at least one of the intrusive thoughts you wrote down earlier. In our next session we will discuss what you have learned. (See Appendix H for the *Five Whys Exercise*.)

In our next session, Courtney was prepared to discuss what she had learned from her journaling throughout the week. She had gained even more awareness. She indicated that her mind had been racing for a long time, even before she found out about Adam's sexual behaviors. She recalled worrying a lot in high school and college. Adam's behaviors had triggered deeper worrying than she had previously encountered, but this wasn't the first time it had occurred. This was helpful for her to understand and important for our work together.

By going through the *Five Why Exercise*, she also identified that she had come to truly believe that she "didn't matter." She had identified another time in her life when she had felt that way. She remembered that were times growing up that she felt that way with her parents. This insight was valuable as it helped her understand that her trauma now was tied to an earlier life experience. Based on her insights and awareness, we then proceeded to do EMDR therapy to heal those traumatic experiences and painful memories. (For more about EMDR, see Chapter Eleven.)

After completing a few more sessions she gained greater control over her racing mind. However, I also wanted to introduce her to another tool that has been scientifically proven to help with anxiety, depression, and traumatic symptoms. She realized how much she loved learning and wanted as much help as I could give her, so I introduced her to another solution that helps slow down a racing mind.

Step #4: Mindfulness Based Healing

Take a few deep breaths. Start by breathing in for a four to six count. Then hold it for a second and then push hard and let your breath out for six to eight seconds. Once you have done this a few times, I would like to invite you to put your book down and do this simple breathing exercise for three minutes. Set a timer and practice breathing in and out as described above. As you do the breathing, try to focus on your breaths going in through your diaphragm and down deep into your stomach. Then follow your breath out. Try to stay focused on your breathing as much as possible during the three minute time. If your mind wanders, as it inevitably will, don't worry about it. Just gently guide your attention back to your breathing.

This is a basic beginning mindfulness exercise. I invite you now to take a few minutes to write about what you just experienced by answering the following questions: How often do you pay attention to basic body functions like breathing, muscle tightness and tension, or pain you may be feeling? Did you feel more relaxed after doing this exercise? I challenge you to do this breathing exercise at least once a day for the next week.

Drawing your attention to your breathing is one of the methods designed to help you slow down and listen to yourself. Mindful breathing promotes a mindful state, or "the awareness that emerges through paying attention on purpose, in the present moment, and nonjudgmentally, to the unfolding of experience moment by moment." (8)

When I introduced mindfulness to Courtney, she struggled to understand how it would benefit her when she dealt with thoughts that felt uncontrollable. I emphasized that in the beginning some of these ideas wouldn't necessarily make sense. I then encouraged her by saying, "Some of the best researchers in the world who study how to help people just like you have found that mindfulness is effective in treating anxiety and that if you practice this simple exercise, you will gain better control over your mind."

I also shared with her two definitions of mindfulness in an effort to help her understand more about mindfulness. In the first, Dr. Daniel Siegel in his book *The Mindful Brain* described it this way: "Mindfulness in its most general sense is about waking up from a life on automatic, and being sensitive to novelty in our everyday experiences." (9) The second way of describing mindfulness comes from Scott Bishop and his colleagues who wrote that mindfulness is "1) the self-regulation of attention so that it is maintained on immediate experience, thereby allowing for increased recognition of mental events in the present moment"; and 2) "a particular orientation toward one's experiences in the present moment, an orientation that is characterized by curiosity, openness, and acceptance.'" (10)

Slowing down the mind (by using breathing exercises as suggested above or by completing the *Five Whys Exercise*) gives clients like Courtney a greater sense of control over their unwanted intrusive thoughts. Over the next few weeks, Courtney did gain more control over her mind. She reported four specific things as helpful. Initially, when the unwanted thoughts came she would try to distract herself by thinking about something else. Sometimes it was effective because she allowed the thought to come and then was able to shift her attention to something else happening in her life. However, when that didn't work, she would try the *Five Whys Exercise*, which helped her gain a deeper understanding of what was happening in her mind. She also found that by focusing on her breathing, she was learning more about the unhealthy breathing patterns she had established. Her tendency was to breathe shallowly. By taking long, deep breaths in and pushing hard out, she was able to relax. She also reported that by breathing and paying closer attention to her thoughts, feelings, and body sensations, she was learning more about herself and how tense and uptight she had been. Her overall self-awareness was rising. She was making great progress.

Sometimes at our weekly meetings, Courtney came in and found that she hadn't been able to get rid of a memory quickly. In those sessions, we would slow down the process and identify what it was about that memory that plagued her. Usually, the *Five Whys Exercise* helped her get deeper and identify the belief hidden in the memory, but there were times when she couldn't work through the belief on her own and needed therapeutic help.

I share her struggles to emphasize that her growth took time and it wasn't a simple, easy, or linear evolution for her. The process of implementing each of the steps outlined in this chapter can help you, but it is important to be patient with yourself when the tools don't work right away or intrusive thoughts continue. It has been my experience that when I tell stories, it is common for people to think, "That was her success, but that can't happen to me." All I am asking you to do is to recognize that the few paragraphs above do not describe Courtney's day to day struggles, so please avoid comparing yourself to her or any other person, and simply try the activities and exercises outlined in this chapter. They will require work and effort, but over time you will see that your mind will slow down. (If you would like more information on the benefits of using mindfulness, see Chapters Twelve and Fourteen.)

Chapter Summary

Intrusive thoughts are common after sexual betrayal. They often manifest in dreams, anxious feelings, and reliving the painful events. Usually, just telling yourself to stop thinking about those thoughts doesn't work, but actually makes matters worse. In this chapter specific steps were introduced to help you work through intrusive thoughts or memories.

The specific suggestions include 1) recognize obsessive thoughts will come; 2) openly acknowledge the unwanted thoughts when they come; 3) implement the 5 Why's exercise to discover the beliefs behind the painful memories; and 4) a mindfulness based exercise was introduced to help you practice how to slow down your mind. While it is difficult to completely stop unwanted thoughts, by using the four steps outlined in this chapter you can gain greater control over your mind.

In the next chapter we will address avoidance. If you find that you are avoiding people, places, and other situations that you used to enjoy, the next chapter is written for you.

Chapter Ten

Start Living Again: Strategies for Facing Your Fears

DSM-5 Criteria C for PTSD: Persistent effortful avoidance of distressing trauma-related stimuli after the event.

"I stopped being myself. I used to spend time at the mall shopping and having a good time with my friends. Now I avoid going with them. My kids loved the local pool in the summer but I can't even go close to it now, even if my husband is not with me. I can't see other women dressed in bikinis without feeling like I am going to have a panic attack. I can't go anywhere without feeling anxious."

When I hear experiences like this from women, it seems to me like they are living in their own prisons. Their husbands' behaviors have triggered fears that are limiting their potential for joy and meaningful connections. Over the years, I have published many blog posts about the effects of sexual betrayal, and one of the common critiques of my work comes from individuals who believe that sexual relations outside of marriage are common and ordinary. These individuals believe that if we all listened to our inner drive we would not be so threatened by sexual relations outside of the marital bond.

However, the truth is actually that people thrive in healthy, committed relationships. Dr. Susan Johnson, founder of *Emotionally Focused Therapy*, believes that we are genetically designed for intimate bonding with one person. (Note: See my audio interview with Dr. Johnson on Love Rice on iTunes.) Fear in relationships stems from our fear of love being taken away. We fear abandonment and rejection. Betrayed spouses feel tremendous fear and end up avoiding distressing, trauma-related memories and experiences.

What are You Avoiding?

Chapter Two includes some of the results from the avoidance section of the TIPSA. Below is a complete list of questions from this section:

1. I spend a lot of energy trying to avoid thinking about my partner's behaviors.

2. I engage in behaviors that distract me (i.e., excessive reading, sleeping, eating, drinking) from thinking about my partner's behavior.

3. I avoid going to places or locations where people could be dressed scantily (e.g., mall, swimming pool, parks).

4. I avoid sexual contact with my partner since discovering his/her behavior.

5. Since learning of my partner's behaviors, I have a hard time participating in things that I previously enjoyed.

6. I have to keep busy to avoid the thoughts I have about my partner's behaviors.

7. I plan activities or run errands when I know my partner will be at home.

8. When other people talk about their partners or relationships, I either leave the conversation or walk away.

Find the complete results from more than 1300 research participants regarding these questions at www.discoverandchange.com/tipsa/assessment (view "Criteria C Results").

As you can see, these questions explore areas associated with avoiding thoughts, actions, people, and sex. In the results, you will find that avoidance is a common symptom that manifests itself in over 70% of the participants who completed the trauma assessment. It deeply concerns me to see the high number of individuals who are feeling the need to avoid activities, events, and people that they used to enjoy. The need for effective coping skills and social support to face this natural defense mechanism is critical. This chapter will help you understand how to face your desire to avoid fearful stimuli (e.g. locations, events, people) so you can feel free to start living your life again.

Reasons for Avoidance

If you slow down enough to understand the story of why you are avoiding things you used to enjoy, you will gain tremendous insight into yourself. Many years ago a friend and colleague of mine taught me a valuable lesson when he said, "There are always reasons for behaviors. We just have to watch and observe and the reasons will eventually manifest themselves." This was sage advice as I have found that there is always an explanation for any behavior we observe. This is true in ourselves and in others. There are always reasons for addiction, trauma, depression, and anxiety. Unfortunately, we seldom take time to ponder the reasons for why we do what we do or feel what we feel.

When it comes to avoidance, I have observed that those who are betrayed often avoid people, places, activities they used to enjoy, and sex with their spouse. This behavior is predictable in many cases. However, understanding why these behaviors are common in those who have experienced sexual betrayal has taken me some time. I understand that when we don't feel safe, we will avoid the person who hurt us, but why were people reporting that they were avoiding friends, family, and even their own children?

Here are a few specific examples that will help explain what is happening to people when they turn to avoidance:

One woman reported the following: "I feel that it effects me emotionally so I often disconnect from my children."

Another woman commented, "I am always trying to hide the pain I am feeling from everyone. I can't concentrate at work and I can't pretend to be happy when spending time with family and friends."

In the first case, the woman was afraid of her own emotions when she was around her children. In the second case, she couldn't hide her emotions from her family and friends. In both cases, these women felt that they had to disconnect from people from whom they would normally gain support and connection as a way to protect those same people from their emotions. In other words, "I don't want them to see my pain."

Another common explanation for avoidance sounds something like this: "I don't believe others want to hear about my problems. After all, they have their own challenges and I don't want to burden them with mine."

As I have pondered the reasons people turn to avoidance to deal with their trauma, I am convinced that the primary purpose is protection of self and others. When they say, "I don't want to be a burden on others," or, "Others don't want to hear me complain," I believe there is a deeper explanation. What I hear them really saying is, "I don't believe anybody will be there for me and I can't handle it if there is nobody there for me." In essence, the statement, "I don't want to be a burden," may be saying, "It would hurt too much to try to let someone in because I am afraid they too will reject or hurt me."

While it is often hard to be this vulnerable, this deeper expression is more true and often resonates with my clients. As they look below their reactionary thoughts and seek to understand their core pain, I often hear statements such as, "I think you're right. I am afraid to let anyone in because I don't trust anyone. I placed my complete trust in my husband and if I can't trust him, who can I trust?"

When they express their true suffering, I can often see the pain on their faces and feel their discomfort at being vulnerable with me as they express their deepest pain. I express appreciation to them for letting me see into their inner world and help them make sense of their emotional reaction. They have been betrayed in a most profound way. Their minds and bodies are confused. There are so many unanswered questions. They are overwhelmed in their interactions with their spouses and they have started generalizing their lack of trust into their relationships with others.

Whether they can see it or not, people who have suffered as a result of betrayal trauma often begin asking themselves questions like, "Who is trustworthy?" and "Will everyone hurt me?" If we were tracking their conscious thoughts, we might hear them answer their own questions by concluding, "I can't trust anyone. Nobody is there for me."

If I thought this way, I too would avoid people and places that used to be comfortable and enjoyable to me.

When betrayal trauma occurs, our brains are affected in ways that can contribute to avoidance behaviors. The human brain is designed to categorize all of our experiences so that we don't have to judge every individual situation. By doing this, the brain doesn't have to work so hard. For instance, if someone asked you about your husband before discovery, you might have replied, "He's a good husband and father." Your brain accepted this analysis and while things probably weren't perfect, you didn't question the accuracy of how you described your husband until you discovered his sexual betrayal. After discovery, your brain has no set answers. There is no default or family past experiences to help categorize the experience of discovery. Your brain now questions everything you thought you knew about your husband.

The brain struggles to categorize people and events that it used to categorize easily prior to the betrayal. It begins questioning more than just the relationship with the spouse. In many instances, everything and everyone is re-evaluated. The question, "Can I trust my spouse?" can easily shift to, "Can I trust anyone?"

Over the years, I have seen individuals generalize their inability to trust in ways that affect their relationships with loving and caring family and friends. Their mind begins wondering whether other people that they used to trust will also hurt them. One woman described her experience to me this way: "I used to share everything with my family. They knew what was going on in my life. Now, I share very little with them. They don't know me anymore. I have begun questioning their love for me. I'm not sure I trust anyone." The loss of trust in people as a whole is one of the most disturbing consequences of sexual betrayal. What used to be known, no longer is, and the brain has to learn how to reorient itself so that it doesn't have to question every aspect of life.

Loneliness

When individuals are not able to overcome their lack of trust, they often begin to experience incredible feelings of loneliness. This truly is one of the most disturbing outcomes associated with sexual betrayal. When loneliness settles in, people are seen differently. According to Dr. John Cacioppo, this is enormously stressful on our minds and bodies, and it doesn't get better on its own, nor with the simple passage of time. (1) In outlining these challenges, Dr. Cacioppo suggests that lonely people struggle with self-regulation. (2) As a result, they have a harder time avoiding activities like alcohol abuse, drug abuse, bulimia nervosa, and even suicide when they are lonely. (3) He believes that "long before feelings of isolation manifest themselves in these serious health problems, impaired self-regulation causes lonely individuals every day, everywhere, to act in ways that, sadly, do nothing more than reinforce their loneliness." (4)

Dr. John Gottman comments on the relationship between trust and loneliness as follows: "[Lonely people] focus on the potential threat in social situations and expect rejection. Their ability to detect treachery is also greatly compromised. Although they are more attentive to social cues than non-lonely people, they tend to misread these cues. Lonely people tend to let themselves be treated unfairly in order to be liked, but they also react with extreme suspicion about potential unfairness. Lonely people are therefore caught in a spiral that keeps them away from others, partly because they withdraw to avoid the potential hurt that could occur from trusting the wrong person. So they trust nobody, even the trustworthy." (5)

For the reasons outlined above, it is imperative that trust issues and established patterns of loneliness be addressed in the healing process. In order to do this, we must identify the core reasons for loneliness.

Avoidance: How We Hide Our Unmet Needs

In Chapter One, I shared my belief that we are all born with a strong natural desire to connect to other human beings. This is a core inner desire that never goes away. When we reach out to others, regardless of our age, we are seeking to be connected. Ultimately, when we are attuned to our inner voice, we long for connections. If we are fortunate, we have experienced this type of bond with a parent, grandparent, other family member, or friend. We all need at least one person in our life with whom we can feel connected. This person is someone who we know will be there for us no matter what. We fully trust them and know that they genuinely understand and care about us. It is in this type of relationship that our deepest human needs for connection are met.

Dr. Rebecca Jorgensen, relationship expert, believes that if we break down our most basic relationship desires, we all need:

1. Acceptance/attention
2. Belonging
3. Comfort
4. Safety

She refers to these as the *ABC's of Secure Attachment.* (6) When our relationships provide these key elements, we feel safe and secure. In contrast, after discovery of sexual betrayal, each of these four elements are ripped away, and it feels like trust is no longer an option. When the most important person in our lives is not available to us due to their behaviors, we usually protest in a variety of ways. According to Dr. Johnson, when we cannot connect with our partner or they are not responsive to our pain, we turn to the following behaviors:

- Angry protest
- Clinging
- Depression
- Despair

These behaviors are simply manifestations of our desire for connection. However, according to Dr. Johnson, these behaviors actually cover up our deeper desire for connection. When we realize that being angry or clingy is not resulting in the connection for which we long, depression and despair sink in. We begin to avoid others in an attempt to lessen interaction and regulate our fears of rejection. Avoidance then is how we hide our deeper unmet need to be loved, validated, and cared for. (7)

Assignment:

Take time to review your answers to the questions from the beginning of this chapter. Analyze the extent to which you have used avoidance since discovery. If you have turned to avoidance as a coping mechanism, how is it influencing your life? Use your journal to explore the answer to this question.

Heal Avoidant Patterns by Creating Connecting Bonds

While it may sound painful to try to trust again, the most effective path to healing is through connection. I am not suggesting that this connection has to be your spouse; he most likely is not safe right now. In fact, as you heal, deep relationship closeness is usually not an option. However, experiencing meaningful care and support from others is a key part of healing. In fact, the single most powerful healing for you will occur through human connection.

In Chapter One, I shared Alecia's story of sexual betrayal by her husband John. Her journey illustrates the power of healing through connection. After seeking to understand the depth of her pain it became obvious that she really didn't trust anyone, including me. When I see this level of pain in my clients, my hope is to create an environment where, at least in therapy, they feel like they can open up and share without reservation. This process took time for Alecia since she had been hurt by most of the men in her life.

In the beginning of our therapeutic relationship, she was hesitant to share much about her past. She primarily wanted to focus on her husband's behaviors. However, as time progressed and she felt like I truly wanted to understand her, she began sharing more about her life. This is when she told me about having sex with her first boyfriend, how lonely she felt growing up, and how disconnected she felt from her parents.

She had a lot of shame surrounding her first sexual experience. She felt like that was the biggest mistake of her life because it changed her so much. She shared with me that she felt like she had to "pay for her sin." As she worked through this, she discovered that her initial sexual experiences with her boyfriend, followed by his rejection, had made her feel like no one could ever love her again. This was a core belief that she had carried with her since that relationship.

After her boyfriend's painful dismissal, her wall came up and she really never resolved that hurt. Even though she thought she'd moved past that experience by the time she married John, she realized that she had never really let him in. She had shut herself off emotionally to others. She eventually discovered her deepest desire: she wanted John to love her. She longed for John to reach out and love her.

She couldn't tell him that due to his betrayal, but that was her biggest desire. She did love John, but she hadn't really been able to let him know because he had hurt her so badly. He had lied to her and deceived her in so many ways.

Therapist Note: When clients share with me that they really want to be closer to their spouse, but they are scared to share that information with their spouse, I try to understand that fear. In this case, by sharing that information, Alecia would have made herself very vulnerable to John who had not expressed his full commitment to trying to save their marriage. I have learned to never push clients to share their core desires with their spouses until such vulnerable information can be heard and validated. If their spouse isn't ready or doesn't want to hear it, sharing only opens someone like Alecia up for more hurt. My hope was that with time, John would be able to work through his own fears and truly commit to Alecia. But he too had to work through his issues and seriously evaluate his commitment level to their relationship. He also had to be willing to work through his deceitful behaviors so he could recover. Only then would he be safe enough for Alecia to share her deepest desires with.

Now that Alecia had shared her core desire with me, we needed to continue to help her heal by developing safe bonds with others. These relationships helped her face her fears of being unlovable. These meaningful connections were empowering to her as she waited to see if John was going to engage in the healing and recovery process. For the first few weeks, John said he wanted to save their relationship, but he was non-committal when it came to doing a full self-disclosure. He felt like it would just bring up old issues and was afraid if Alecia really knew it all, she would not want to stay with him. In truth, Alecia didn't know how she would respond if she knew everything, but she told us in a joint session that she wanted to try if he was willing to be completely open and honest.

It was at this point that John fully committed to try and save their relationship. He began preparing to do a full disclosure. This was a very painful time for Alecia because she didn't know what was coming. She was very anxious and worried that she wouldn't be able to handle it. Her mind naturally started thinking of worst case scenarios. Through all of this, John's attitude changed. He began working on his recovery and realized how deeply he had hurt her; he wanted their marriage to be better but wondered if he had done too much damage. He also expressed the feeling he'd had throughout their marriage that Alecia had "never really let him in."

This became a focus of Alecia's therapy over the next few sessions. Alecia knew that John was right. I shared with Alecia something that I knew about John: he too wanted their relationship, but he was scared. He wanted her to let him in. She was surprised, "Really, you think that?" I encouraged her to listen to what he said again, "She has never really let me in." Inherent in that statement was his desire to be let in. This got Alecia thinking.

In therapy, she began to focus on her avoiding tendencies and recount her history of avoidance. She realized that she had cut herself off from almost everyone who could help her. Her early life trauma had broken her natural attachment bonds with her parents. Since her first sexual experience, she was very hesitant to try and build a trusting relationship with anyone.

As her trust in me developed, we began discussing in more depth her fears of being hurt and rejected by others. She thought back to high school when she tried confiding in her parents but felt like they didn't understand her. As an adult, she saw that experience through a different lens. She realized her parents had done the best they could given their busy schedules and their own upbringing. This was an important step because she felt guilty for holding resentment toward them. Much of her adult life she had kept them at a distance because she had tied them to her relationship trauma with her high school boyfriend.

Her self-awareness grew and we began working through her fears. She had never really reached out to others for support, so that became a focus for her. Her goal was to share something she needed with someone else. She was attempting to be vulnerable by reaching out to another for support. It was scary for her to even think about asking for help. We talked about who she might feel safe enough to ask for help. Then we role played, practicing and discussing how this type of conversation might go. I knew that she had deep fears that needed to be slowly resolved so we took each week based on what she felt she could do. As she practiced, she began working through some of her fears and her avoidance strategies lessened. She began to get more in tune with her inner desire to connect with others.

Model for Reaching Out

In my work with her, we discussed the difference between having an open relationship or only having a surface-level relationship. As I explained to her, "There is a difference when we communicate from a place of vulnerability compared to communicating from a place of little depth." Here is an example that shows no-depth versus vulnerability in conversation:

No Depth

Person 1: Hi, how are you?

Person 2: I'm fine.

Person 1: Just fine?

Person 2: Yeah, I'm okay.

Person 1: Can I do anything to help?

Person 2: No. Thanks, though!

Vulnerability

Person 1: Hi, how are you?

Person 2: Honestly, I'm struggling today.

Person 1: Oh. I'm sorry to hear that; what's up?

Person 2: I need some help. I'm having a hard time. I don't feel like I can handle my own feelings some days. I think I am losing my mind.

Person 1: Thank you so much for letting me know. I'm here. Do you want to talk about it?

Person 2: I'm scared to ask for your help; I don't want to burden you with my problems.

Person 1: You're taking a risk to talk with me and I want to be there for you. Thanks so much for letting me in and sharing what is happening. I'm here to support you.

As we talked about these examples, Alecia said, "I can't talk like that to others." I said, "I don't expect you to do that right now, but I would like you to think about someone you think might respond that way to you."

I shared with Alecia the idea that we all need a healing hand. Usually these individuals help us regulate ourselves when we can't do it on our own. This type of person is a healer, someone who genuinely cares about you. It took some time, but eventually Alecia identified her old college roommate as someone that cared about her. The idea was sparked when, out of the blue, Meredith, her roommate, suddenly reached out to her. She said that Meredith had periodically reached out to her throughout the years and every time she did it was so good to talk and catch up.

This was the connection I was looking for that might help Alecia while she prepared for John's disclosure. Knowing that she struggled with trust issues, this would be a big step for her. It took a few weeks, but Alecia called Meredith and asked if they could talk. Meredith was surprised but agreed. Alecia reported that she reluctantly began talking about what she and John were going through. Meredith listened and in her kind way said, "Oh, Aleica, I am so sorry." This response was so soft and validating that Alecia began to cry. They had a great conversation; this was an important turning point for Alecia. She had never been that open with anyone. Not like that. Meredith's response was exactly what Alecia needed. It was a significant event that facilitated Alecia's healing process.

I have found that even one deep and meaningful connection can help people through difficult circumstances. Fortunately, Alecia had Meredith. Not all of my clients have someone that can be there. When my clients feel they have nobody, we begin by identifying as many options as possible. If there truly is nobody, twelve-step support groups, neighbors, co-workers, and religious leaders have been sources where clients have started to build relationships of trust again.

While connecting with Meredith was a great start, it was also important for Alecia to have additional support, so I encouraged her to begin attending a support group for partners of sex addicts. She was hesitant because she didn't want to be triggered by their stories. However, I had a group of women I knew focused on their healing and not on what their husbands had done. This group became another refuge for her. She found supportive women who understood her and what she was experiencing.

Between Meredith, her support group, and therapy, Alecia began developing a support team. One day she came to my office and said, "I can't believe I waited so long to reach out for help. For so long, I carried this burden inside of myself. I am beginning to feel free, . . . like I am going to be okay. I know that I will be okay regardless of John. I want things to work out, but I am no longer waiting on him. I am going to be okay. I will be okay regardless of John."

This statement represented a huge transformation: Alecia had gone from wondering at a basic level, "Does anyone really care about me?" and, "Will anyone be there for me?" to a place where she felt others genuinely cared about her and understood her suffering. Her uncertainty regarding the answers to these questions had triggered much emotional pain, but as she created meaningful connections and healthy support, the pain and fear went away.

Reaching Out to Safe People

When we reach out to others for support, we are really asking them to comfort us. This is such a vulnerable behavior and yet it is something that we all need: to hear a comforting voice of support or feel a soothing touch or hug. When clients discover the value of these connections, they usually turn the corner toward healing and their initial avoidance strategies go away.

In an effort to reinforce what Alecia had been doing, we stopped and processed what had changed in her life. We identified her shift from feeling alone to feeling connected. This power of connection is well described by Dr. Johnson in *Hold Me Tight*: "The people we love are the 'hidden regulators' of our bodily processes and our emotional lives." (8)

As we talked, she outlined key components of what I refer to as healing and recovery capital. The concept originates in addiction recovery literature. When researchers, Dr.'s Robert Granfield and William Cloud, interviewed individuals who had maintained sobriety for years at a time they discovered common elements in those in recovery. Their research reveals both drug addicts and alcoholics are more successful in their recovery attempts when they have multiple systems of support. The authors coined the term "recovery capital." They found that the more recovery capital a person had, the better their chances of maintaining sobriety. (9)

I have found that many of the same elements that are effective for individuals dealing with addiction are also helpful for individuals experiencing sexual betrayal. The four key recovery capital elements are: 1) 12-step support groups; 2) a sponsor; 3) motivation, and 4) spiritual/religious conviction. I have added to the list and share these with my clients when we develop their healing strategy: 5) emotional regulation (see Chapter Twelve for more information); 6) healthy habits (see Chapter Thirteen); 7) self-compassion (see Chapter Thirteen).

As we reviewed this list, Alecia identified that she was doing well in many of the areas, although she hadn't been using spiritual support and she wondered about emotional regulation. I informed her that we hadn't spent much time discussing emotional regulation, but we would in future sessions. She then said that she felt like she needed to figure out how to reconnect with God. She reported that for years she felt like He had abandoned her because of her own actions, but now as she attended the 12-step groups and reconnected with Meredith, she realized she wanted to renew her relationship with God again.

It has been my personal experience that when individuals begin their healing process, they often return to their spiritual roots. In Alicia's case, as she reconnected with others, her relationship with God improved too. A key part of healing usually includes healing spiritual wounds. Over the next few months Alecia worked on her relationship with God. She discovered her early sexual experiences had triggered shame in her and that she felt unworthy of God's love. As she resolved her shame and discovered God's love for her, she built another meaningful connection. In resolving her "God" issues she reconnected with her religious organization and found additional relationships and connections. She was making great progress.

From Avoidance to Expressing Unmet Needs

As Alecia continued working through her fears, we began identifying deeper needs that she wanted met in her relationship with John. Prior to this time, she hadn't allowed herself to have wants in a relationship because she didn't feel like she deserved them. Her mind didn't allow her to even explore let alone express what she wanted. In an individual session, while discussing the process of identifying her needs in her marriage, she became scared. "What if he doesn't want to be there for me and meet my needs?" she asked during one session.

"That's a good question. It's good that you are expressing that feeling. Let's explore that fear...you are afraid he doesn't want to be there for you?"

"Right," she said. "I'm scared he doesn't want to be with me anymore."

Therapist Note: Alecia was making it clear that her biggest fear was being abandoned by John. I believed that her next step was for her to share this fear with John. However, I wasn't sure how Alecia felt about sharing this fear with him. I asked her if she felt like she could share that fear with John. I could tell she was getting strong when she said, "I couldn't have said that to him in the past, but while I still don't fully trust he can hear my needs, I want to have the courage to tell him the truth." Fortunately, I knew that he did want to be there for her based on the work he was doing in his groups and conversations he was having with his therapist.

During the rest of that session, she began identifying additional things she was hoping for in her relationship. I had her address the following question in writing:

What are my needs, hopes, and desires for my relationship?

She wrote, "Know what your needs are; you have to identify what you really want."

Then she wrote, "First, I have to have honesty and truth, complete fidelity. If that is happening, then I want this in our relationship: I want connection. I need to know I am loved. I really long for John to care for me."

She felt anxious about sharing these desires with John, so we talked about her fears. She concluded that she had seen many good changes in John. John had given her a full disclosure of his behaviors in an earlier session which was incredibly hard for both of them, but she reported that it was helpful. However, she had never been this vulnerable with anyone and expressing her true desires to John was going to be difficult. I told her how impressed I was that she was able to identify her needs and be able to share them with me. Our next step was to have John join us and have her discuss these desires with John, if she felt like their relationship was at that point.

In our next session, Alecia and John had a meaningful conversation. In the session, Alecia was able to discuss her fears of sharing her feelings with John. He was prepared well and listened to her and validated her fears. He said, "I get it. I haven't known how to respond and that is on me." He continued, "I don't know if together we have been very successful in having these hard conversations." His response opened her up. She continued, "I suppose I have two primary fears. First, for years I have feared that you would leave me. I now see that fear has been with me for years, long before I met you. My second fear is related to dishonesty and your sexual behaviors. You have lied to me repeatedly and I can't live with that. I won't accept lying to me."

When clients are able to be this open with their spouse, it is usually because they want their relationship to work and they have established some trust. These types of conversations come after extensive work by both parties. It is not recommended that individuals be this vulnerable without first establishing a foundation of safety. John was prepared to hear her. He had done a lot of recovery work so he could understand what she was saying without becoming defensive. For example, when he acknowledged that he hadn't known how to respond and that was on him, he showed ownership and that he was open and ready for this important discussion.

Since John had shown a willingness to be vulnerable himself, vulnerability felt much easier for Aleicia. She was able to express her desire for a deeper connection and she told John she was aware that she had kept him at a distance but that she really did want him to show his love. She told him that she longed to have him care for her. John had never heard her speak this way and he too opened up. He said, "I really do want to be there for you. I've felt like a failure to you. I didn't know you really wanted me this way; I feel hopeful."

Alecia and John reached this point after a slow process and developing openness and willingness in their hearts. I believe that when both partners are willing to put in the work required to achieve deep intimacy, they will reap the rewards. As an author, what I can't explain on paper is the many sessions where feelings of helplessness, being overwhelmed, and complete hopelessness were also present. That is, despite the hopefulness felt by both John and Alecia after several sessions and group attendance, there were many moments of despair.

As you read, please be careful not to compare your relationship to John and Alecia's. My hope is that you will understand that healing is possible. The goal of this chapter is to help you identify the key principles behind healing, especially when avoidance behaviors have been developed.

Chapter Summary

Avoidance is one of the five behaviors associated with PTSD. Based on my research, sexual betrayal triggers common behaviors associated with avoidance in more than 70% of research participants. Some of the common avoidance behaviors include: 1) avoiding activities previously enjoyed; 2) avoiding anything that reminds individuals of sexual betrayal (e.g. swimming pools and malls); and 3) avoiding a sexual relationship with the spouse.

Soon after discovery, many individuals begin questioning their mental model of trust and safety. If meaningful connections cannot be made, trust in others and all of society is questioned. As a result, solutions for avoidance begin with reestablishing relationships with individuals that are available and supportive.

Some of the specific solutions include identifying people that are able to help you feel accepted, provide you comfort, and are emotionally safe. Additional ideas included identifying your needs and learning how to express them. This process was demonstrated by sharing Alecia's story as she reached out to an old friend, attended a support group, and, over time, developed the strength to communicate her needs openly and honestly with her husband.

It has been my experience that when individuals heal from sexual betrayal, their avoidance behaviors go down significantly. Instead of feeling lonely, they feel connected. They refuse to fight the battle alone. As you work through your recovery, please continuously evaluate whether you are connecting or avoiding. Creating long-term connections is a valuable solution that heals wounded hearts. May you find connection in your healing journey.

In the next chapter, we explore negative self-beliefs and moods that often manifest after sexual betrayal. We will discuss how to face these challenges and why it is essential to resolve them as you heal.

Chapter Eleven

Facing Negative Self-Beliefs and Mental Health Challenges

The great lie: "If I was prettier, taller, thinner, or sexier, he wouldn't act out in the way he does."

When individuals turn to friends for support after sexual betrayal, they often hear something like, "I can't believe he did that to you. What a jerk!" This response is natural and is an expression of friends' belief that "he" is the problem. He's a jerk. However, I have learned through my research that something quite different is happening inside the minds of those experiencing sexual betrayal. On a cognitive level they are able to say, "Yeah, it's his problem. I can't believe he did this to me." But, when we look deeper at the emotional level, we discover something completely different.

When we begin exploring the deeper emotions, we discover another set of feelings of fear and worry. Usually, beneath the initial fear and anxiety are thoughts of self-doubt and negative self-beliefs. When clients let down their walls and allow me into their inner world, I hear statements like, "What is wrong with me? Everyone I am with seems to hurt me," or, "It was my fault! I wasn't sexual enough."

In its development of the current criterion for PTSD, The American Psychiatric Association (APA) altered the current diagnostic conditions to include self-blame, which refers to internalizing the traumatic event by assuming blame for it. The professional clinicians and researchers who make up the APA believe self-blame occurs frequently enough in the aftermath of trauma to include negative self-cognitions and mood alterations as new criteria for diagnosing PTSD. They made these changes to the diagnostic requirements for PTSD in the DSM-5, published in 2013.

This additional component for diagnosing PTSD pushed me to rethink sections of my original assessment. It also helped me explore how much individuals experiencing sexual betrayal were internalizing what was happening in their relationships by blaming themselves. The added criteria also got me thinking about the prevalence of depression and anxiety in those who experience betrayal in their relationships. These issues are addressed in this chapter as we explore the extent sexual betrayal both triggers negative self-beliefs and creates alterations in mood (e.g. depression, anxiety) as well as how to treat these challenging thoughts and emotions.

Assessing Negative Alterations in Cognitions and Mood

Below is the list of questions from the TIPSA designed to identify the extent to which you feel your partner's sexual betrayal altered your cognitions (self-beliefs) and mood:

1. I feel like my partner acts out because I am not good enough.

2. I feel like it is my fault that my partner sexually acts out.

3. After what my partner has done, I feel like it is hard to trust anyone.

4. I feel ashamed because of what my partner has done.

5. Since I discovered my partner's behavior, I hold back from people who used to be close to me.

6. I am still able to enjoy things since learning of my partner's behavior.*

7. I feel like I am a bad person because of what my partner has done.

8. When I am in social settings, I don't feel like I belong anymore.

9. Since discovering my partner's behaviors, I feel like I am different than everyone else.

10. I feel like my spouse would not be this way if society was not so bad.

11. I feel like I am stupid for not seeing what he/she was doing behind my back.

You can find the summarized results at www.discoverandchange.com/tipsa/assessment under "Critera D Results."

If you review the results for the criteria associated with negative cognitions (e.g. self-beliefs and shame) and mood, you will see that elevated traumatic symptoms are often present after sexual betrayal. In fact, many of those who completed our survey indicated that they were experiencing the symptoms listed above.

Here are a few of the findings:

Negative Self-Beliefs and Shame

- 78% reported that they felt like their partner acted out because they were not good enough.

- 62% reported that they feel like it is their fault that their partner sexually acts out.

- 84% reported that they felt ashamed because of what their partner had done.

- 41% indicated that they felt like they were a bad person because of what their partner had done.

- 74% reported that since discovering their partner's behaviors, they felt like they were different than everyone else.

Alterations in Mood

By including the sixth question on the previous page, I hoped to understand if participants were still able to enjoy their lives since learning of their partner's behavior. Seventy-nine percent reported that they were able to enjoy things about half the time or less. In other words, most of the participants were finding it difficult most of the time to enjoy things that used to be fun for them. Sixty-nine percent indicated that they felt like they didn't belong in social settings anymore. This is a common symptom of depression. People who don't feel like they belong usually begin to isolate themselves away from others and a depressing loneliness sets in.

Why Negative Alterations in Cognitions and Mood?

I have spent much time pondering "why" this happens. While there are many potential factors, I believe that negative self-beliefs form for the following reasons. First, when something bad happens to us we naturally look inside and think that we should have somehow foreseen what was going to happen. In other words, if we had foreseen it, we would have acted differently, and things would have turned out differently. Therefore, the way things turned out becomes our fault. When this happens, I hear statements like, "I knew this would happen. I should have known better," or, "I must be stupid for not seeing what was going on." These statements reveal the negative self-beliefs that often play in the background of our minds. When beliefs like this are accepted as truths without being questioned, the end result is usually depression and anxiety. The belief is: "I am flawed."

The second reason we blame ourselves after trauma is we somehow think that if it is our fault, we can change the outcome. If it's your partner's fault, you can't do anything about it; his behavior is totally out of your control. But if it's your fault, then it's in your control to change. This concept relates to learned helplessness. In contrast to learned helplessness, which suggests that believing we cannot affect change leads to less and less effective responses, when we believe that we *can* influence an outcome, we gain strength. Researchers refer to our perception of being able to influence an outcome as locus of control. Locus of control is the extent to which individuals perceive that their actions have influence on the life conditions they face and the extent to which they attribute their circumstances and rewards to fate, luck, chance, or powerful others, instead of believing that their circumstances and rewards are influenced by their own actions. (1)

Interestingly, in a 1999 study, married couples were asked about their perceptions of being able to influence an outcome in their relationships. The researchers found "higher levels of marital locus of control was associated with reports of higher positive marital quality and reports of lower negative marital quality. Spouses with lower levels of marital locus of control were more likely to report the presence of marital strains that were linked to lower levels of marital quality." (2) That is, relationships in which individuals reported that their behaviors could influence their spouse were happier overall.

The research suggests that we do better and are more motivated when believe we can determine ultimately what happens to us. As explored in Chapter Eight, learned helplessness is the bi-product of a belief that no matter what we do, we can't change the outcome.

Unfortunately, for sexual betrayal victims, this backfires. If one way to combat the feeling of helplessness is to take ownership for the problem, then I therefore blame myself in order to control the outcome and fix things.

This is a common problem that I see in many clients who have experienced traumatic events. For example, when I work with individuals whose parents have divorced, they often admit to blaming themselves for the divorce. They express having thoughts like, "My parents wouldn't have divorced if I had done something different." Usually, they make comments like this in passing, because they don't realize the power these types of beliefs have had on their relationships as they grew older. For many, they have carried the weight of their parents' divorce with them for years. As we pause to explore the burden they have felt, they realize they have taken the load of their parents' divorce upon themselves. Their core belief sounds something like, "If I were better, this wouldn't have happened or I could have stopped it."

Ultimately, when the marital outcome proves unchangeable by one partner alone, negative self-beliefs are internalized. This is when we hear statements like, "I'm just not enough," or, "It's my fault this happened." Fortunately, as we increase our understanding of our internalized beliefs, we have powerful solutions that can help create the ability to confront these negative self-perceptions.

However, before we move toward ideas to help resolve the negative alterations in self-beliefs and moods, there is a third reason individuals blame themselves for sexual betrayal. The third reason is related to experiences from their family background. Some individuals grew up in homes where their "job" was fixing problems or where they were blamed when things went wrong in the family.

I had such a client; Kelly shared her story with me:

"While growing up, my mom told me that I was the cause of the problems that she was having with my dad. She accused me of coming in between them because my dad would spend time with me when he came home. If my dad spent any time with me, she would become jealous and accuse him of loving me more than her. There was lots of fighting and arguing and eventually dad and mom divorced. I wanted to live with my dad, but he was in a situation where he couldn't take care of me, so I ended up with Mom. She would remind me that I was the reason for their divorce."

When she described this experience, she knew cognitively that the divorce wasn't her fault, but emotionally, she couldn't help feeling like her parents divorced because of her. The carryover from this childhood experience was a belief that when something bad happened, it was her fault. She would often apologize for things that were not her fault. Even in our sessions, she would often say, "I'm sorry for being so emotional." Unresolved childhood experiences often manifest in negative self-beliefs in adult relationships. If true freedom and healing are going to occur, these beliefs have to be resolved and rewritten.

Rewriting Negative Self-Beliefs

While working on my doctorate degree, I had the privilege of meeting and working with two talented therapists, Ken and Sharon Patey. These two incredible people opened my mind to the power of understanding how our beliefs guide our actions. Ken would often say, "Show me someone's behaviors and I will predict their beliefs. Give me someone's beliefs and I will predict their behavior." Over the years, I have used this wise advice as a guide in my clinical work.

When clients tell me about their anger, anxious mind, or feelings of helplessness, I focus more on the core beliefs they have about themselves than on these specific behaviors. As I work with them, I am trying to identify the beliefs they have about themselves and others as a result of their experiences. For example, in the TIPSA, I provide this question: "Since discovering my partner's behaviors, I feel like I am different than everyone else." Nearly 74% reported feeling this way. When I explore these types of beliefs, those that promote feeling different, I generally follow-up by identifying memories or experiences that accompany those beliefs.

The value of seeking a deeper understanding of your beliefs is that you will likely gain additional insight into your behaviors and why you act the way you do in certain situations. Sometimes, as you explore your self-beliefs, you will discover how they are related to specific experiences or memories that may not be resolved and are still disturbing you.

In Kelly's case, she was able to identify that when her husband cheated on her, she had become numb. At the time, she didn't see the link between what her husband had done and how her mother blamed her for her parents' divorce, but as she talked, she found the connection. As a child, she felt ashamed that she couldn't save her parents' marriage. Now in her marriage, she was again feeling at fault when her husband had cheated on her. She acknowledged that she had simply assumed that his behaviors were due to her inadequacies. She said, "It was easy for me to take the blame and accept that it was my fault. That was what I learned growing up when my parents divorced."

Clearly, the work she needed in therapy revolved around her self-beliefs and her understanding of why others do what they do. Over many sessions, we began unraveling her negative beliefs. As we worked together, her insights about herself, her parents' divorce, and her husband's betrayal grew. She realized that she was living her life based on the beliefs she had accepted as a little girl when her mom blamed her for her parents' divorce. At this point, her insight was elevated, but insight alone doesn't heal. It was time to help her rewrite her negative self-beliefs.

EMDR: A Powerful Tool for Healing

As a counselor who has been practicing therapy for over twenty years, I have read countless books, attended many workshops, and spent thousands of hours in therapy with my clients. I desire for my clients to have the best treatment I can provide them. However, even with all of my experience, there are times when I think to myself that I could be better. I realize that I am missing something, so I read and study hoping to discover new and better treatment strategies. For years, the topic of treating trauma was difficult for me. I questioned if I was providing the best treatment available when I worked with traumatized individuals. Then in the Spring of 2015, while reading Bessel van der Kolk's masterful book *The Body Keeps the Score*, I found myself excited as I listened to him describe Eye Movement Desensitization and Reprocessing therapy (EMDR). I was mesmerized by the stories he shared about helping individuals heal using this specialized treatment. I read as much as I could about EMDR and signed up for the next training available.

A few months later, I attended a conference to learn all about EMDR therapy. On the second day of our training, we began practicing with each other. I had chosen a difficult memory from my childhood when my mother discovered that my dad was cheating on her. I had identified my belief related to that experience as, "I didn't matter." The person working with me asked me to go back to the details of this experience. As I brought it to my mind, I saw myself in an intersection. Our car was heading south and my dad's truck was heading north. I was in the backseat of the car that my mom was driving when my dad stopped at the same intersection with another woman in his passenger seat.

I followed the index finger of the person I was practicing with as she moved rapidly from side to side about twelve inches from my eyes. EMDR therapists call this bilateral stimulation (BLS). As my eyes tracked her fingers I found myself triggered with the deepest rage I had ever felt. I felt my head burning and the vivid sensation of wanting to scream. I saw myself getting out of the car and stomping out to the middle of that intersection enraged. I was yelling at my dad and saying, "What are you doing? You are ruining our family!"

That is when my colleague's finger stopped. I was crying and the tears were running down my cheek. By this time, the supervising therapist was there. "Just stay with those moments and let me know what are you noticing," he told me. I reported what I had just seen. I was thinking to myself, "Didn't you see it too?" After reporting what I experienced and what I felt in my body, we continued.

During the next set of eye movements, I saw the little boy (me) being loved by his family. I saw my grandparents, aunts, and uncles. Then the boy saw his dad at his baseball game supporting him. Here my colleague stopped again and asked me to take a deep breath and let it out. She asked me, "What are you noticing now?" I related what I had experienced.

We went through one more series where I felt this tremendous weight on my shoulders. I found myself thinking, "My dad is a good man who had a problem." At this, the weight lifted and I felt free. My original belief, "I didn't matter," no longer felt true. In fact, I knew I was loved. Within a few short minutes, I had processed a very painful and disturbing memory from my past and had changed my belief. When I started the processing, I had ranked the memory as a six or seven in terms of how disturbing if felt to me (on a scale of 0-10, on which zero is completely peaceful and 10 is the most disturbance possible). After processing the memory using EMDR, the emotional pain and level of disturbance was completely gone. The memory felt like a zero.

My mind was buzzing. I thought to myself, "This experience is very powerful; I'm sure it could help my clients." Since that time, I have experienced multiple life-changing sessions with my clients through EMDR therapy. They are healing from traumatic memories that, in the past, I could not have helped them work through. My clients are healing in ways beyond my comprehension.

Kelly's Story with EMDR

When Kelly shared the memory of her mom blaming her for her parents' divorce, her lip quivered and her voice shook. While she had sought my help to cope with her husband's infidelity, she saw the wisdom in identifying how her past experiences were limiting her ability to respond to her husband now. Together we explored the relationship between her past experiences with her parents, her other dating relationships, and her subsequent marriage to Tim. Each of these relationships involved hurt and betrayal in one form or another. However, when we discussed which memory felt the most disturbing to her, she felt like her mom blaming her for the divorce was the most painful; that is where we began to work on her healing.

I introduced her to the process of EMDR and we began. I asked her to think about the memory and what negative belief she felt about herself now. She thought for a moment and said, "It doesn't matter what I do, I can't stop bad things from happening." I followed up and asked, "What does that mean about you?" She said, "I am worthless." I followed up that question by asking if she had had recent experiences where she felt that way. She said, "Sure. When I caught my husband cheating, I again felt like I'm worthless. Nobody wants me. Even my dad who loved me, left me with my mom." She was surprised at what she was saying.

I continued by following the EMDR protocol which included a series of additional questions that explored what she wanted to believe about herself, what emotions she felt when she thought about the memory of her mom blaming her, and where she felt those emotions in her body. Then I asked her to focus on the memory with her mom, the negative belief (I am worthless), and what she was feeling in her body. Then I began moving my fingers from right to left about 12 inches from her eyes for a little more than one minute.

When I stopped moving my fingers, I asked Kelly to take a deep breath and then let it go. I asked her what she noticed. She described being in the kitchen with her mom pointing her finger at her and saying, "You know it's your fault that we're getting divorced." I told her to notice that and we moved to the next set.

While doing the next set, Kelly looked visibly upset. When I stopped, she said, "I'm not sure if my mom tried to stop me from seeing my dad, but I didn't see my dad as much. I was told he was so busy with his new life that he didn't have time for me." Again, I asked her to focus on that and moved my fingers for another set. We continued to do this process a few more times. On the sixth or seventh series, something inside Kelly's mind began to shift. After I stopped moving my fingers and she had taken a deep breath, she blurted out, "My mom was doing the best she could. She grew up in a home where she was abused by her dad. She didn't know any better. She has never been able to trust men, so how could she have trusted my dad?"

At this point, it would be natural to stop and talk about that insight; however, EMDR therapy is about the brain processing and following the specific protocol is important. I could tell she had found relief from her mother blaming her, but we needed to continue her processing to make sure that all of the pain associated with that memory had been resolved in her mind.

I asked her to pay attention to her thoughts, and we moved on to another set of bilateral eye movements. As a therapist, I have learned to watch for shifts in facial expressions or shifts in body movements. Kelly's facial expressions were revealing something important was happening in her mind. When I stopped, she couldn't wait to tell me what she had experienced, "I saw my dad leaving and his eyes. He looked at me with a deep love. He wanted to bring me with him, but he couldn't. He loved me. He didn't abandon me."

She began to cry.

"All along I thought he had stopped loving me, but I think my mom kept me from him because she felt like she needed to protect me." I told her to go with that and we continued to the next BLS set. When I was done, she said, "My mom was trying to protect me the best she could, and my dad loved me but didn't want to fight against my mom."

That was it. Kelly had processed through one of the most painful memories of her past. When I again asked her to identify how disturbing that original memory was for her, she said, "It's gone. There is zero disturbance with that memory." Then she wondered aloud, "How does that work? It's gone. That memory has been haunting me for years and now it's just gone!"

I confirmed that this is how EMDR works. It helps you process through painful memories and once they are resolved, you can move on freely without fear that they will come back. I then continued with the rest of the EMDR protocol to reinforce what she had learned. One of the steps is to help clients shift their beliefs. Her original belief was "I am worthless." Before beginning her processing, I had asked her what she would prefer to believe about herself and she had identified, "I am of worth." As we followed through the steps of the EMDR protocol, I asked her to bring up the original memory with her mother and think about the statement, "I am of worth." When I asked her how true that felt to her, she said, "It's true. I am of worth." Her self-belief had shifted.

Kelly's experience is not unique. Individuals often get stuck emotionally after they experience trauma. Kelly's self-belief from that memory was "I am worthless." She had carried that belief for more than twenty years. Now, realizing that she was of worth and that she was loveable, we turned our attention to her marriage.

When I share stories like Kelly's, I often get asked why the EMDR processing was focused on this experience rather than Kelly's husband's sexual betrayal. To answer that question, I turn to the EMDR literature, which suggests that we listen to the needs of our clients rather than using our agenda. (3) For Kelly, the memory with her mother was the *most* painful, so we processed it first. Processing another painful but less painful trauma may have helped Kelly, but as long as the most painful memory of feeling worthless is still unprocessed, other experiences with worthlessness are likely to reactivate it. The pain remains active until the first or worst memory associated with worthlessness is integrated.

In my subsequent work with Kelly, she was stronger and able to create boundaries with Tim. She had completely stopped blaming herself for his behaviors and had the strength to express what she wanted out of their marriage if they were going to stay together. By changing her self-beliefs, she had also freed herself from the depression that had plagued her for years.

The Effectiveness of EMDR

One of the most important advances in the treatment of trauma stems from our awareness of treatment protocols that are effective. In *The Body Keeps the Score*, Dr. van der Kolk cites research on the effectiveness of EMDR in treating PTSD. His work was funded by the National Institute of Mental Health to compare the effects of EMDR with standard doses of Prozac or a placebo. Below are his findings:

"Of our eighty-eight subjects, thirty received EMDR, twenty-eight Prozac, and the rest on a placebo sugar pill. As often happens, the people on placebo did well. After eight weeks, their 42% improvement was greater than that for many other treatments that are promoted as "evidence based.""

"The group on Prozac did slightly better than the placebo group, but barely so. This is typical of most studies of drugs for PTSD: Simply showing up brings about a 30% to 42% improvement; when drugs work, they add an additional 5% to 15%. However, the patients on EMDR did substantially better than those on either Prozac or the placebo: After eight EMDR sessions one in four were completely cured (their PTSD scores had dropped to negligible levels), compared with one in ten of the Prozac group. But the real difference occurred over time: When we interviewed our subjects eight months later, 60% of those who had received EMDR scored as being completely cured." (4,5)

While EMDR may not work for all people, it is clearly the leading form of therapy available now to treat trauma. "Once people started to integrate their traumatic memories, they spontaneously continued to improve. In contrast, all those who had taken Prozac relapsed when they went off the drug. This study was significant because it demonstrated that a focused, trauma-specific therapy for PTSD like EMDR could be much more effective than medication." (6)

As research expands, trauma treatment continues to improve. Fortunately, EMDR now provides a treatment protocol that is clinically proven to be one of the most effective treatments available. (7) I have seen it heal emotional wounds and help individuals overcome negative beliefs that would have likely lasted a lifetime. Watching my clients process through their traumatic memories and seeing their negative self-beliefs drop away has been very rewarding.

The Benefits of Addressing the Root Problems

When we are able to address the root of a problem, we usually see significant changes in many areas of our clients' lives. One of the most common benefits we see is an improvement in mental health. In my research addressing sexual betrayal trauma, I asked participants if they had ever been clinically diagnosed with common mental health challenges such as depression and anxiety.

Here are the five most common mental-health challenges research participants reported:

- Depression   48%
- Anxiety   45%
- PTSD   18%
- ADHD   10%
- Bipolar Disorder   4%

Nearly 50% of those who completed the survey reported that they had been clinically diagnosed with depression while 45% reported an anxiety diagnosis. For some, they may have marked themselves as having both depression and anxiety. It's not uncommon for someone with an anxiety disorder to also suffer from depression and vice versa. Nearly one-half of those diagnosed with depression are also diagnosed with an anxiety disorder. (8)

Regardless, these are very high numbers considering that at any point in time, 3-5% of adults suffer from major depression; the lifetime risk is about 17%. (9) Anxiety disorders are the most common mental illness in the United States, affecting 40 million adults nationally, or 18% of the population. (10)

Those who completed the TIPSA reported significantly higher rates of both depression and anxiety than the national average. I believe this is related to the specific relational stressors they were facing due to sexual betrayal. The good news is that when we begin dealing with the root issues, negative self-beliefs, and relationship trauma, we begin to see mental health challenges like depression and anxiety diminish and often disappear all together.

Dr. van der Kolk writes, "As the great psychiatrist Milton Erickson said, once you kick the log, the river will start flowing. Once people started to integrate their traumatic memories, they spontaneously continued to improve." (11) To further explore the powerful effect of EMDR therapy in trauma recovery and treatment of depression and anxiety, let's turn to the research.

EMDR and Depression

In a 2015 study on the effectiveness of using EMDR to treat individuals with depression, Dr. Michael Hase and his colleagues' findings are encouraging. In the study, the researchers recruited a group of 16 patients with depressive episodes in an inpatient setting. These 16 patients were treated with EMDR therapy, in addition to treatment as usual (TAU), in order to reprocess memories related to stressful life events.

Through their research, Hase et al found that "68% percent of the patients in the EMDR group showed full remission at end of treatment. The EMDR group showed a greater reduction in depressive symptoms as measured by the SCL-90-R depression subscale. This difference was significant even when adjusted for duration of treatment. In a follow-up period of more than one year, the EMDR group reported fewer problems related to depression and fewer relapses than the control group." (12)

EMDR and Anxiety

As aforementioned, the American Psychological Association updated its manual, the DSM-5, in 2013. Prior to that time, PTSD was categorized as anxiety disorder. Now, PTSD has been removed from that class and is now considered a trauma and stressor-related disorder. Because of this recent shift, much of the research on PTSD equates it to anxiety rather than trauma. That said, there are studies that show the effectiveness of using EMDR therapy to treat anxiety.

For example, a 1997 study on the effects of EMDR in treating 67 individuals reveals those who received EMDR treatment showed significantly greater improvement with greater rapidity than those in the standard care treatment group on measures of PTSD, depression, anxiety, and general symptoms. Those who received EMDR treatment required fewer medication appointments for their psychological symptoms and needed fewer psychotherapy appointments. (13)

Treating Beliefs Associated with Complex Trauma

When you picked up this book, you were likely experiencing a lot of emotional pain. There is a high probability that throughout your life you have had multiple traumatic experiences. In addition, some of these traumas have probably been repetitive. In this chapter, we have discussed using EMDR as a treatment for healing the negative self-beliefs that usually accompany such trauma. It has been my experience that when clients have been through recurrent trauma, they begin to feel overwhelmed and hopeless. Please understand that if you have experienced multiple traumatic relationship events, the process of healing and recovery as outlined above can still work for you.

I have witnessed individuals with deep emotional wounds regain their sense of confidence in themselves and in their abilities to build connecting relationships. The process is slow due the the complexity of the trauma, but the journey is possible and worth it. In order to treat complex trauma, it is best to find an expert who understands the delicate nature of your trauma. Usually this type of work takes months and sometimes years of effort. The cases above are illustrations of what is possible through EMDR therapy, but even in these cases, months of preparation were necessary to develop a trusting therapeutic relationship and safe therapy environment. EMDR, or any treatment, is not easy, but when it is done right, healing is possible. I believe all wounds can be healed.

Chapter Summary

One of the common side-effects of sexual betrayal is negative self-beliefs and alterations in mood. It's common for individuals to turn their trauma inward and blame themselves for their spouse's behaviors. The three thoughts that drive self-blame are 1) "I should have known better;" 2) "If I believe I can control the outcome, I feel better about what is happening to me, but when I realize I can't determine the outcome, I feel helpless (locus of control)"; and 3) "I grew up in a home where I was blamed for problems, so naturally I take current relationship issues upon myself."

Fortunately, there are solutions for turning away from self-blame. As seen through Kelly's example, the realization that early life experiences influenced how she was responding to her husband can be utilized and reprocessed through EMDR work. By using EMDR, Kelly was able to move beyond her early life's negative beliefs and begin her healing. As cited above, research is encouraging regarding the overall effectiveness of EMDR in helping ease depression and anxiety.

In the next chapter, we discuss strategies for slowing down the angry, anxious, and overwhelmed mind by learning how to regulate difficult emotions.

Chapter Twelve

Discover How to Regulate
Difficult Emotions

Sleep was elusive. I couldn't eat. Day and night my heart felt like it was go-
ing to jump out of my body. The slightest change in my husband's demean-
or would set me off. I felt like at any moment I would explode.

The human body is not designed to be in constant battle. In fact, it functions best when it has time to relax and calm down. Yet, in today's fast-paced society, it's hard to take time to intentionally slow down. As if day-to-day stress is not enough, sexual betrayal triggers a warning sign to the body that even more adrenaline and cortisol needs to be released. When it releases these chemicals, the body is preparing for the battle that lies ahead. These hormones are good for meeting our short-term needs, but when there are large amounts of these hormones in our system, they become quite harmful. (1) Unfortunately, with sexual betrayal, the countless questions, fears, and worries usually don't end in a few days, weeks, or even months. This makes the mind get stuck in "on" mode and, as a result, it becomes hypervigilant: constantly on the lookout and ready to protect itself. This hypervigilance floods the brain with too much adrenaline and cortisol.

When the siren warnings of threat or danger are relentless, normal functioning begins to deteriorate. Usually, sleep patterns are disrupted, eating becomes a burden or a crutch for comfort, and experiences that used to bring joy seem unappealing. The worn-out body becomes easily triggered; irritability and anger come easily. Everything from intense panic attacks to suicidal thoughts can also become the norm. These are just a few ways that sexual betrayal hijacks the fear center of the brain.

In the DSM-5, the fifth criteria for diagnosing PTSD is "arousal that is marked aggressive, or self-destructive behavior; sleep disturbances; hypervigilism; or other related behaviors." When these behaviors are present after betrayal, they reveal that a person is in fight mode. While in fight mode, it is nearly impossible to regulate emotions; consequently, it is natural to feel like you are out of control.

Assessing Marked Alterations in Arousal and Reactivity

How prevalent are these behaviors after the discovery of sexual betrayal? In order to assess this, we designed questions to identify specific behaviors that manifest heightened arousal symptoms like sleep difficulty, irritability, and anger. We also explored the extent individuals feel compelled to monitor their spouses' behaviors. Finally, we asked hard questions about self-destructive desires, hurting oneself, and feeling suicidal. Below is the list of questions designed to identify the extent to which you feel these things as a result of your partner's sexual betrayal:

1. Since learning of my partner's behavior, I have difficulty falling asleep.

2. After discovering my partner's sexual behaviors, I find that I am increasingly angry in response to my partner.

3. I find that I am more critical in conversations with my partner since discovering his/her behavior.

4. I feel like I am emotionally on edge more now than I used to be before all this happened.

5. I have been surprisingly calm since discovering my partner's behaviors.

6. I find it harder to focus on what is going on around me since I discovered my partner's behavior.

7. I find that I lose things since I learned of my partner's behaviors.

8. I feel the need to monitor my partner's behaviors.

9. When I am around my partner, I am constantly trying to read his/her emotions.

10. I feel like I need to check up on my partner.

11. I feel more anxious since I learned of my partner's behavior.

12. I am worried that I may follow through on an impulse to hurt myself.

13. I feel suicidal due to this experience with my partner.

A summary of these results is available at www.discoverandchange.com/tipsa/assessment under "Criteria E Results."

If you review the results for the criteria associated with marked alterations in arousal (e.g. anger, being on edge, monitoring behaviors, and anxiousness), well over 70% of participants reported experiences of elevated traumatic symptoms after sexual betrayal. The only exception for this was question twelve that asked about harming oneself, which was disturbingly high at 18%.

Below is a specific breakdown of the findings:

- 74% have a hard time with sleep.

- 87% are increasingly angry.

- 95% are more emotionally on edge.

- 87% feel a strong need to monitor their partner's behaviors.

- 90% try to read their partner's emotions.

- 18% were concerned that they might follow through and hurt themselves

Note: I only included the participants who marked this as having happened to them at least half of the time or more.

In reviewing the numbers above, it is clear that the fight response is one of the most common reactions to trauma. It makes sense that individuals who feel threatened by the loss of love and relationship stability would respond with intense emotions. Ironically, these responses usually represent a person's desire for relationship connection. We generally fight for what we want. However, when clients respond to sexual betrayal with apathy, this might indicate a lack of interest in saving the relationship. Therefore, when I hear the offending spouse complain about their spouse's anger, I try to gently share that it would be more concerning if their spouse had no response at all, telling them, "At least when your partner is fighting, they are showing signs that they may still want your relationship."

Recently, while I was working with a couple dealing with sexual betrayal, I had them enact a role play to help them understand their patterns of conflict. As they began talking about how they see each other's position during conflict, I asked the husband what physical stance represents his role in their conflict. He got down on his knees. I asked him where he would put his wife, and he had her stand on a chair. When I turned to her and asked what it was like being on the chair, she said, "I enjoy being angry. It is the only time I feel empowered enough to take a stand for what has happened to me." Then she thought for a minute and said, "But I go back and forth between being angry and feeling ashamed for my behavior." At one point in the role play, she looked at me and said, "I like being angry because it protects me from being hurt again. The problem is that I don't want to be this way."

She was expressing sincere confusion about her emotions. On one hand, she believed that her anger was protecting her and she acknowledged that she had started to enjoy the powerful feeling she felt. It helped her feel like she was taking control of her life. And yet, the more she thought about it, she realized she felt guilty for liking her anger. "I shouldn't be this way," she said.

As we continued the role play, she started understanding more about her anger. She had experienced a controlling father while growing up and resented the way he treated her. Now as an adult, she was not going to let anyone else hurt her. After discovering her husband's betrayal, she had had enough. She felt empowered by her anger and the powerful feelings associated with it. She wasn't sure she wanted to let it go because she was afraid of being hurt again.

This insight was valuable for both her and her husband to hear. She was able to identify the root of her anger and realize that it was simply there to protect her from being hurt again. She began to recognize that she had stopped letting others in after discovery and it was not just her husband she was keeping at a distance. She kept most people at a distance. For years she had avoided thinking about what she was doing and had got into the pattern of being angry to protect herself, which was followed up with feelings of shame for being so angry. It was emotionally draining for her to vacillate between her anger and her shame. After the role play, both she and her husband had a better understanding of the root of her anger.

When clients become aware of their patterns, sometimes their awareness alone will help them make changes. However, more often than not, awareness by itself is not enough to make lasting change. The powerful emotional habits of anger and self-shaming require intentional efforts to create change.

Since we can become addicted to our own emotions, it is helpful to understand that in order to heal, change needs to be more than just behavioral. In other words, the hormones associated with stress (e.g. adrenaline and cortisol) need to be lowered as well. Regarding this challenge, Dr. Joe Dispenza writes, "At first you only need a little of the emotion/drug in order to feel it; then your body becomes desensitized, and your cells require more and more of it just to feel the same again. Trying to change your emotional pattern is like going through drug withdrawal." (2)

Two Methods to Slow Down Your Racing Mind

While under threat, your mind has to be ever-vigilant to protect you. This sign that you are able to protect yourself is a good thing. However, when your fire alarm is always going off, it can become distressing and debilitating. The stress eventually wears down the body. The end result is usually a weakened immune system and increased risk of developing illnesses and potential diseases.

The solutions are not as simple as taking a pill or telling yourself to slow down. After being under perceived threat for extended periods of time, the mind needs to be trained in how to slow down. It needs a quiet place where it can find peace and refuge. Fortunately, there are valuable skills that you can practice to aid you in slowing down your anxious mind. Below is a list of three steps that can help as you learn how to regulate difficult emotions:

Method #1: Increase Your Window of Tolerance

When you are faced with a stressful experience, what happens to your thoughts and emotions? How does your body respond while you are stressed? Can you battle through the pressure or do you feel like shutting down and curling up in a ball until the pressure is gone? Your answer to these questions reveals a lot about your current ability to deal with difficult circumstances.

When you are not able to deal with your own emotions, what we refer to as your affect, you will likely try to escape in one form or another. Your ability to regulate your affect is largely dependent on your ability to shift emotional states. For example, if you find that you are constantly angry and can't slow down your mind, you may find the emotion comparable to putting a car in neutral and pushing on the gas. The engine revs up but you don't go anywhere. In contrast, being able to shift emotions by transitioning out of anger and toward a place of calmness is an example of effective affect regulation.

According to Dr. Daniel Siegel, a leading neuroscientist and mindfulness expert whose work we introduced in Chapter Nine, each of us has a tolerance level for dealing with stress. He refers to this as our window of tolerance. In his book *Mindsight*, he discusses the idea that we all have a personal window of tolerance. The smaller the window, the more difficult it is to deal with seemingly simple daily events. He believes that when we expand our window of tolerance, we are more capable of dealing with day-to-day stressors. By learning how to face difficult emotional experiences, our window of tolerance increases and we gain a greater internal strength.

Regarding this concept, Dr. Siegel writes the following: "Personal change, both in therapy and in life, often depends on widening what I call a 'window of tolerance.' When that window is widened, we can maintain equilibrium in the face of stresses that would once have thrown us off kilter. Think of the window as the band of arousal (of any kind) within which an individual can function well. This band can be narrow or wide. If an experience pushes us outside our window of tolerance, we may fall into rigidity and depression on the one hand, or into chaos on the other. A narrow window of tolerance can constrict our lives." (3)

Most individuals who have experienced sexual betrayal have a smaller window of tolerance. Slight shifts in a partner's behaviors can trigger unexpected anger, irritability, shutting down, or avoidance behaviors. These responses are all symptoms of a decreased window of tolerance. Fortunately, by learning new methods, you can widen your bandwidth. As you practice the skills outlined below, you will naturally increase your ability to deal with stressful events. Imagine finding yourself upset by something your spouse said or did and, instead of reacting with anger, you step back and take a few minutes to identify your core hurt. As you think about what is happening inside of you, you come to the realization that his facial expression reminds you of a time earlier in your marriage when your spouse was hiding his behaviors. His look was your trigger. Now with this new awareness and personal insight, you are able to communicate clearly with your spouse. You say, "When you gave me that look, it reminded me of when you were hiding behaviors and I realized it is a big trigger to me." This type of response would be an indicator of a widening your window of tolerance. As the window gets bigger, new options become apparent and challenging emotional experiences are more readily resolved.

Increasing Tolerance for Difficult Emotions

One of the skills associated with increasing your window of tolerance comes when you discover how to be "with" your emotions. While most people tend to escape from difficult emotions by running or hiding from the discomfort, those who widen their window of tolerance evaluate their deep sadness or anger. Instead of eating for comfort, spending money they don't have, or numbing out in front of a computer, they pause and reflect on their experiences. They ask themselves questions like, "Why am I feeling this tension inside?" or, "I wonder what triggered this response inside of me?" By exploring these thoughts and body sensations, their insight increases.

This process leads to an understanding like what my client identified above in our role play: she wanted her anger to protect her from her husband because as a young girl she had promised herself she would not be hurt again by a man. By gaining this type of insight, she no longer thought of her anger as shameful. She saw it for what it was, a protecting source from hurt she had experienced earlier in life and again from the hurt of her spouse's sexual betrayal. This awareness helped her to stop shaming herself and ultimately aided her in responding without anger to her husband. She became more capable of identifying and thus tolerating her emotions.

The ability to both be "with" and understand your emotions is referred to as affect tolerance. This skill is crucial and is linked to the capacity to modulate the intensity of affect. When you can enter a state of high arousal (anger, irritability) or low arousal (sadness, boredom) without becoming overwhelmed by your own emotions, that is, when you can tolerate your emotions well, it becomes possible to develop the skill of affect modulation as well. As you increase in your capacity to deal with difficult emotions, your sense of self-trust increases and you feel a strength to handle whatever emotions may arise. In contrast, without affect tolerance and modulation, dysregulation, or the inability to cope with your own emotions, can occur.

Many people have asked me how they can increase their window of tolerance so that they are not upset all of the time. A good beginning step is to accept that when you are upset, you are having a normal response that needs to be understood and evaluated before you try to stop it. For example, if you find yourself angry all the time, realize that what you are feeling is serving an important purpose and can teach you if you pay close attention to what is underneath it. Anger is a secondary emotion driven by other emotions like hurt or sadness

Method #2: Pay Attention to Your Inner Self

If possible, stop reading and do a quick body scan. Pay close attention to the sensations you feel throughout your body. Start with your head and work your way down to your neck, shoulders, arms, and your hands. Now shift your attention to the upper torso and core of your body. Gradually work your way down to your stomach, buttocks, and continue working down your body to your upper and lower legs. Finally, feel your feet and toes. As you explored your body in this way, what did you notice? Did you feel tension? Tightness? Any unusual sensations?

This simple exercise illustrates how the process of paying attention can help you become more attuned to your own body. Similar exercises can be done with your thoughts and emotions. Recent discoveries on how you can change your thoughts, emotions, and behaviors has come from research in the field of neuroscience; these discoveries demonstrate how paying attention alters the brain. The researchers have found that by simply paying attention to what is happening inside your mind, you alter or rewire the neural pathways of your brain. Dr. Siegel, in his book *Mind*, writes this regarding how paying attention can change the brain: "With shifts in external attention, the opportunity is created to alter the internal neural firings that shape not only the activity in the brain in the moment, but also alter the structural connections in the brains of those engaged in the interactions, in the communication, among people in the world." He continues by saying, "Where attention goes, neural firing flows and neural connection grows." (4) In other words, the more attention we give to our own thoughts and emotions, the more they change.

During highly stressful experiences like discovering sexual betrayal, it is very common to become misattuned to self. The fear of uncertainty triggers protection mode. In this mental state, the mind races to look for clues of how to respond. Should you fight or flee? Since it is usually in one or the other of these two responses, your digestive system is likely to get upset, your muscles will become tense, and you will be ready for any potential threat that comes your way. While you are "always" ready for the what is coming next, your mind's attention is focused on survival and can't focus on other things. By slowing down the mind and paying attention to thoughts, emotions, and body sensations, you can discover more about yourself and your internal experiences. This insight will help you create new neural connections that can be used for your healing.

The process of learning to pay attention to your thoughts, emotions, and physical sensations can help you and will be a crucial piece to your healing process. Below are two strategies to help you slow down your anxious mind. Later, in Chapter Fourteen, you'll find a case study that illustrates how one client learned to pay close attention to her inner world and how this helped her heal

Now we turn our attention to what it takes for the mind to slow down and relax. We focus on why this process is an indication that healing is happening.

Integration

In a practical sense, anger is the mind's way of protecting itself from a real or perceived threat. It is the natural fight response in all of us. However, when the mind gets stuck in anger, it is usually because it cannot integrate the painful experience or memory. In other words, it cannot make sense of separate elements to provide a harmonious, interrelated whole. An example of non-integration is what happens to you after discovering sexual betrayal. Your mind wants to understand how your spouse could lie to you while saying that he still loves you. These two contradictory thoughts are very difficult to integrate because our mind cannot readily say, "He still loves me even though he is lying to me." Consequently, your mind is not able to integrate these opposing thoughts. Your mind then gets stuck in a loop asking questions like, "How can he say he loves me but still cheat on me?" The lack of understanding usually wears on you to the point where emotional states like depression and anxiety are common. Then, as time progresses and you face new stressors, the unintegrated experiences or memories more readily trigger the unintegrated thoughts and emotions. You become quick to anger or escape or both. The weight of the unresolved trauma coupled with new stressors overwhelms the mind, and anxiety, or other difficult emotions, become the norm.

When individuals heal from any trauma, it is usually because they have discovered how to integrate painful experiences and move beyond them. Therefore, it could be argued that healing from trauma is really integration. Furthermore, when individuals are able to integrate their trauma, they naturally widen the bandwidth of their window of tolerance. That said, the natural next question is: how can we help the mind integrate experiences that make no sense to the mind? Usually, this occurs when your mind is able to make sense of what it is experiencing and you gain a greater sense of how to respond. For example, when I have observed clients healing from sexual betrayal, I have seen how they have integrated their experiences. Often there is a significant shift in their self perception, including new self-beliefs such as, "It's not my fault," or, "I am strong and will be okay with or without this relationship," or, "If things don't change, I will leave." These seemingly simple statements are usually filled with a quiet calmness and internal resolution. The integration process includes a shift in thoughts, emotions, and behaviors.

Unfortunately, the process of integration is not easy. This is especially true when we can't regulate difficult emotions. For example, my client who enjoyed her anger and then felt shame for being angry clearly hadn't integrated her experience. Her hijacked brain lived between anger and shame which prevented her from responding effectively to her husband. Being caught between the anger and shame consequently made her feel helpless and depressed.

Regarding this pattern, Dr. Daniel Hill, author of *Affect Regulation Theory* wrote that when we enter "hyperaroused states of love or hate, we tend to regard others as part objects — idealized or demonized. We lose the ability to reconcile contradictory representations of the same person. The same is true of one's sense of self. In depressed states, we are unable to integrate positive self-representations into our sense of self." (5) When we cannot integrate our experiences with people who have hurt us, we naturally see their bad traits. They become the enemy. This is one reason why when you see them, your stomach turns over.

Dr. Hill continued by explaining, "When affect is dysregulated, the representational system becomes dissociated and loses its integrative capacity". In other words, when we are not able to regulate our emotions, we also cannot integrate our experiences. For example, while in anger, you cannot see your spouse's attempted apology as anything other than an attempt to manipulate or hurt you, regardless of whether he was genuine or not.

In contrast, when your affect is regulated, you are able to see your spouse's attempted apology as an effort to make amends. Even though you still may not want to be close nor do you trust your spouse, you can see their effort as an attempt to improve things. When you are able to integrate this experience and respond flexibly (e.g. "I will watch and see if you continue to make progress," versus a firm-held belief, "You can't change."), you begin to experience a sense of self-mastery, and indeed, when regulated, you are optimally functional. (6)

Dr. Hill believes the process of integration is critical for us to have optimal mental and physical healthy. He believes in the idea that our mind emerges from the body into what he calls the bodymind. Regarding this he wrote, when affect is regulated and the bodymind become integrated. When affect is dysregulated, the bodymind is dissociated. The goal then is to learn how to shift from a dissociated to an integrated self-state which follows a shift from dysregulated to regulated affect. (7)

When individuals move through their trauma, they integrate difficult experiences and see a significant shift in three key areas. First, their thoughts change. For example, instead of obsessing about what their spouse is doing, they focus on things that they can control. I know this is happening when I hear clients say things like, "I don't obsess about what he is doing anymore. I have other things I want to do with my life and I am not going to let his behaviors change me any longer." Second, we see a shift in emotions. Fear and anxiety are reduced and there is a greater sense of calmness. And third, there are physical changes in the body. The biggest manifestation of this is seen in relaxation. In some sessions, I have observed the physical changes in my clients as they have processed through their trauma. Over time, what was once a sense of helplessness shifts to more consistent states of being calm and hopeful for the future. This is what happens when individuals are able to integrate their experiences.

Now that we have discussed two important elements to healing (increasing your window of tolerance and learning to pay attention to your inner self) as well as introduced the idea of integration, it is time for you to learn two of the most effective strategies researchers have found for helping you in your healing and recovery process.

Two Strategies for Helping the Overwhelmed Mind

While in trauma, individuals lose track of their inner selves. In fact, it is common for individuals to become so used to their stress that they don't recognize how chaotic their lives have become. This fact and other research outcomes point to the reality that trauma survivors are deeply disconnected from their core being -- the feeling of being embodied. This seems to be a great source of the suffering associated with complex trauma and PTSD. In essence, research on the brain suggests that traumatized people do not have a reliable self, a feel-able self, a foundation from which to safely experience themselves, relationships, and the world around them. (8)

Strategy #1

Yoga: A Tool for Healing Mind and Body

Have you ever participated in some form of yoga? If so, you have likely experienced powerful emotions while doing some of yoga's most common postures. So how can yoga help with trauma? The primary purpose of yoga is to help an individual get back in touch with their body. Today there are many forms of therapy that now emphasize intervention through a somatic experience. Somatic refers to any clinical intervention that includes, indicates, or acknowledges the body in some way. (9) These methods usually include learning through the body. Some methods believe that trauma is stored in the body and healing occurs by releasing that trauma through movement.

More importantly, there is growing evidence that trauma cannot be "talked out" through traditional talk therapy. New neuroscience findings suggest that traumatized people are alienated from their bodies and that they may be unable to talk about their experience because of the impact to Broca's area, the expressive speech center of the brain. (10) The suggestion here is twofold: we need to pay more attention to what it really feels like to live in a traumatized body and we need a broader range of treatments for traumatized people in addition to those that are talk-based or strictly cognitive. (11)

Over the years, I have gained great respect for the practice of yoga. The center where I work has an outstanding yoga therapist who provides a safe place for clients to navigate through their trauma by using specific postures and movements. As they participate in yoga, they focus their attention on their breathing and on their body sensations moment to moment. According to research, yoga helps individuals begin to notice the connection between their emotions and their bodies; for example, they may notice how anxiety about executing a pose actually throws them off balance. People who practice yoga begin to experiment with changing the way they feel. They explore whether taking a deep breath can relieve that tension in their shoulder. They question whether focusing on exhalations will produce a sense of calm. (12)

According to Dr. Bessel van der Kolk, author of *The Body Keeps the Score* as mentioned in Chapter Eleven, "simply noticing what you feel fosters emotional regulation, and it helps you to stop trying to ignore what is going on inside you. As I often tell my students, the two most important phrases in therapy, as in yoga, are 'Notice that' and 'What happens next?' Once you start approaching your body with curiosity rather than with fear, everything shifts." (13) You are giving attention to a part of you that has been storing your trauma.

Dr. van der Kolk and other researchers have found that "body awareness also changes your sense of time. Trauma makes you feel as if you are stuck forever in a helpless state of horror. In yoga, you learn that sensations rise to a peak and then fall." Yoga is a powerful form of meditation that has been found to help in physiological self-regulation. (14,15)

In van der Kolk's research, he found that moving into certain yoga positions has to be done slowly since some postures have the potential to bring significant emotional discomfort. Regarding this Dr. van der Kolk wrote, "Any posture that involved the pelvis could precipitate intense panic or even flashbacks to sexual assaults. Intense physical sensations unleashed the demons from the past that had been so carefully kept in check by numbing and inattention. This taught us to go slow, often at a snail's pace. That approach paid off: In our most recent study only one out of thirty-four participants did not finish (the treatment protocol)." (16)

Yoga is one form of intense meditation. If carried out in a comfortable environment, it can be a powerful tool for healing. It can also be helpful in developing self-regulation skills.

Strategy #2

Mindful Awareness

While yoga is one form of mindfulness, there are other mindful awareness activities that can be done sitting, walking, or even while eating. Researchers have discovered that mindfulness is one of the most effective tools available to help slow down the racing mind.

So what exactly is mindfulness? Some of the leaders in the field of mindfulness describe it this way: "Being mindful, having mindful awareness, is often defined as a way of intentionally paying attention to the present moment without being swept up by judgments." (17) Dr. Jon Kabat-Zinn views mindfulness as a way of paying attention, on purpose, non-judgmentally to the present moment. (18) While other mindfulness experts like Shauna Shapiro and her colleagues "see mindful practice as how we pay attention to the present moment in 'an open, kind and discerning way.'" (19)

When I initially present these ideas to clients, they often give me a look that says, "What are you talking about?" So, I can only imagine that as you are reading this book you too might be thinking, "What does it mean to pay attention to the present moment without judgement?" I begin by telling my clients whose minds are racing that by practicing what I am teaching them they will learn how to slow down their minds. However, experiencing mindfulness is really the only way to make sense of the definitions above, so I often have them practice mindfulness exercises that include simple things like intentional breathing. (See Appendix I to practice using a basic Mindfulness Exercise).

Mindful Awareness Can Help Heal the Mind, Body, and Relationships

Dr. Daniel Siegel describes what mindfulness can do for those who practice using it in the following way: "Mindful awareness, as we will see, actually involves more than just simply being aware: It involves being aware of aspects of the mind itself. Instead of being on automatic and mindless, mindfulness helps us awaken, and by reflecting on the mind we are enabled to make choices and thus change becomes possible...Studies have shown that specific applications of mindful awareness improve the capacity to regulate emotion, to combat emotional dysfunction, to improve patterns of thinking, and to reduce negative mindsets." (20)

Other researchers have found mindfulness to be effective in treating anxiety, addiction, anger, depression, trauma and much more. (21,22,23,24) Mindfulness can also improve physical health problems: "A range of studies now show that mindfulness meditation can help improve the medical condition of those with psoriasis, fibromyalgia, multiple sclerosis, and hypertension. Mindfulness has now been shown to improve immune function and even raise the level of the enzyme telomerase, which maintains and repairs the ends of chromosomes." (25)

While there are many benefits of practicing mindful awareness, one of the most important is that while dealing with trauma, mindfulness will increase your ability to face the stressors of life. Since experiencing too much stress is one of the most damaging things that can happen to our minds, learning to respond to stress is one of the most valuable skills we can develop. Below is a short list of the benefits of how using mindfulness can help people deal with stress in their relationships:

Less conflict in relationships

One of the more interesting outcomes in research is that individuals who practice mindfulness develop greater self-kindness. This internal shift helps people see others with more kindness as well which helps them when potential conflict arises. In one research outcome exploring how individuals who practiced mindfulness dealt with conflict in their relationships, the authors discovered the following: "The capacity of mindfulness to inhibit reactivity to conflict was also evident in the cognitive judgments that each partner made: those higher in trait mindfulness showed a more positive (or less negative) pre-post conflict change in their perception of the partner and the relationship." (26) This critical finding provides insight into a possible solution to help regulate the typical fight response many people face while dealing with trauma in their relationships.

Better reported quality in relationships

Another benefit of practicing mindful awareness is the ability to improve the quality of relationships. This is one of the most beneficial outcomes for individuals who have been betrayed. Researchers now believe that mindful awareness improves our capacity to attune to ourselves and may reinforce those mental capacities and corresponding neural circuits that support a healthy relationship with other people in both personal and professional settings. (27).

There is great healing power in learning how to attune to ourselves, and because recovery from sexual betrayal requires close supportive connection with others, mindfulness practice is an essential recovery tool. Mindfulness of self supports better quality relationships, and better quality relationships translate to the kind of safe, healing connections needed to heal from trauma.

Understanding nonverbal emotional cues

In my research with individuals who had experienced sexual betrayal, I found that nearly 50% were constantly trying to read their partner's emotions. More than 90% felt at least half of the time like they were trying to understand their partner's emotional output. These statistics show how important understanding their spouses' emotional state is to betrayed partners. The good news is researchers believe that by practicing mindful awareness, individuals can improve their ability to understand the emotional signals of others. "Our relationships with others are also improved perhaps because the ability to perceive the nonverbal emotional signals from others may be enhanced and our ability to sense the internal worlds of others may be augmented." (28)

In my work with clients, I have found that mindfulness is one of the most powerful strategies I can help them develop especially when they haven't been able to slow down their racing minds. I know that when they practice mindfulness, my clients will feel less overwhelmed by internal emotions (e.g. depression and anxiety) and external factors (their relationships). There are many mindful awareness activities available. I encourage you to begin practicing mindfulness by doing the basic breathing exercise found in Appendix I, where you will also find additional resources that I often suggest to my clients.

Chapter Summary

Traumatic symptoms of arousal and reactivity (e.g. anger, fear, monitoring, etc.) are common when sexual betrayal has occurred. When this happens, the mind can easily get stuck in protection mode, constantly ready to protect itself. Two methods for helping regulate intense emotions are 1) increase your window of tolerance;

and 2) slow down and pay attention to thoughts, emotions, and body sensations.

Integration occurs when all of the parts of the traumatic experience are brought together and an individual is able to make sense of what has happened. The outcome of integration is healthy living. Thoughts, emotions, and even physical sensations improve as integration occurs.

Two strategies which can help with integration are yoga and mindfulness. Researchers are finding these two methods extremely helpful in promoting emotional regulation. Additionally, when these two practices are implemented, mind, body, and relationships all benefit.

Ultimately, all five criterion associated with PTSD (threatening experiences, intrusive memories, avoidance, negative mood and cognition, and emotional arousal) can manifest and be treated in the aftermath of sexual betrayal. In the next chapter, the focus will shift to how you can regain confidence by developing self-compassion.

Part Four

The Essentials of Healing

Chapter Thirteen

Self-Compassion: A Hallmark of Healing

If we can find ourselves in the midst of suffering and acknowledge the depth of our struggle, the heart begins to soften automatically. We stop trying to feel better and instead discover sympathy for ourselves. We start caring for ourselves because we're suffering.

Christopher Germer

I looked at the one hundred and fifty women who were waiting for me to say something. They were attending this particular conference looking for help to deal with their spouses sexual betrayal. This annual event brought women together from all over the country. They were hoping for something, anything, to help them with their pain. Together they were strong and united; alone they felt weak and worn out. This was the third year in a row I had been invited to be with them to share what I was learning about sexual betrayal trauma.

Before I could say anything, I was overwhelmed by who they were, their life experiences, and what they were hoping to get out of my presentation. The feeling was so strong inside of me, I found myself tearing up. As I quickly gathered my thoughts and emotions, I found myself saying to them, "I want you to say with me, 'I am awesome.'" They looked at me hesitantly and as I said out loud, "I am awesome," I heard a few repeat after me. Not satisfied, I said, "Let's do that again." The second time we did it together and it was a little better, but I still wanted them to hear themselves and others say, "I am awesome." The third time they said it with more passion in their voices. Once we were done I said to them, "You are awesome, but right now you probably don't believe or know that is true." As I now remember looking out at the faces in the audience, I can still see the tears in some of the women's eyes. I knew they had forgotten this basic truth. They are of infinite worth and value, regardless of life's experiences.

Through painful events, many of the women had gotten lost in their pain. They once felt energetic and were filled with hope for what life could offer. Now, they were each seeking refuge from being with their own self. They hated the way that they felt. Their anger, their inability to focus, and the challenge they had just getting out of bed some days was overwhelming them. They had lost their sense of self. And yet, there they were in the audience, looking for refuge from the chaos of the world they were facing.

During the past twenty-two years of working as a therapist, I have observed many basic truths about us humans. First, we all need someone who genuinely understands us. We need someone to believe in us regardless of whether we are weak or strong, happy or sad, angry or calm. We need someone to believe in us no matter what. One of my favorite authors, Thich Nhat Hanh described it this way, "Without understanding, love can't be true love. We must look deeply in order to see and understand the needs, aspirations, and suffering of the ones we love. We all need love." (1)

While it is true that we all need someone, the most important healing you will do will come from within you. Let me explain. A few years ago my four-year-old daughter had put on a dress that was so cute. I said to her, "You look beautiful in that dress." Her reply was priceless: "I know!" At the time, I thought that her beauty was much deeper than her dress, but realized that she knew of her beauty inside and out. I have thought a lot about that four year old girl. How did she know? What is it inside of us when we are children that seems to know the truth? And what happens to that knowledge? Where does it go?

I have come to realize that life's experiences have a way of attacking that sense of worth. Negative events usually begin long before most children understand what is happening to them. It begins on a playground or in a classroom or even in a child's own home. It can come from being bullied at school or laughed at when you made a mistake. Sadly, it doesn't matter much where self-worth is lost or where the trauma begins; what seems to matter the most is that it happens.

The loss of self-worth is really a loss of self-compassion. When individuals forget who they really are -- a person of infinite worth and value -- they lose their true identity. Therefore, all authentic healing is a restoration of self-beliefs, a reestablishment of the sense of who you are and who you can become. Self-compassion is a requirement for true healing. *So name calling causing*

Why Self-Compassion? H/words /degregation.

The idea of having compassion for self is a novel concept for some people. They can easily feel it for others, but having self-compassion feels strange to them.

In some cases, almost as if they are doing something wrong. They feel guilty or weak because they are not being strong enough. Our society has focused so much on being strong and holding it together that we seldom discuss or explore our own suffering. We simply don't take the time to be with our own suffering. One of the most powerful ways to understand compassion is to look at the roots of the word: "'Compassion' is composed of *com* ('together with') and *passion* ('to suffer')." (2) Through this lens, we realize that when we are compassionate with others we are with them in their suffering. In relating to ourselves, we find that we need to be with ourselves in our suffering and to do so without self-judgment.

In her book *Self-Compassion,* Dr. Kristen Neff suggests that "...we stop to recognize our own suffering. We can't be moved by our own pain if we don't even acknowledge that it exists in the first place." (3) In my work with partners who have experienced sexual betrayal, I have discovered that it is very likely that they feel ashamed by what has happened to them. They have internalized their experience so much that they become ashamed by what their spouse has done and, in some cases, believe they are to blame. Since these were common findings as a result of my research, I began to realize that healing after sexual betrayal would likely not happen without my clients developing self-compassion. Try as you might, you simply cannot heal yourself if you don't like yourself. However, when my clients began having more self-compassion, I discovered that their healing accelerated.

The idea of having self-compassion is not just a feel-good idea. Researchers are discovering that individuals who are self-compassionate "tend to experience fewer negative emotions -- such as fear, irritability, hostility, or distress -- than those who lack self-compassion. These emotions still come up, but they aren't as frequent, long lasting, or persistent." (4) Additional research reveals that individuals who train in self-compassion not only experience decreases in depression and anxiety, but also experience increases in happiness and relationship satisfaction. (5,6) There are additional benefits of practicing self-compassion that are related to having a greater motivation to improve. (7) There are wide-ranging benefits to training your brain with self-compassion. While the research is clear regarding the benefits of practicing self-compassion, it's important to understand why it is so helpful.

Your Brain on Self-Compassion

In one of the most powerful studies on the influence of self-compassion on the brain, neuroscientist Dr. Richard Davidson studied the brains of Tibetan monks who had more than 10,000 hours of practice in various meditations. When he watched their brains, "he found that when they were engaged in compassion meditation — sending compassion to themselves and all beings — they showed the highest readings ever recorded in the happiness centers of their brains." (8)

monks

After completing this study, Davidson wondered how the monks would compare to others who had never practiced meditation. Would they show similar levels of happiness as the monks had? In a second study, "He put [participants] in fMRI tubes to observe their brain activity and taught them the same compassion practice the monks had used. He observed that the practice had a strong effect on the happiness centers of their brains, but not nearly as strong as it did for the monks, who had been training in this practice for decades." (9)

Compassion meditation

In the final phase of Davidson's research, he brought in a third group of people who had never meditated before. He wanted to measure how an intensive 8-week meditation course would influence their brains' levels of happiness. "When he measured their brains at the end of the course, he confirmed his theory. This intensive training had resulted in the subjects having a much stronger happiness response when they meditated, as well as a significantly greater level of happiness while resting. The training had not only improved their ability to create happiness using compassion meditation, they had also developed a happier temperament. This study was an empirical demonstration of Davidson's core message: Well-being can be learned, but it requires practice." (10)

There are two very important findings that stem from Davidson's work. First, the single best intervention for creating happiness is self-compassion. And second, the more individuals train and practice using self-compassion strategies, the happier they will become.

Barriers that Prevent Self-Compassion

When I introduce the idea of self-compassion to my clients and the people who attend my classes, they like the idea, but they struggle to see how it applies to their healing from sexual betrayal. In fact, some believe that it can't help them at all because they have a difficult time accepting the idea that they deserve any kind of compassion. They are facing very painful experiences and yet cannot seem to find a way to have compassion for self. They are suffering deeply and their most difficult barriers come from within. Here are some of the most common barriers I have observed:

Barrier #1: Negative self-talk *NEVER Do This*

This often manifests in individuals who for years have had a negative inner voice that puts the self down. Statements like, "Nobody really likes you," or, "You aren't as good as others," or, "You deserve the bad things that happen to you," or, "You have to work harder than everyone else because you aren't as good as they are." These types of statements may be motivating initially, but eventually they wear you down. In fact, researchers have found that self-criticism is one of the biggest predictors of serious mental health problems (11).

Sarah encourage my kids to stop criticisms themselves & start encouraging

Barrier #2: Lack of awareness

When the mind becomes encompassed in the battle between fighting and flee-ing, much personal insight is lost. This is especially true when it comes to paying attention to personal thoughts, feelings, and body sensations. I often ask clients to slow down and pay closer attention to their inner self. Often, as they learn to listen to their own inner thoughts and body sensations, they discover how out of tune they have become to their own self.

Barrier #3: Treating oneself poorly

There are some individuals who stop taking care of themselves. They so to speak "let themselves go" in various ways. They may stop eating or they may eat to comfort themselves in their pain. Others turn to drugs or alcohol in an effort to soothe their hurt. Still others are so devaluing of self that they punish themselves physically. Some refer to this as self-hatred. *"You are a fool!"* *"Are you crazy!"*

Barrier #4: Unhealthy environment   *"Any woman—for"* *"You didn't do anything"*

Some individuals have a difficult time experiencing self-compassion due to the negative environment in which they live. It is hard to believe in yourself if you are constantly being told that there is something wrong with you. While many people do not fully appreciate the importance of living in a safe environment, it may be one of the single most important elements behind long-term healing and recovery. It is hard to heal in an environment where there is regular negativity. "Constant dripping weareth away the strongest stone." It is hard to stay strong when you are being barraged with negativity. *"F-Y—?!" "You are not a good christian"* *"you are not my blood," "you are not sexy"*

Assessing Your Level of Self-Compassion *"you don't appreciate me,"*

"You don't love my dad," "you were not good..."

In an effort to understand how much or how little individuals have compassion for self after sexual betrayal, I created a short assignment for one of my online classes. I asked partners if they were able to feel compassion for self or if, in-stead, they were critical toward self when discovering sexual betrayal. As you read through the questions and the individual responses, I invite you to think about the amount of compassion you feel for yourself.

Question: As you reflect on your story, are you able to feel compassion for self or are you critical toward yourself?

Responses:

#1: I do feel some compassion, but I am very critical toward myself.

#2: I don't feel critical toward myself. I also don't feel critical or angry with my husband. We were both uneducated and uninformed. I'm glad that we have been able to get education and individually feel the desire to heal.

#3: There are times when I feel very negative toward myself. I feel like I had so many signs over the years that I let slide. How stupid was I to have let those pass by. I didn't get it. I allowed the cheating and lies to continue because I wasn't able to see reality.

Assignment:

As you read the three responses above, identify which of the three most represents your approach regarding self-compassion. Of the three examples above which feels the most compassionate to you?

If you would like to see your personal level of self-compassion, you can take a free assessment written by leading researcher on self-compassion Dr. Kristen Neff. Find the Self-Compassion Assessment at her website: www.self-compassion.org/test-how-self-compassionate-you-are/.

Cultivating Your Compassionate Mind

When I met Amber, she told me that she had always had low self-confidence. For years she had felt inadequate around others and was self-conscious about her appearance. When she discovered that her husband had been viewing pornography and visiting massage parlors for sexual experiences, she was devastated. His behavior was evidence to her that something was wrong with her. She was struggling with depression and heightened anxiety.

In my mind, as I reviewed Amber's case and the many other cases of clients who had experienced sexual betrayal, it became clear to me that to have any form of self-compassion after betrayal was a challenge. In Amber's case, she had struggled with self-compassion for many years even before discovering her husband's betrayal. She had worked hard to make her marriage better. Religion was important to her and she felt that she needed to be forgiving toward him when they had problems. He was kind to her most of the time, but when he held back she interpreted it as her not being good enough for him. Then she would get upset at herself because she didn't know if he was really holding back or not.

In our work together, I introduced her to the aforementioned concepts of cultivating a compassionate mind. My hope is, as it was with Amber, these research-based ideas will aid you in your healing as well. There are specific concepts that have been found to be very effective in helping individuals who are struggling to develop self-compassion. They include 1) learning to befriend painful emotions; 2) watching for negative self-judgments; and 3) increasing self-kindness. Each of these will be discussed below.

Befriending Painful Emotions

In my conversation with Amber, I began by discussing the value of being with her pain. For years she had tried to ignore how her husband's behaviors had hurt her. She had assumed that somehow it would go away if she just tried harder. She somehow thought if she was a better wife and more patient person, he would change. As we talked, I introduced her to one of the steps taught in mindfulness training. One of the first steps is to attune to what is happening inside yourself. "Mindfulness is the ability to feel our pain — if there's pain to feel — and stay out of the drama. That's step one in metta (or loving kindness) practice. When we're aware of and open to discomfort, kindness and compassion flow more easily." (12)

While this was a hard step for Amber to take, she embraced the idea of being with her pain rather than trying to ignore or hide from it. We began practicing this together. I asked her to think about a recent or past experience that represents some of her pain. It wasn't hard as she readily recounted one of her last interactions with her spouse. He had discounted her fears, telling her he was not acting out and it was time for her to "get over it."

As she recounted this experience, it was one of countless memories where she felt like she wasn't being heard by her husband. Instead of focusing on his behaviors, I asked her to gently look inside of herself, to attend to the memory of her experience and listen to how she felt about what had happened. As she looked, she indicated that she felt sad. I asked her to just be with the sadness and listen to what else she felt. She indicated that she was feeling really alone, like nobody knew her. We continued with tracking her emotions as well as her body sensations. She reported that she felt sad in her eyes. She felt a pit in her stomach and chest.

As she identified her deeper thoughts, emotions, and body sensations, we began to transition to having compassion for them. I asked her to attend to the suffering she was experiencing. By attending to it, I was asking her to just be with the hurt and pain and invited her to do so with loving kindness. This is an important point in developing self-compassion. As we sit in hurtful memories, it is so important to do so with loving kindness. As we do so, we honor our own suffering. This is a form of self-comfort. From your brain's perspective, comforting yourself is almost identical to being nurtured by someone else. (13)

Watch Self-Judgments

The next step for Amber was to help her identify how her critical self-talk was hindering her ability to experience self-compassion. We began by attending to the thoughts she had about herself. She easily identified two of her most common core beliefs: "I am not lovable," and, "I am not pretty enough." While she could see these thoughts and knew they were not true, she felt them. It has been my experience that even though we know something may not be true, if we feel it is true, that feeling needs to be addressed.

As we worked together, Amber began to pay more attention to the times these thoughts came into her mind. Instead of just accepting them as truths she started simply observing them without judgment. She was surprised at how often they came into her mind. In fact, in the beginning she was surprised at how often negative thoughts in general would come. "I can't do this," and, "Nobody cares about you," were just a few of the myriad of thoughts that would enter her mind. With practice, she was able to see them more clearly. They were part of what was wearing her down.

The more she saw these thoughts and just observed them, they began losing their power over her. Her self-awareness was increasing and she began to understand herself more fully. Author Tim Desmond wrote, "When we understand someone deeply enough, compassion arises naturally." I believe that someone can be ourselves; the more we deeply understand ourselves, the more compassionate we can become with ourselves. This is what began happening with Amber. Instead of the old patterns of judging herself, she began discovering how to shift her focus from the negative thoughts to a more compassionate view of herself.

This brings us to the third part of cultivating a compassionate mind.

Increase Self-Kindness

In the next step, Amber began focusing on increasing kindness for self. It is not enough to simply remove the negative self-talk. Powerful healing comes when loving kindness is given to oneself. As I discussed this with Amber, she initially was resistant to the idea. Her whole life she had been taught not to be prideful and, consequently, she had a deep belief that she would be prideful if she loved herself.

At this point I asked her what the two great commandments were from Holy Writ. She said, "To love God and to love your neighbor." I responded, "You are right. But you're missing an important part found in those scriptures." We then turned to the Bible and read together. "Thou shalt love the Lord thy God with all thy heart, and with all thy soul, and with all thy mind. This is the first and great commandment. And the second is like unto it, Thou shalt love thy neighbor *as thyself*." (14)

Before she finished reading the last line, Amber realized aloud, "I have never paid attention to that last part." Inherent in the two great commandments is the expectation that we love ourselves. This insight provided her the freedom she needed to begin practicing loving-kindness meditations. It was as if she had been given permission to finally love herself. This was not easy for her. She had felt so inadequate and had been so judgmental of herself for so long that she would catch herself thinking negatively about herself and then gently with loving kindness say, "Oh, there's that thought [the self-critical thought]. I understand you now." Then she would say a little mantra she had developed that went something like, "I have been suffering. I am doing the best I can with what I have. I am not alone." Then she would recite the following loving-kindness meditation:

May I be safe.

May I be happy.

May I be healthy.

May I be at ease.

While these words were not natural for her to say in the beginning, they did offer a good starting place for healing. In *The Mindful Path to Self-Compassion*, Christopher Germer writes the following about the power of our words: "Most of the words we hear are actually going on inside us. Even if you're not generally a talkative person, your mind is constantly chattering away." He suggests that if you say unkind things (e.g. "I am worthless.") to yourself, you will suffer. In contrast, when you say nice things about yourself (e.g. "I did a good job."), you will be happy. "Words shape our experience. That's the rationale behind using words as the focus of attention in loving-kindness meditation." (15).

To fully understand loving-kindness, we need to more fully know ourselves. Thich Nhat Hahn wrote this regarding this process: "To know the real situation within ourselves, we have to survey our own territory thoroughly, including the elements within us that are at war with each other. To bring about harmony, reconciliation, and healing within, we have to understand ourselves. Looking and listening deeply, surveying our territory, is the beginning of love meditation." (16)

As we learn this process, we can begin by coming up with our own loving meditations. Christopher Germer suggests that individuals come up with their own phrases and practice them throughout the day. Some of my favorite loving kindness phrases include:

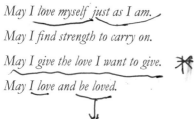

May I love myself just as I am.

May I find strength to carry on.

May I give the love I want to give.

May I love and be loved.

May I be kind to myself.

May I be patient with my imperfections.

Self-Compassion Leads to Self-Care

I knew one client had turned a corner when she said, "I finally went back to college after years of putting my life on hold. I don't know what I was waiting for, but it wasn't going to happen the way I was thinking. I decided that if my life was going to be what I wanted it to be, I had to enroll now and get started." Far too often, when I first meet with clients, they have stopped doing the essentials that help them stay strong through their adversity. As a result, they are worn out physically and emotionally. I have had clients who have lost or gained too much weight. Others can't sleep more than two to four hours a night. Still others have completely stopped going outside and are isolating themselves from others, including family. These behaviors might work temporarily, but over the long-term, they are devastating to one's well-being.

Due to the chaos that takes place after discovering sexual betrayal, in all of the educational classes I teach, I try to focus on how to implement self-care. One of my favorite activities that we have our group participants complete is a self-calming kit (see appendix J). This exercise includes creating a collage of images that represent self-care to the participant. What many of the group members tell us when they complete this exercise is that they had forgotten what it is like to let their hair down and take care of themselves. As they find pictures that represent self-care to them, they also begin implementing self-care when they feel overwhelmed. This self-care helps them through difficult times. Some individuals have a hard time putting into action self-care exercises, so I encourage them to choose one self-care activity each week and make it happen. Soon I begin to hear stories about them getting massages, facials, pedicures, attending a yoga retreat, or having a getaway weekend with friends.

The Essentials of Self-Care

One of the most common things I see in clients right after discovery is that they are in shock. Naturally they go into survival mode. Unfortunately, they can be in this emotional state for months and even years. By the time they come to my office, many have suffered for so long that they struggle to do even basic self-maintenance behaviors. They struggle to sleep, eat, and find time to exercise. Is this you?

Here's a quick quiz for you to take. When was the last time you did the following:

Slept at least 7-8 hours in a given night? No

Ate three healthy meals in one day? No (1 or 2)

Exercised more than twice in a week? ✓ Yes

While few people can say that they often do all three of these things, I have found that my clients are rarely doing these things when we meet for the first time. Unfortunately, while under stress, they stop doing the essentials of good self-care because they are in survival mode. When the basics of eating healthily, sleeping adequately, and exercising regularly are ignored, the body has to work even harder to deal with all of the pressures of life. What I tell all of my clients is if they want to increase their chances of better physical and emotional health, healthy eating, sleeping, and exercise are the essentials.

When I talk with my clients about incorporating these essentials into their lives they readily agree that these are good ideas, but they don't know if they can do them. Usually, they report that sleep is hard to come by and that they aren't hungry. And exercise seems like an impossible luxury with all that is happening in their life.

At this point, that I tell them that healing begins with seemingly small and simple things. I try to help them understand that these are not just good ideas, but that they truly are the essentials of a healthy lifestyle. Below I share with them the science of why these things matter.

Essential Self-Care #1: Sleep

When I meet with clients I often ask them about their sleep patterns. I want to better understand their sleep habits. How many hours a night are they sleeping? Are they taking a sleep aid? How has their pattern of sleep changed since discovering their partner's sexual behaviors? Sleep is critical for all of us and has been found to be one of the most essential elements behind healthy physical and mental well-being.

"Sleep deprivation at its worst is literally torturous; even mild chronic sleep deprivation changes brain chemistry and physiology, leading to deterioration of cognition, memory, and mood." (17) The critical interplay between sleep, physical health, and mental functioning is difficult to overstate. Unfortunately, under extremely high stress and pressure, most people do not know how to effectively shut down their elevated stress, and consequently, they become sleep deprived.

Healthy, restorative sleep is vitally important to our overall functioning, yet most people do not know what to change to improve their sleep habits. For this purpose I have created a short video that my clients can view that will help them understand how they can develop healthy sleep hygiene. (This video is available at www.discoverandchange.com/tipsa/video (see Sleep Hygiene.)

One of the most effective ways to improve sleep is to be intentional about how you approach it. Good sleep habits, or what many refer to as sleep hygiene, include many commonly recognized behaviors. Below is a list of suggestions I give clients based on what researchers have found effective in aiding restorative sleep; many of these suggestions come from a valuable journal article by Dolores Puterbaugh on how professionals can help their clients overcome poor sleep habits. (18)

1. Develop evening rituals that help you slow down before getting into bed. For example, listen to calm, relaxing music or do a mindful meditation.

2. Exercise regularly but not within a few hours of bedtime. (19) Restorative sleep is just one of many benefits to exercise.

3. Reduce or stop using caffeine. Researchers have discovered many negative consequences associated with caffeine consumption.

4. Minimize the use of all electronic media for about one hour before bedtime. Research shows that blue light from these devices reduces melatonin output in the body. (20)

5. Minimize the use of very bright lights before bedtime and regularly expose yourself to bright morning light or very bright artificial light indoors during morning hours to help regulate circadian rhythms (21).

6. Use progressive relaxation techniques before bedtime to help alleviate any tension. Gentle movement will also help reduce stress by activating the parasympathetic nervous system (22).

7. Restrict use of the bed and bedroom to sleep and sex in order to avoid the bed becoming a conditioned stimulus for work, anxiety, lying awake, etc. (23). Note: For some individuals who do not feel safe having sex with their spouse, it may be advisable to sleep in different beds to make the bed a place of relaxation rather than stress. Given that the bed is frequently related to sex, it is important to assess whether the bed can be a safe place or not. The bed should be equated to sleep, not stress.

Essential Self-Care #2: Healthy Eating

The Mental Health Foundation in the United Kingdom reports the following: "Recent evidence suggests that good nutrition is essential for our mental health and that a number of mental health conditions may be influenced by dietary factors." (24) Nutritional psychiatry is a rapidly growing field; the president of the International Society for Nutritional Psychiatry, Felipe Jacka writes, "A very large body of evidence now exists that suggests diet is as important to mental health as it is to physical health." (25)

Given this research, it is clear that healthy dietary habits are important to establish and maintain. Some of the most basic habits can determine our overall health patterns. Here are a few questions for you to consider about your eating patterns:

- Do I eat regular meals throughout the day? Regular eating helps maintain consistent blood sugar levels. Missing meals, especially breakfast, leads to low blood sugar and this can cause low mood, irritability, and fatigue. If you feel hungry between meals, a healthy snack like fruit, nuts, or cereals are a good alternative to sweets or high carb snacks.

- Do I consume a lot of sugary foods? Food with high sugar content, or high glycaemic index foods, is absorbed quickly into the bloodstream. This may cause an initial 'high' or surge of energy that soon wears off as the body increases its insulin production, leaving you feeling tired and low.

- Do I include protein in each meal? By including protein and a healthy carbohydrate at each meal, you ensure a continuous supply of the amino acid tryptophan to the brain. Tryptophan is converted to 5-hydroxy-tryptophan (5-HTP), which is then converted into serotonin, a neurotransmitter essential in regulating appetite, sleep, mood, and pain. Tryptophan is a natural sedative and present in dairy products, meats, brown rice, fish, and soybeans. (26) Unfortunately, most people tend to be unbalanced in their protein intake and are likely to eat more protein with dinner. A more effective approach is balancing out your protein intake throughout the day.

- Do I eat fruit and vegetables throughout the day? According to researchers, nearly two thirds of those who do not report daily mental health problems eat fresh fruit or fruit juice every day compared with less than half of those who do report daily mental health problems. This pattern is similar for fresh vegetables and salad. Those who report some level of mental health problems also eat fewer healthy foods (fresh fruit and vegetables, organic foods, and meals made from scratch) and more unhealthy foods (chips and cookies, chocolate, frozen meals, and fast food). (27)

- Do I drink enough water? Seemingly simple things like dehydration can impact our mental health. The early effects of even mild dehydration can affect our feelings and performance, often characterised by restless or irritable behaviour. (28)

This information is only a small percentage of what is available regarding healthy eating and its benefits to mental health. The single most important thing for you to remember is the connection between diet and mental well-being needs to be seriously considered. While under great stress, you need every advantage you can get to maintain your health and energy. As you review your answers to the questions above, I encourage you to complete the following assignment:

Assignment:

Read and answer the five questions above about your eating habits. Evaluate how you are doing. Are there areas you need to improve on? If so, make a list of things you can work on. Track your progress by observing how you feel physically and mentally for a week. After the week, reevaluate and again identify areas upon which you can improve. Continue this assignment as you work through trauma and recovery.

Note: If you would like to learn more about healthy eating and your mental health I have recorded a short video; visit www.discoverandchange.com/tipsa/video (see Healthy Eating).

Essential Self-Care #3: Exercise

We hear about the physical benefits of exercise all the time and yet few people realize that it is an essential element behind good mental health as well. In *Spark: The Revolutionary New Science of Exercise and the Brain,* Dr. John Ratey wrote, "If exercise came in pill form, it would be plastered across the front page, hailed as the blockbuster drug of the century." (29) In my experience, I have found that clients who regularly exercise report significant benefits. Some believe that it is the only thing that keeps them going when things get difficult.

How does exercise benefit our mental health? First, exercise leads to the release of endorphins, feel good chemicals that help us to relax and feel happy. Exercise has been found to be especially helpful for individuals dealing with stress, anxiety, depression, addiction, hormonal changes associated with menopause, and aging-related issues. (30) If you want a deeper understanding of how exercise helps in all of these areas, I recommend reading Dr. Ratey's exceptional book.

It is safe to say that even small doses of daily exercise are associated with improvements in mental health. That said, how much should you exercise? Research on exercise indicates that 20 to 40 minutes of aerobic activity results in improvements in anxiety and mood that persist for several hours. (31) However, it is also important to understand that too much exercise can be detrimental as it can wear down the body. Furthermore, when you have been through high levels of trauma or abuse, researchers have discovered that it may take your body more time after exercise to regulate back to a calm state. (32)

With the benefits of exercise in mind, please consider the following questions:

- How many times each week do I exercise (e.g. get my heart rate about 1.5 times its resting rate)?

- When I exercise, what benefits have I experienced?

- If I struggle to exercise on a regular basis, what is preventing me from exercising? How could I overcome that obstacle?

- Do I exercise by myself or with others? Researchers have found that individuals who exercise with others are more likely to maintain their exercise routines.

Assignment:

Take a few minutes and evaluate your current exercise routine or lack thereof by answering the questions above. Identify your patterns; identify what is working for you and what is not. If you have not been exercising, begin with a basic plan (e.g. walking 7000-9000 steps each day). Having a specific goal in mind will help you achieve a positive outcome. (I have recorded a short video on how to implement exercise into your healing and recovery; see www.discoverandchange.com/tipsa/ video (see exercise.)

Chapter Summary

After years of therapy with individuals experiencing sexual betrayal trauma, it has been my experience that those who make the most improvement increase their levels of self-compassion. There are four common barriers to self-compassion: 1) negative self-talk, 2) lack of awareness, 3) treating yourself poorly, and 4) being in unhealthy environments. Specific suggestions for improving compassion for yourself include the following: 1) befriending painful emotions, 2) watching self-judgments, and 3) increasing your loving kindness. Taking care of the basics of sleep, healthy eating, and exercise are other ways to show love to yourself. I cannot emphasize enough the value of doing these basic forms of loving kindness for yourself.

In the final chapter, we discuss a case study that illustrates how to implement the strategies discussed in this book.

Chapter Fourteen

A Case Study: Four Key Elements of Healing

New patterns are hard to establish and old patterns are hard to break, but those who pay the price to create lasting change simply act no matter how difficult the journey may be.

The following case study reviews the key elements of trauma treatment as outlined in preceding chapters and explores the different phases of recovery from sexual betrayal. I will begin with the onset of the therapy process, and I will share how I conceptualize this case and what the treatment plan looks like. I will also share this client's assessment outcomes, symptoms, stated goals, the treatment plan we created together, and my personal notes.

Note: Parts of the case outlined below has been changed to protect the confidentiality of my client. In some areas, I have included elements from another case that illustrate a key concept. My hope is this case will serve as an example to demonstrate the process of therapy from beginning to present day.

Misty's Case:

Client Phone Intake:

Client seeking help to cope with recent discovery of husband's sexual betrayal after 14 years of marriage. Client reports that spouse has had multiple affairs over the years that she discovered through a forced disclosure four months ago.

The following are the results of the assessment the client completed before attending her first session:

Client's Trauma Inventory for Partner's of Sex Addicts (TIPSA Scores):

PTSD Criteria	Category
Criteria A--Life Threatening	Moderate
Criteria B--Reliving	Extremely high
Criteria C--Avoidance	Moderate high
Criteria D--Negative Cognitions and Mood	Moderate high
Criteria E--Emotional Arousal and Reactivity	Moderate

Assessment Results for Depression, Anxiety, and Stress

Depression	Extremely severe
Anxiety	Extremely severe
Stress	Severe

Critical Areas Based on Assessment Results:

Early Life Relationships

Client reports emotional and physical abuse as a child. No other form of abuse as a child.

Addiction was a part of her family growing up.

Mother had serious mental health challenges including depression and anxiety.

Dad absent most of the time.

Often left to care for herself.

Current Relationship

Client does not feel safe being with spouse and asked the spouse to leave a few weeks ago.

Client has worried about possibility of getting an STD.

Very low trust in partner.

Client's Current Mental State of Mind

Client has been suicidal in the past, but does not feel this way now.

Physical Symptoms:

Sleep deprivation

Physical exhaustion

Physical pain (ulcers)

Miscellaneous symptoms (high blood pressure, hair loss (client believes due to stress)

Reported symptoms:

Client reported high depression and anxiety which is supported by her assessment results (both were extremely elevated). She said she feels numb most of the time. She said, "I could barely get out of bed when I found out about his affairs. I felt like I didn't know myself anymore. I was a stranger in my own world. I experienced multiple panic attacks each day during the first few weeks. Even now, four months later, I am in shock. I can't stop the obsessive thoughts running through my mind, and I am constantly sad. I wake up in the night startled. I have had nightmares about his sexual affairs."

Client's Stated Goals

Client wants to learn how to overcome her anxiety and depression. She said, "I'm not sure about my marriage. I would like to see if my marriage can be worked out for the children's sake." She reports that she still has feelings of love for her spouse, but is scared of being hurt so she is very hesitant to try and connect.

Her anxiety is wearing her down. She reports being too tired to be angry all of the time, but she has felt angrier now than at any other time in her life.

Other findings from our initial appointment include: 1) not sleeping more than 3-4 hours a night; 2) avoiding friends; 3) distancing herself from her family; 4) having a hard time trusting anyone.

My Notes (Session #1 and #2):

Assess for client's negative self-beliefs based on depressive symptoms and Criteria D (Negative Alterations in Cognitions and Mood). Discuss suicidal thoughts from her past to understand what was happening when she was feeling suicidal. Also, have her consider visiting her physician to discuss the possibility of being prescribed medication for anxiety and depression to stabilize her mood while she works through trauma. She appears to be very motivated in her healing and willing to do whatever it takes. She was open and honest, displaying a depth of trust that surprised me. Assess and observe trust she has with self and others.

A Model to Address Sexual Betrayal: The Essential Tools for Healing

Over the past few years, I have tried to develop a working model in my mind for what healing and recovery from sexual betrayal looks like. Originally, the model was designed to help me remember the key parts of healing in my own work with betrayed partners, as it was easy for me to get lost in the process. The Model to Address Sexual Betrayal below stems from my research and clinical practice. Most of the key areas that I have identified have been discussed throughout this book.

Four core treatment solutions are identified; these are the four general areas clients suffering from betrayal trauma will need to address throughout their healing process. Each core treatment solution is broken down into five specific treatment components; these are the therapy interventions, recovery skills, psychoeducational topics, and healthy living habits I have found essential to healing from betrayal trauma.

While Core Treatment Solution #1 is usually the first step, the other solutions may be introduced at any given time in the therapy process. Furthermore, solutions one through four are not always completed in that order or one at a time, and the components within each solution are not completed linearly. In other words, clients may be working on two or more components under two or more solutions at any given time (e.g. inner circle work (component #4 of solution #3) and the Key Life Events Inventory (component #1 from solution #2) may be addressed concurrently).

A Model to Address Sexual Betrayal: The Essential Tools for Healing

	Core Treatment Solution #1: Seek Genuine Understanding and Create a Safe and Trusting Environment	Core Treatment Solution #2: Internal Exploration: Resolve Difficult Emotions and Hurtful Beliefs	Core Treatment Solution #3: Creating a Positive Support Network While Reducing Negative Interactions	Core Treatment Solution #4: Strengthening Your Inner Self
Component #1	Model compassion	Explore new and old wounds (Key Life Events Inventory)	Boundaries	Self-trust
Component #2	Understand client/ help them feel felt	Identify triggers	Establish close connections	Self-care
Component #3	Provide education and clear guidance	Find core beliefs about self and others	Build a support team	Mindfulness/ Yoga
Component #4	Help client listen to their inner voice	Process painful memories and difficult emotions	Inner circle (identify who's where)	Resiliency
Component #5	Establish working goals to help client feel hope	Treat PTSD symptoms	Understand spiritual connections	Create genuine happiness

Core Treatment Solution #1
Seek Genuine Understanding and Create a Safe and Trusting Environment

After presenting at a recent conference in Las Vegas, a nice woman approached me and introduced herself. She expressed deep gratitude for the website *Bloom for Women* (www.bloomforwomen.com), which I co-founded. She said that she thought she was going to die from her betrayal trauma. She had been searching for answers to what was happening to her mind and body. Then she found our website and started watching our educational videos on trauma. She said to me, "This site saved my life. I truly thought I wasn't going to make it, and then I happened onto one of your videos and it resonated with me. I found myself watching your videos everyday." I took this opportunity to ask her what specifically had helped her. She said, "For the first time, I felt understood, like I wasn't crazy. You made me feel like I was genuinely understood." I often hear this from individuals who participate in our educational classes or watch videos regarding the treatment of sexual betrayal.

After observing my clients for the past twenty years, I have found that the single most important thing I can do for them is create a safe environment where they can be completely open and honest. This is a key indicator that they trust me. When our relationship is built on trust, together we can help them create the lasting change they desire. However, their trust is not easily given after they have been betrayed and hurt by people who should have protected them. Therefore, my goal is to earn their trust. In order to do this, I have identified five key components that aid in building trust in these relationships:

1. Model compassion.

2. Understand client/ help them feel felt.

3. Provide education and clear direction.

4. Help client listen to their inner voice and feel safe with self.

5. Establish working goals to help client feel hope.

Let's look at each of these five components.

Model Compassion

A few years ago, I watched my neighbor sit by the bedside of his elderly wife while she was in a care center. When I was visiting with them, I watched how he loved her. I found myself drawn to the tender care he gave to her. He was by her bedside even though she couldn't talk or say much the last few months of her life. It didn't matter to him that she wasn't able to respond; he just wanted to be with her. This tender example of love taught me a valuable lesson. He modeled for me what genuine compassion looks like: to be with someone in their suffering.

I have found as a therapist that in order for my clients to trust me, they need to know that I am willing to sit with them in their suffering. This means that I try to genuinely understand their heartaches and pains. As I try to genuinely listen, they learn that what they say matters and what they have felt is real. I have found that when I am effective at doing this, our work together leads to positive outcomes. Sometimes we have to sit with people in their pain, and when they know they are not alone in their suffering, they are able to heal.

Understand Client/ Help Them Feel Felt

When any of us seek help with our pain, there are usually so many unresolved issues that it can feel completely overwhelming. Sometimes just being able to describe intense fears, how hard it is to slow down your racing mind, and discuss how alone you feel can be helpful. As a result, a critical step to creating a safe environment is to feel heard and listened to. This is essential if you are talking with a friend, religious leader, family member, or therapist.

Since you will be sharing your deepest and most painful experiences, your trust in this person is vital. Usually when clients seek my help, I know that their trust levels are very low due to what they have experienced. Earning their trust is critical. Anyone who works with someone in trauma should begin by seeking a deep understanding of what is happening without judgment or offering premature advice. It is best to simply listen and try to understand; we need to genuinely seek to understand the suffering of those who come to us in need, without relying on assumptions and while putting aside our own preconceptions regarding the pain of betrayal trauma. We cannot assume we know what they are experiencing. We as clinicians may be the perceived experts on betrayal trauma in general, but we need to be open to learning about each client's specific betrayal trauma experience. Each client is the expert on their own pain. When we are able to openly listen and genuinely try to understand their individual hurt, they feel heard and understood to depths that they may not have experienced before.

When we feel like someone is genuinely listening to us, we naturally let down our protective guard. As we are able to determine that there is no threat, it feels safer to open up. One way we decide that we are safe is when we feel we are understood by others. The term we use for this form of being understood is "feeling felt." The concept of feeling felt comes from Dr. Daniel Siegel who asked one of his clients, "'What was most helpful to you?'" "'Oh, that's obvious,'" she replied. "'Yes,'" I [Dr. Siegel] said, "'I know, but if you had to put words to it, what would you say?'" She paused for a moment, looking at me with moist eyes, and said,

"'You know, I've never had this experience before. I've never had this experience of feeling felt by anyone. That's what helped me get better.'" Feeling felt. I had never heard of such an eloquent way of expressing the connections we have with another person when we are felt, understood, and connected." (1)

Once safety and true understanding have been established, it is important to provide a clear pathway and guidance for what recovery can be like.

Provide Education and Clear Guidance

When I first meet with clients, I want them to understand that there are solutions to help them overcome their suffering. Therefore, once I know that they feel safe (e.g. they are opening up and sharing with me), I then turn my attention to helping them understand what the healing and recovery process looks like. I know that they are looking for someone who not only understands them, but someone who can provide clear guidance through the healing process. If progress is going to occur, they need to both feel that healing is possible and understand the steps they need to take to make it happen. Providing this type of guidance is one of the core pieces of how trust is created between us.

That is, while I know that depression, anxiety, and PTSD symptoms are present, I usually don't focus on these issues in the first session or two. Instead, I begin by understanding the suffering and pain that they are experiencing. This helps me identify their real needs and provide specific guided solutions to meet their needs. Then, in follow-up, I review with them the trauma and other symptoms they are experiencing and then introduce to them how we are going to treat their trauma using The Essential Tools for Healing Model as outlined above.

Help Client Listen to Their Inner Voice

I have discovered that when individuals have been experiencing sexual betrayal, they often question their own instincts. Therefore, early in the treatment process it is imperative to help them realize that the seeds to the solutions to their problems are within themselves. While I can teach, aid, support, and guide them, the key to long-term healing is for them to understand that they know how to heal; they simply need to learn how to once again listen to their inner voice. This is the same voice (or feeling) that has been telling them that something was missing or wrong in their relationship. When I explain to them that they have the answers within themselves and they realize that this is true, their trust in me increases. My message to them is clear: I believe in them.

In order for them to hear their inner voice, they need to stop beating themselves up (see Chapter Eleven), take action (see Chapter Seven), create boundaries (see

Chapter Eight), and realize their true worth and value (see Chapter Thirteen). I have a fundamental belief about people. I believe that we are all of infinite worth and value. If any of us question our worth, it is usually because life's experiences have made it easy for us to question it. We are born with infinite worth and potential. When we learn to listen to it, our inner voice confirms this.

Establish Working Goals to Help Client Feel Hope

The final way I discovered to build trust with my clients is to give them goals to work on. I have found that my clients do best when they know what they are working toward. For example, if I show them the model to treat sexual betrayal above and give them assignments to complete, they begin to see the pathway to healing. By establishing this type of pattern within therapy and through homework between sessions, they begin practicing the skills it takes to heal and recover. This is best done through the creation of a treatment plan that is guided by their current pain, their assessment results, and their expressed goals.

Let's now look again at Misty's example to see how to implement each of these five components.

Misty's Case and Core Treatment Solution #1

By the time I met with Misty, I probably knew more about her struggles than most of the people around her. In her assessment, as outlined above, she was experiencing PTSD symptoms and extremely elevated depression and anxiety. She'd had a very difficult childhood and her husband had betrayed her trust by having multiple affairs. Because she completed the assessment she was asked to take, I knew all of this before we ever met.

Therefore, when we did meet, I needed not focus on information gathering and was prepared to let her explain how she was doing and what she felt like she needed to discuss. She was very open and, after formal introductions, I let her know that I had reviewed her assessment and would like to go over the results, but before we discussed that, I wanted to understand what she was going through in her own words. This is where I learned about her husband's affairs, her painful discovery of his hidden behaviors after nearly 15 years, her response of going numb, having panic attacks, angry outbursts, and subsequent depression. She thought she was "losing it."

Usually, when I hear that, I say something like, "I know it feels like you are losing it. What if I told you what you are experiencing is explainable and that many people who have experienced sexual betrayal respond just like you? Would that be helpful?" When Misty heard this, she replied, "Really? What I'm feeling happens to others?" This gave me the chance to say, "Not only is it common, but it's a natural response." Most people tell me, "I didn't know that. I thought it was just me."

At this point, I explain that I have been gathering data on this for the past ten years, and in my research, sexual betrayal triggers posttraumatic stress in a majority of people. For Misty, I felt it was especially important for her to know that I had seen many women experiencing similar issues and that solutions are available. When I told her this, she said, "What do I need to do? I can't live this way anymore."

It was at this point that I knew she had some trust in me and that she felt safe to move forward. The next step was to seek a deeper understanding of her current pain. I wanted to genuinely understand how her husband's affairs had influenced her thoughts, emotions, and behaviors. When I asked her about her experiences, she said, "I can't think of anything else throughout the day. It has been four months and I should be getting better, but instead I feel like I'm getting worse. I am always anxious and I feel depressed." While I knew this information from her assessment, her description of it helped me understand how deep her feelings ran.

Next, I asked her where she felt the stress in her body. She said, "I feel it in my chest, stomach, and shoulders. Especially in my stomach." I replied, "Is that from the ulcer you described in the assessment?" To which she replied, "Yes. I've had it for a few months." I let her know that the stress she has been experiencing has likely made her feel that she isn't safe, so her body is constantly on guard. I told her that when this happens, her body produces adrenaline and cortisol beyond what it needs. When these chemicals are released, our bodies go into protection mode, which makes it so our digestive system doesn't work very well. I told her it would be normal for her to either not be hungry or to get an upset stomach because her body isn't able to process food the way it normally does when it's relaxed.

She reported that this awareness helped her understand more about herself. Up to this point in our first session, I was just starting to understand small pieces of her suffering. In the next two sessions, Misty began talking more about her relationship with her husband. She described how he had deceived her and lied to her over the years to hide his infidelity. As she opened up, she was able to discuss how it made her feel stupid, as if she was "being played." As she talked about these things, her anger increased and I encouraged her to let the anger out. She was surprised when I asked her to just let the anger come. She had never been allowed to express her true feelings growing up, so my encouraging her to express her anger caught her off guard. She said, "I haven't ever been able to say how I really feel."

As a therapist, I have found that only when clients are able to say whatever they are feeling and express their truest emotions do we get to their core hurts. For this reason, I encourage my clients to learn to give all thoughts and emotions a voice. Often they are afraid to express emotions like anger or shame because our society usually discourages the discussion of feelings. As a result, they have buried these emotions rather than explored them. I encourage them to explore these emotions by having them do it in my office and in a journal at home.

In the third session, Misty reported that she was feeling less depressed, but she was still experiencing quite a bit of anxiety. It was in this session that I talked with her about the model above and we began discussing her healing and recovery game plan. I explained to her that everything I do is usually supported by scientific evidence and that if she ever wanted to ask me why I was doing something, I would explain it. While we had a long way to go in establishing safety in her home environment, she was opening up to me and trust in the therapy process had begun to grow. As I will explain later, her trust in me was a critical step that became even more essential as she progressed.

Below is the treatment plan we created.

Treatment Plan:

Based on Misty's assessment and our first two sessions, we both felt that the primary goal should be to reduce the panic attacks and heightened anxiety that she was feeling. Her PTSD symptoms for Criteria B (reliving) were especially high, and I felt that by focusing on reducing her anxiety she would benefit in this area as well. The second goal we identified was helping her reduce her severe depression. I believed that as we worked on her depression, Criteria D (negative cognitions and mood) symptoms would be reduced. In addition, Misty wanted to make an informed decision regarding her relationship. Additional issues that we agreed to track throughout the therapy process included sleep problems, avoidance of friends and family, and rebuilding trust in others.

Core Treatment Solution #2
Internal Exploration: Integrate Difficult Emotions and Hurtful Beliefs

The five components that I have found helpful in resolving difficult emotions and hurtful beliefs include:

1. Explore new and old wounds.

2. Identify triggers.

3. Find core beliefs about self and others.

4. Process painful memories and difficult emotions.

5.   Treat PTSD symptoms.

In Chapter Twelve, I discuss the idea of healing through integration. Integration is the bringing together of all the parts of your experiences, which allows your mind to begin to make sense of what is happening and what has happened. The chaos of your life turns into organization, structure, and balance. As this happens, you will begin to see depression, anxiety, and other challenges reduce. They do not go completely away, but your window of tolerance has increased. I believe that the earlier we can accomplish integration in therapy, the more hope clients will feel. Addressing the five components listed above is essential to the integration process.

Misty's Case and Core Treatment Solution #2

In order to begin the integration process with Misty as quickly as possible, I needed to understand the experiences that made her feel "non-integrated." In order to deepen her self-awareness and aid me in understanding her, at the end of our third session I asked her to start working on the *Key Life Events Inventory* (See Appendix A). The purpose was to help her identify new and old wounds (Component #1). She came to our fourth session with her worksheet completed. She had gained tremendous personal insight by simply completing the assignment on her own.

Here is the list of key events she identified:

1.   Throughout my entire childhood, my mom was distracted due to health problems and severe depression. The first time I remember knowing something was wrong was coming home from school in first grade and my mom was in her room. At one point, I didn't see her outside of her room for weeks at a time. I thought she was going to die.

2.   My dad was busy and had little time for me and my younger siblings. Once mom got sick, I was her primary caregiver and the primary caregiver for my siblings, too.

3.   At age 10, others made fun of me because I was dressed in old clothes. I was embarrassed to go to school after that.

4.   From age 11-13, there were a lot of conflicts at home and my parents were talking about getting a divorce. I worried about them getting a divorce. They stayed together, but their marriage was not good.

5.   I was lonely throughout junior high school and felt like I was different than others. I spent a lot of time alone when I wasn't taking care of my younger siblings and helping around the house. There wasn't much time for play.

6. In high school, I met Sarah who saved my life. She and her family were so caring and loving; I wanted to live with them. Their home was a safe haven from what I was experiencing at home. This may have been the best time of my life.

7. In college, I met my husband Tim when I was a freshman. He gave me a lot of attention. I thought he was everything I didn't get growing up. He was caring, he made me feel loved, and he made me feel like I was important. We married in 2002. In the beginning of our marriage, I thought he was sent to save me.

8. One year into our marriage, I discovered Tim had been lying to me about his time on the computer. I found that he was viewing pornography. He told me it was a one-time incident and promised it wouldn't happen again.

9. In 2005, we had our first son, Justin.

10. Year five of our marriage, I found that Tim had been chatting with other women online. Again he promised me he wouldn't do it again. I was scared but chose to believe him. I think this was a big turning point for me. I didn't know how big of a problem he had but sensed something was going on. I didn't dare talk about what I was feeling. I didn't trust him.

11. Over the next nine years, I questioned him often about the people he was working with and others. He promised me nothing was happening. In the 14th year of our marriage, I received a phone call from an anonymous person telling me that my husband was cheating on me with another woman. I confronted him about it and he confessed this affair. When I asked him if there was more to tell me, he said there wasn't.

12. A few weeks ago I found out that he had had two more affairs that he hadn't told me about.

As we reviewed the inventory together, she reported that she had never looked at her life this way before. She told me that completing it was helpful, but as she worked on it she realized she had felt alone most of her life. As we talked, she listed some of the key experiences that made her feel like she was by herself. We discussed which of these memories were most painful to her. She said, "It hurts me to think about my relationship with my parents. They were fighting and angry at each other all the time. Mom was depressed and Dad was absent. They weren't there for me." She began crying. "I have never been important to them. They try to show love to me now, but even now, they don't really know me."

Identify Triggers

This awareness provided us the window into identifying the difficult emotions that she had felt but had previously been unable to identify. As we continued talking, I asked her how she responded to others when she felt like she wasn't important to them (Component #2: Identify triggers). She said, "I usually just avoid them. For example, I have gone months at a time without contacting my parents. More recently, I have been distant from my husband. I don't want to connect with him." I pointed out that these are the triggers that we are looking to better understand.

Find Core Beliefs about Self and Others

Next, I wanted to understand more about her core belief, "I am not lovable." (Component #3: Find core beliefs about self and others). She was able to quickly find and make sense of this core belief by drawing on memories from her childhood with her parents. Identifying these memories opened the door for processing (Component #4: Process painful memories and difficult emotions). In the EMDR process, we focus on the first or worst memories that validate the core belief. For Misty, she was able to identify a time when her mom was only out of bed long enough to fight with her dad. On her way back into her bedroom, she turned to Misty and said, "This is all because of you kids." This painful memory was interpreted by young Misty as, "I am not wanted. I am not important." There were other examples that she was able to identify that also made her feel unimportant, but the most recent was the discovery of her husband's affair. It had only validated the belief that she was not important.

Process Painful Memories and Difficult Emotions

Using the EMDR protocol, we began processing her painful memories as well as the emotions associated with those memories. She chose the memory of her mom saying, "This is all because of you kids." As we worked through this memory, other experiences of her parents came up that also reinforced her belief that she was not important. This is typical for EMDR therapy; while Misty processed through her initial memory, additional painful memories emerged. As we continued the processing, she suddenly focused on a very different memory. She remembered being with her grandma who made her feel loved. Then she remembered her closest friend, Sarah. She began crying. After one more eye-movement set, she reported, "God loves me. I am important to God." At that, she stopped crying and firmly said, "I am important. I matter."

At this point, Misty reported significant relief and exhibited a sense of calmness that I had not yet seen in her. At this point I wanted to reinforce her positive self-belief so I encouraged her to begin attending a Mindfulness-Based Stress Reduction (MBSR) class. She left the session relieved and optimistic about herself. We hadn't dealt specifically with her husband's betrayal, but we had helped her establish a stronger sense of self. She knew she was important.

(Note: In this session, Misty began the integration process. She received significant relief from her negative self-belief of "I am not lovable." This is a critical step in the healing process. I introduced a mindfulness class to help reinforce her new belief: "I am important; I matter." This is an example of how solutions from two different categories overlap. The categories listed above are not linear, but designed to help you see the different components of the overall healing process.)

Treat PTSD Symptoms

In our next session, I reviewed what Misty had experienced in our last meeting and we went over additional thoughts she had had since then. She reported that she was experiencing much less anxiety and that she'd had a good week. During this session, I reassessed the PTSD symptoms she reported in our initial session; she now had significantly fewer intrusive memories (Criteria B), less self-loathing (Criteria D), and less anger (Criteria E). However, she was still avoiding interaction with others, especially her husband and friends who had been reaching out to her.

We next shifted our attention to helping her create a meaningful support team.

Core Treatment Solution #3
Creating a Positive Support Network While Reducing Negative Interactions

One of the most important elements in the healing process after betrayal is learning to connect with others in meaningful ways. As discussed in Chapter Ten, when trust is lost in others it is common for individuals to begin avoiding people and social activities that they used to enjoy. Therefore, a crucial element of healing is re-learning how to reach out and create a healthy support network. Even one meaningful close relationship can provide strength.

As I got to know Misty, it became clear that this would be a challenge for her. She had felt different from others for much of her life and connecting with others had proven difficult for as long as she could remember. Establishing support was going to be a big step for her, but not because she didn't want to build close relationships; she simply hadn't had very many good experiences with friends or others.

When clients struggle in their relationships, I usually let them know that we will move slowly and not push them. With Misty, I discussed the key components that I have found helpful with my clients over the years. They are:

1. Inner circle activities (see example below)

2. Creating effective boundaries

3. Building a support team

4. Establishing close connections

5. Address spiritual connections

In my early sessions with Misty, it became clear that she had very little trust in others. While we discussed her lack of connection to others in earlier sessions, I intentionally did not make it the focus of our work together because I felt it would overwhelm her with the other issues she was working on. Instead, I wanted to help her address her other challenges (e.g. PTSD, depression, and anxiety) first.

After her productive EMDR session, I knew that we could start exploring her approach to relationships. Usually after sexual betrayal, clients want to focus on their relationship with their partner. However, I have found it is helpful to understand all of my client's relationships. One way to do this is to do the inner circle exercise. This activity is designed to help clients understand the key people and activities in their lives, and it helps me understand how my clients see themselves in relation to others.

Inner Circle Activity

I encourage you to complete the following activity yourself.

Step 1:

Begin by using 3x5 cards or cut a few pieces of paper in half. On each card or piece of paper, identify one key person or animal (e.g. husband, Mom, Dad, friends, dog Rowdy) present in your life. Next, list the important activities in your life (e.g. work, school, church activities, reading books, shopping, traveling, etc.), each on its own 3x5 card or piece of paper.

Step 2:

Imagine you are in your own little circle. Then, like an onion, different layers surround you and extend out from you. Place each card down where it fits in relation to you in your life today. This is what it looked like for Misty:

Me:

Layer 1: My daughter Caitlyn, eating, reading

Layer 2: Work, church responsibilities (leading a group of teenagers), my son Scott, shopping

Layer 3: My friend Sarah, God

Layer 4: My husband Tim, my mom and dad

Step 3:

Write down in your journal or share with someone your initial thoughts about this inner-circle activity.

Here is Misty's initial response to her inner circle:

I am all alone. I don't have anyone close to me. The closest person to me is my daughter, Caitlyn, but she's young and I wouldn't tell her what's happening in my life. Then there is Scott, but I am having a hard time with him lately. It is interesting that I put Tim and my parents the furthest away from me. I use food and reading books to escape.

In my Layer 2, my work and church responsibilities keep me so busy. I like my job but it's hard to stay focused with what's happening at home. I like the responsibilities I have at church, but again, it's hard for me to focus.

In Layer 3, I was surprised that I put God there. I think this shows how little I trust anyone including God.

Step 4:

Rearrange the cards as needed to reflect how you would like them to be.

Initially this was hard for Misty. She struggled with where to put Tim and God. She wanted to put God in her inner circle, but she recognized that she was mad at Him for not warning her about what Tim was doing. She wanted to move Tim a little closer, but again she was scared of being hurt.

When she was done, this is what her layers looked like:

Me (God, if I can work out my hurt)

Layer 1: Sarah, Caitlyn, Scott, reading

Layer 2: Tim, Work, church responsibilities

Layer 3: my parents, exercise

Layer 4: eating, shopping

Misty was a very spiritual person and wanted to resolve her anger at God. She identified that she wanted to reach out to Sarah, her old friend from high school. She wanted Tim a little closer, but still not too close. She added exercise and moved her parents up to level three. Finally, she moved eating and shopping to the outermost circle. She felt that they were unhealthy coping mechanisms for her.

This exercise was valuable for both of us as it gave us a better idea of what we needed to work on in therapy in regards to her relationships. After completing this exercise, I helped Misty create a gameplan for how to initiate the changes she had just outlined. She wanted to begin with her relationship with Tim. My suggestion was to slowly work on all of them. Her relationship with Tim was complex; in contrast, reaching out to Sarah would be simpler. They had talked periodically throughout the years, so reaching out to her would not be too difficult. We could also begin to address her lack of trust in God.

Over the next few weeks and months, Misty started creating changes. She established some boundaries with Tim (see Misty's boundaries below). She also reached out to Sarah, and began attending a support group. Finally, she addressed how hurt she felt by God. It took effort and time to accomplish all this. In an effort to help you understand how this can happen, I will describe how Misty worked in each of these areas.

Create Clear Boundaries

When Misty initially discovered Tim's behaviors, she didn't know how to respond. She thought about asking him to leave, but instead she had him sleep in a guest bedroom. Other than that, she hadn't established any boundary with him. She had a hard time being around him and when she looked at him, she often would think about what he had done. She felt sick to her stomach when he was close to her. I explained to her that it was normal to have this type of physical response.

As I gathered more information, I asked how Tim had responded after discovery. She said that, in the beginning, Tim was all over the place. One moment he was contrite and apologetic, the next moment he was upset and blaming her. By the time Misty first came to see me, Tim said he was willing to work on his recovery and their relationship but he hadn't really started. After discussing the importance of creating a safe environment in their relationship, Misty identified a few things that she needed from him to rebuild trust.

She created the following boundaries that she discussed with Tim and then he discussed them with his therapist. He agreed to the following:

1. Start regular counselling with someone who specializes in sexual addiction. Tim responded and started his own counseling with another therapist. They worked on preparing a full disclosure.

2. Attend at least two 12-step group meetings a week. He began attending 12-step meetings and reported that he was comfortable with them.

3. Find a sponsor; he found a sponsor at his 12-step meetings and was reporting daily.

4. Give a full disclosure; he prepared his full disclosure with his therapist

5. Sexual boundary: do not push for sex when I say no.

6. Any contact with the other woman needs to be reported immediately. (This was included because a prior affair partner had reached out to him through social media.)

7. Any relapse with pornography had to be disclosed within an hour. Tim also agreed to avoid any social media apps since it had been a way for him to talk with the women he'd had affairs with.

8. She wanted his support if she decided to attend a group.

These boundaries were effective and helped stabilize their relationship. It wasn't always easy, but they both knew what to expect. Misty still didn't trust Tim, but as he continued to live by these boundaries and work on his own recovery, their relationship slowly began to improve.

Building a Support Team

While boundaries were being set and worked on, Misty decided that she wanted to get more support. She let me know that this would be hard for her, but that she wanted to try. I told her that I expected it would be a gradual process due to her life experiences of being hurt in relationships by people she thought would be there for her. She asked me why I thought that. I told her that her Key Life Events Inventory had revealed some potential issues with trust in others that we would eventually need to address. She said, "I see it is time to deal with my past hurts." I replied that it was important to do so if she wanted to change how she approached relationships now.

As we began discussing some of her life experiences, one in particular stood out. Misty referred to an experience she had when she was in fifth grade. Her father didn't make a lot of money so her clothes were worn out and well-used. One day at school, some of the other girls made a negative comment about what she was wearing. From that day forward, she felt isolated from girls her age. That experience was a game-changer for her as she recognized that she had pulled back from others. When she met Sarah, she thought her discomfort with others was gone. However, not long into her first semester at college, she met Tim. Sarah had gone to another college so all of her attention turned to him. When they started having problems, she didn't have anyone to turn to. In fact, her insecurities had come back and she didn't know where to turn for support.

We did two things to address the isolation these events had created for Misty. First, we used EMDR therapy to deal with her experience as a fifth grader. She was able to process through the negative belief, "I'm not as good as others." Through EMDR, she realized that the girls were unkind, but their response was due to their own insecurities. Her belief changed to, "I am a good person." This was an important first step because it allowed her to see herself as someone who is a good person and that others would want to be around. This was especially critical for Misty because she had felt inferior to others since that experience in fifth grade. Having worked through that difficult memory, it was now time to start building her support team.

Second, we identified people that she would like to be closer to. She readily identified Sarah, but she lived in a different state. Then she said, "I don't have anyone else!" I encouraged her to begin attending an educational support group at our center. She started and began bonding with other women in her group. This group was a powerful support to her. They began going out to lunch with each other, supporting each other on their birthdays, and when they were going through something hard, they would reach out to each other. She had built a support team. As an observer of her experience, I was impressed with the way she and the other women reached out to each other.

Establish Close Connections

Even though Sarah lived in a different state, Misty still reached out to her and plans to visit. While there, they caught up and Misty shared with her what was happening in her relationship with Tim. Sarah was very supportive and said that she could call her anytime. This bond created an extra support for Misty, one she had been missing for years.

Misty also started making more connections with the women in her church congregation. For the first time since high school, she was connecting with others. She became especially close to one woman from church who she discovered was experiencing similar challenges with her husband. Misty really bonded with her and they became each other's supports during very difficult times.

While Misty's experience may sound like it was easy for her, it was not. In the beginning, she was hesitant and held back in her group. It took her a few months to reach out to Sarah. She had a hard time at church until about nine months into her work, when she observed another woman struggling and she asked her if everything was okay. It was at that time the woman opened up to her what was happening in her marriage and the two began building a true friendship. All in all, it took about sixteen months to establish deeper bonds and friendships.

Address Spiritual Connections (or Disconnections)

After a few months (about our 15th session together), Misty came to therapy and said, "I think it is time for me to deal with my God issue." She had given much thought to why she was upset at God. She said, "After I discovered Tim chatting with other women, I was going to leave. But when I prayed asking for guidance, I felt impressed to stay. So I did. I think that is when I started questioning God and why He would tell me to stay even though He knew Tim would eventually cheat on me."

As we talked, it became apparent that Misty had a belief that God didn't care about her or He would have protected her from this hurt. And yet, even with this core belief in place, she still longed for a deeper connection with God. She was a very spiritual person and this disconnect with God was very distressing to her.

By this time, she had had enough positive experiences with EMDR that she asked if she could do a session of EMDR to deal with this belief. She even was able to identify her belief on her own: "God doesn't love me. I'm not important to Him." Within the first five minutes of doing EMDR, she stopped me because she was giggling. She said, "What was I thinking? God has been there for me. He can't stop my husband from doing what he did, but He has comforted me countless times. Of course He loves me."

Resolving that painful disconnect with God was very important to her overall healing. She was a very spiritual woman who had lost this important connection. It wasn't long after resolving her belief that God didn't love her that she had that initial connecting conversation with her newfound friend at church.

In my experience, many individuals are like Misty. They believe in God, but they become confused because of the sexual betrayal. They question whether God is trustworthy. They wonder if He too has abandoned them. Often because of their anger they believe God is disappointed in them. In sum, they are confused spiritually.

The solution to these spiritual challenges, as was the case with Misty, is to address the core trauma issues. It has been my experience that when the trauma is reduced, unresolved spiritual questions can be effectively addressed. As trauma decreases, the mind naturally returns to it roots. When spiritual healing occurs this meaningful bond or connection with one's Higher Power heals the deepest wounds.

For Misty, resolving her relationship issues with her Higher Power was important to her long-term healing. I have observed that all individuals, regardless of their spiritual beliefs, benefit by addressing any anger, hurt, rejection, or disappointment with their Higher Power. If you do not believe in a God, you may not have the same spiritual questions or concerns that Misty experienced; however, it will still be important for you to find your place for mental peace. This means identifying something bigger than yourself that you can connect with. In other words, where do you go in times of desperation, when everything else fails? For some, this place is the arts: music, literature, museums, theater, design, writing, etc. For others, peace is found in the natural world: hiking, walking, swimming, running, gardening, getting fresh air, etc. For still others, this place of peace is a hobby: fitness, meditation, yoga, animals, collections, blogging, volunteering, finances, organizing, etc. *What* it is does not matter; what *does* matter is identifying for yourself what helps you feel connected, grounded, and most like yourself. In the end, we all need to find our place of peace. This is where our minds rest and find comfort.

Core Treatment Solution #4
Strengthening Your Inner Self

In working with individuals who have experienced sexual betrayal, it is easy to ignore their core inner strengths. Many have learned to escape into behaviors that do not resolve their pain, but rather leave them feeling out of control. Unfortunately, what most people see is the outward manifesting behaviors (e.g. angry outbursts, lack of interest in others, drinking, etc.). These coping behaviors are efforts to cover up the internal pain, but they don't make the pain go away. In fact, I have discovered that none of us can run fast enough or hide well enough to escape our pain. Sadly, after many failed attempts to resolve their pain, most people no longer feel competent to resolve their problems. In fact, they are right. They can't make their partner stop acting out. However, they *can* gain enough inner strength to make important decisions regarding their own futures.

Misty's Case and Core Solution #4

In the first few weeks of therapy with Misty, I emphasized that we were going to spend time in our sessions working on her inner self. Based on what she had told me, I knew that she not only didn't trust others, but she didn't trust herself either. She felt weak for staying with Tim after she caught him chatting with other women. She felt out of control when she got angry. She was upset that she couldn't get what he did out of her mind. She hated how she coped by eating. She simply didn't trust herself.

I let her know that one of the most critical steps to her long-term healing would come from strengthening her inner self. I outlined the following areas (Components #1-5 under Core Treatment Solution #4) that I believe are essential to healing:

1. Self-Trust

2. Self-care

3. Mindfulness/Yoga

4. Resiliency

5. Discovering your happiness

Here is how we implemented these five important parts of her recovery:

Self-Trust

When I used the word self-trust, Misty quickly said, "I don't trust myself. How is that even possible?" At that time in the therapy process, I validated her feelings but encouraged her to please put in the back of her mind that one of our goals would be to help her trust herself again.

Self-trust, I explained to Misty, comes when you learn to listen to your inner voice again. It is this voice that usually drives you to take action when you need to. In *Trust: Mastering the 4 Essential Trusts*, Iyanla Vanzant describes it this way: "Self-trust is about having an inner voice, being connected to that inner voice, learning how to hear and follow that voice, and doing the personal healing work required to make sure that the voice you hear brings your best interests to the forefront of your mind." (2)

As we discussed this concept, Misty asked, "I haven't learned how to do that. I don't trust myself. Where do I start?" We began with a simple concept: "What do you want to change?" By the time we had this conversation, she was doing better with her depression and anxiety, but she still found herself getting angry with Tim and with others. So we decided to focus on reducing her anger.

I taught her a simple practice described by Mark Reiter in *Triggers*. He suggests that one way to make lasting change is to ask yourself daily questions. Reiter suggests that first a person should decide what they want to change, then track their progress by asking themselves daily questions.

When I introduced this concept to Misty her focus was on reducing her anger. Here's how she began implementing this process:

Goal: Reduce my anger

Daily question: Did I do my best to…not get angry?

Daily tracking (scoring 0 = no and 10 = absolutely)

I had Misty track her anger this way between our appointments. At the end of each day she would give herself a score. By simply monitoring her anger at the end of each day, she felt like she was getting less angry at home. When she scored a ten, she was happy to see her progress. When she scored a five, she reported what had happened and why she fell short. As she did this, her awareness increased and she was able to gain more control over her anger.

Misty liked this idea so much that she began implementing it in other areas of her life. She used it with eating and exercise. She was gaining good traction by simply identifying what she wanted to change and then asking herself the daily question, "Did I do my best to…"

I have found that clients like this exercise as it helps them gain more confidence in self. It also helps them establish healthy habits that create lasting behavioral changes. For Misty, this activity was very helpful and was significant in helping her feel a greater sense of self-trust.

Exercise: What do you want to change? Be specific and then ask yourself the daily question "Did I do my best to…" Track your score for at least two weeks by giving yourself a score between 0 (not at all) and 10 (completely).

Self-Care

In our earliest sessions I asked Misty if she was taking care of herself. She replied, "Not really. I don't have much energy to do anything." In our early sessions I evaluated her sleep, eating, and exercise habits. She wasn't doing well in any of the categories. However, as I mentioned earlier, she was very motivated to heal. Within a few sessions she was working on eating better and she was exercising on a regular basis. Sleep was difficult in the beginning due to her nightmares, but her sleep improved after she had completed a few sessions of mindfulness and processed some difficult emotions through EMDR therapy.

Over time, Misty began implementing other forms of self-care into her routine:

- Receiving regular massages
- Getting a pedicure
- Meeting with a nutritionist to discuss healthy eating
- Giving herself a half day off each week to spend time doing what she wanted to do (e.g. be with friends, read a book, etc.)
- Attending Yoga sessions

Yoga/ Mindfulness/ Find a calm place

In our initial treatment planning, I asked Misty if she had ever participated in yoga or mindfulness training. When she said she hadn't, I shared with her that in order to overcome some of her anxiety and depression, we would need to help her slow down her mind; I had just the perfect thing for her.

As outlined in the initial intake, Misty was constantly dysregulated. She was anxious, depressed, and angry. I told Misty that she could receive some mental relief if we could teach her how to regulate those emotions. She was interested, so I introduced her to the following three healing tools:

Tool #1: Yoga: The Art of Attuning to Self

As we concluded our second session, I introduced Misty to our yoga instructor. Over the next few weeks, she began participating in yoga. She really enjoyed it and reported that while it was hard, her capacity to listen to her body during difficult experiences increased. Her weekly yoga was one of the primary methods she used to discover how to slow down and listen to her body. She reported that after a couple sessions, she had fewer days of heightened anxiety and her panic attacks were gone.

Tool #2: Practice a Mindful Awareness Activity Daily

Not long after starting yoga, Misty had a day where she had very high anxiety and wished that she could do something by herself in those moments. This began a series of discussions about using mindfulness as a daily practice. Initially, I introduced her to the exercise found in Appendix I. Now, I have clients read Chapter Thirteen from this book and watch the video *The Secret Sauce of Healing*. In the video, I demonstrate some basic activities for developing self-compassion. (More information about this and other videos is provided at the end of this book.)

Tool #3: Find a Calm/Safe Place

I explained to Misty what I have said throughout this book: "The human mind needs rest." When it gets stuck in the always "on" mode, we get worn out and overwhelmed. Once we understand this important concept, we realize that one powerful way to get unstuck is to create a safe/calm place where the mind can find rest. Learn how to do this by listening to the audio recording titled Calm/Safe Place at the following link: www.discoverandchange.com/tipsa/audio.

Misty was responding well to yoga and her mindfulness exercises. I encouraged her to begin practicing the mindfulness breathing on her own each day. I then suggested she listen to some guided mindfulness recordings. She began using these strategies when she was feeling overwhelmed. Instead of retreating into panic she learned to attend to her fear and notice her physical sensations. As her awareness increased, her anxiety and fear decreased. She began to have more confidence in her ability to deal with difficult emotions.

Resiliency

One of the key components of people who heal is they are resilient. During the past few years, as I've studied what experts believe make us resilient, I had the privilege of doing a radio interview with Dr. Al Seibert. His book *The Resiliency Advantage* has made a lasting impression on me. After our interview, I was so impressed with him that I asked if he would join me for another show. He politely declined and informed me that he was fighting his own battle with cancer and would likely not survive; he sadly died three months later.

Dr. Seibert spent 35 years studying the lives of resilient people and said to me after our interview, "I have studied the lives of others, but I am now having to do it myself." In his book, he poses a poignant question: "What do you do when your life turns upside down? When the world around you know falls apart, how do you avoid being stuck in the pain?" (3)

As clients like Misty progress, I begin giving additional attention in our sessions to their progress. Many of my client's feel the change but don't take stock of exactly how much change they have made. After nearly a year of individual therapy, group therapy, yoga, and mindfulness practice, Misty had made significant progress.

Near the end of one particular session, I asked Misty if I could review how far she had come. Together we reviewed her initial treatment plan:

Goal #1: Provide strategies to slow down the mind.

Help Misty slow down her racing mind by encouraging her to practice mindful awareness, attend yoga, and establish a safe/calm place.

Goal #2: Explore current relationship trauma and other life experiences that are not integrated.

Give Misty the Key Life Event Inventory. Help her understand her relationship history and how her past plays into her relationships with Tim and others.

Goal #3: Explore beliefs about self and others to help integrate disturbing relationship memories.

Develop strategies to cope with depression and anxiety. Primarily focus on negative self-beliefs.

Goal #4: Develop meaningful connections and a support team.

Help Misty develop meaningful connections. Since Misty has very little outside support and does not feel safe with others, therapy needs to focus on helping her develop more meaningful friendships. Misty also wants to have a better relationship with her two children.

After reviewing these initial goals, Misty realized how far she had come. In every area, she had seen significant improvement. To this I said, "We are resilient human beings. We can do hard things. During this past year, you have done everything I have asked plus some." She truly was demonstrating the characteristics of resilient people.

Near the end of my sessions with clients like Misty, I give them a final challenge.

Create Genuine Happiness

After years of suffering and surviving, healing is not about just getting over the pain. True healing is creating genuine happiness. This is not a concept that can be taught at the beginning of therapy, rather it is one of the last steps to healing that reinforces all of the life changes that have transpired.

For Misty this concept made sense, but she felt a little lost. She had spent so much energy on dealing with Tim's betrayal and her own challenges that she hadn't given much thought to the concept of "being happy." She reported that she was feeling better than she had felt in many years, so she didn't know where to go with this idea. I asked if she would like a few ideas and she said she would. I shared with her the following proven strategies from Martin Seligman's Positive Psychology.

Activity #1: Each day write down three things that you are grateful and why you are grateful for each thing. Do this for at least 30 days in a row.

Example: I am grateful for my friends. Why? For so many years I felt completely alone and isolated. Now I have people that I trust completely.

Activity #2: Write a letter (300-500 words) expressing gratitude to someone who has had a positive influence in your life. Set up a time to visit them and read them your letter.

According to Dr. Seligman's research, these two exercises are very effective in creating positive emotions and lead to increased levels of happiness. (4) Misty took the first challenge and reported in our next session that she found by focusing on what she was grateful for each day, she was feeling optimistic.

It was at this point that therapy with Misty concluded. She had made tremendous progress. I have seen many clients have experiences like Misty. The journey is hard and difficult, but it is worth it.

Chapter Summary

I hope that this case study has provided additional insight into the process of change. In this chapter I introduced the complete model to address sexual betrayal. I have included the *Four Core Treatment Solutions* which include:

1. Seek genuine understanding and create a safe environment.

2. Internal exploration: Resolve difficult emotions and hurtful beliefs.

3. Create a positive support network while reducing negative interactions.

4. Strengthen your inner self.

I believe that these four treatment solutions are the essential tools for healing. Misty's case study shows how each of these four solutions apply to the healing process and demonstrates how to use all four solutions with each of the components in recovery. In Misty's case, she incorporated many of the strategies into her healing.

Thank You

Dear Reader,

I hope that as you have read this book, you have gathered helpful ideas for how you can heal and move forward in your life. While I do not know all of the heartache you have experienced, my desire is for you to find relief from your suffering. As an observer, through research and many hours of therapy with those experiencing sexual betrayal, I feel a deep sense of compassion for your suffering. If this book has provided insight to aid you in your healing process and helped you move toward mending your wounded heart, then it has accomplished its purpose.

I can't express the gratitude I have to you for letting me share with you what I have learned about *Treating Trauma from Sexual Betrayal*. Thank you for letting me be a small part of your life's journey. I hope that you have found my research and clinical experiences to be helpful in your healing.

I need to express gratitude to my clients and others who have trusted me with their lives. They are my heroes. I also need to express gratitude to the thousands of individuals who have completed my online survey. Your responses have made this book possible. I hope that you find this book gives a voice to your pain. My deepest desire is that you have found solutions to your pain as you have read this book.

With my deepest appreciation, I thank you. May you be blessed in your healing journey.

Best regards,

Dr. Kevin B. Skinner, LMFT, CSAT-S

References and Notes:

Introduction:

1. Steffens, B A., & Rennie, R. L. (2006). The Traumatic Nature of Disclosure for Wives of Sexual Addicts. Sexual Addiction & Compulsivity, 13, 247-267

2. Glass, S. (2003). Not just friends: Protect your relationship from infidelity and heal the trauma of betrayal. New York: The Free Press.

3. Johnson, S. (2002). Emotionally focused couple therapy with trauma survivors. New York: Guilford.

Chapter One:

1. Porges, S. W. (2011). The Polyvagal Theory: Neurophysiological Foundations of Emotions, Attachment, Communication, and Self-regulation (Norton Series on Interpersonal Neurobiology). W. W. Norton & Company. New York: New York

2. Vanzant, I. (2015). Trust: Mastering the Four Essential Trusts. Smiley Books. Carlsbad, CA.

Chapter Two:

1. https://en.m.wikipedia.org/wiki/Hypervigilance

Chapter Three:

1. Oxford Dictionary definition of 'gaslighting'". Oxford Dictionaries. Oxford University Press. Retrieved 20 April 2016.

2. Dorpat, T.L. (1994). "*On the double whammy and gaslighting*". *Psychoanalysis & Psychotherapy*. 11 (1): 91–96."

Chapter Four:

1. Sapolsky, Robert M., Why Zebras Don't Get Ulcers (New York: Henry Holt and Company, 2004). Sapolsky is a leading expert on stress and its effects on the brain and body. Also see: Joe Dispenza, Evolve Your Brain: The Science of Changing Your Mind (Deerfield Beach, FL: Health Com-

munications, Inc., 2007). In addition, emotional addiction is a concept taught at Ramtha's School of Enlightenment; see JZK Publishing, a division of JZK, Inc., the publishing house for RSE, at: http://jzkpublishing. com or http://www.ramtha.com.

Chapter Five:

1. Schneider, J. P., Corley, M. D., and Iron, R. R. (1998). Surviving Disclosure of Infidelity: Results of an International Survey of 164 Recovering Sex Addicts and Partners. *Sexual Addiction & Compulsivity, 5 (3): 189-218.*

2. Schenider, J. P., Corley, M. D. (2002). Disclosing secrets: Guidelines for therapists working with sex addicts and coaddicts. *Sexual Addiction and Compulsivity 9: 43-67.*

3. Zeigarnik 1927: Das Behalten erledigter und unerledigter Handlungen. Psychologische Forschung 9, 1-85.

4. Gottman, J. M. (2011). The Science of Trust. W. W. Norton, New York: New York

5. Schneider, J. P. (2015). Back from Betrayal: Recovering From the Trauma of Infidelity, Forth Edition, 2015. Originally published by Hazelden/ Harper and Row.

Chapter Six:

1. Porges, S. W. (2011). The Polyvagal Theory: Neurophysiological Foundations of Emotions, Attachment, Communication, and Self-regulation (Norton Series on Interpersonal Neurobiology). W. W. Norton & Company. New York: New York

2. Ibid Porges, S. W., (2011).

3. Gottman, J. M. (2011). The Science of Trust. W. W. Norton, New York: New York

Chapter Seven:

1. Sherwood, B. (2009). The Survivors Club: The Secrets and Science that could save your life. Grand Central Publishing. Pg. 48.

2. Leach, J. (2004). Why people 'freeze' in an emergency: Temporal and cognitive constraints on survival responses. Aviation, Space & Environmental Medicine, 75, 539–542.

3. Leach, J. (1994). Survival psychology. Basingstoke: Palgrave Macmillan.

References and Notes:

4. http://dictionary.reference.com/browse/perseveration

5. http://neuraptitude.org/2016/06/27/risk-of-relapse-declines-significantly-after-5-years-of-abstinence-from-alcohol/

6. Duhigg, C. (2012). The Power of Habit: why we do what we do in life and business. Random House, Inc.: New York: New York.

7. 1966, The Manufacturing Man and His Job by Robert E. Finley and Henry R. Ziobro, "The Manufacturing Manager's Skills" by William H. Markle (Vice President, Stainless Processing Company, Chicago, Illinois), Start Page 15, Quote Page 18, Published by American Management Association, Inc., New York.

Chapter Eight:

1. Diagnostic and statistical manual of mental disorders: DSM-5. (2013). Washington, D.C.: American Psychiatric Association.

2. Seligman, M. E. P. (1972). "Learned helplessness". Annual Review of Medicine. 23 (1): 407–412.

3. Ibid Seligman, M. E. P. (1972).

4. Carlson, Neil R. (2010). Psychology the science of behavior. Pearson Canada. p. 409. ISBN 978-0-205-69918-6.

5. Nolen, J.L. "Learned helplessness". Encyclopaedia Britannica. Retrieved January 14, 2014.

6. Gallup, G., & Maser, J. (1977). Tonic Immobility: Evolutionary Underpinnings of Human Catalepsy and Catalonia. In J.D. Maser & M.F. P. Seligman (Eds.), Psychopathology: Experimental Models. San Francisco: Freeman.

7. Levine, P.A., 2010. In an Unspoken Voice: How the Body Releases Trauma and Restores Goodness. North Atlantic Books. Berkeley California

8. Ibid Levin, P. A. (2010).

9. Ibid Levin, P. A. (2010).

10. Ibid Levin, P. A. (2010).

11. Ibid Levine, P. A. (2010).

12. Ibid Levine, P. A. (2010).

13. Carnes, S. (2011). Mending a Shattered Heart. Gentle Path Press. Carefree Arizona. (2nd Edition, edit by S. Carnes.) Chapter 5 by Cara Tripodi,

"How Do I Set Boundaries and Keep Myself Safe?"

14. Wallace, A. C. (1997). Setting Psychological Boundaries: A Handbook of Women. Bergen and Garvey. Westport, CT.

15. Levine, P. A. (2010). In an Unspoken Voice. How the body releases trauma and restores goodness. North Atlantic Books. Berkeley CA.

16. Ibid Levine, P. A. (2010).

17. Wallace, A. C. (1997). Setting Psychological Boundaries: A Handbook of Women. Bergen and Garvey. Westport, CT.

18. Mellody, P., Miller, A. W., & Miller, K. (1992). Facing love addiction: giving yourself the power to change the way you love: the love connection to codependence. New York, NY: HarperSan Francisco.

19. Porges, S. W. (2011). The Polyvagal Theory: Neurophysiological Foundations of Emotions, Attachment, Communication, and Self-regulation (Norton Series on Interpersonal Neurobiology). W. W. Norton & Company. New York: New York

20. Gaskin, I. M. (2003). Ina May's guide to childbirth. New York: Bantam Books.

21. Ibid Porges, S. W. (2011).

Chapter Nine:

1. http://www.discoverandchange.com/TIPSA/audio (LeDoux)

2. http://www.toyota-global.com/company/toyota_traditions/quality/mar_apr_2006.html

3. von Bohlen und Halbach, O; Dermietzel, R (2006). Neurotransmitters and neuromodulators: handbook of receptors and biological effects. Wiley-VCH. p. 125. ISBN 978-3-527-31307-5.

4. Amunts, K.; Kedo, O.; Kindler, M.; Pieperhoff, P.; Mohlberg, H.; Shah, N. J.; Habel, U.; Schneider, F.; Zilles, K. (2005). "Cytoarchitectonic mapping of the human amygdala, hippocampal region and entorhinal cortex: Intersubject variability and probability maps". Anatomy and Embryology. 210 (5–6): 343–352. doi:10.1007/s00429-005-0025-5. PMID 16208455.

5. Schacter, Daniel L.; Gilbert, Daniel T. and Wegner, Daniel M. (2011) Psychology Study Guide, Worth Publishers, ISBN 1429206152.

6. Ledoux, J. (2003). "The emotional brain, fear, and the amygdala". Cellular and molecular neurobiology. 23 (4–5): 727–738.

doi:10.1023/A:1025048802629. PMID 14514027.

7. American Psychiatric Association (1994). Diagnostic and statistical manual of mental disorders: DSM-IV. Washington, DC. ISBN 0-89042-061-0.

8. Kabat-Zinn, J. (2003a). Mindfulness-based interventions in context: Past, present, and future. Clinical Psychology: Science and Practice, 10(2), 144–156.

9. Siegel, D. J. (2007). The Mindful Brain: Reflection and Attunement in the Cultivation of Well-Being. W. W. Norton: New York: New York

10. Bishop, S. R., Lau, M., Shapiro, S., Carlson, L., Anderson, N. D., & Carmody, J. et al. (2004). Mindfulness: A proposed operational definition. Clinical Psychology: Science and Practice, 11(3), 230–241.

Chapter Ten:

1. Cacioppo, J., & Patrick, W. (2008). Loneliness: Human nature and the need for social connection. New York: Norton.

2. Ibid from Cacioppo and Patrick (2008)

3. I. Asker Lind and J. O. Hornquist, "Loneliness and alcohol abuse: A review of evidence of an interplay," *Social Science and Medicine,* 34 (1992): 405-414. A. W. Stacy, M. D. Newcomb, and P. M. Bentley, "Expectancy in mediational models of cocaine abuse," *Personality and Individual Differences,* 19 (1995): 655-667. D. Comic and B. I. Murstein, "Bulimia nervosa: Prevalence and psychological correlates in a college community," *Eating Disorders: The Journal of Treatment and Prevention* 1 (1993): 39-51. S. K. Goldsmith, T. C. Perlman, A. M. Kleinman, and W. E. Bonney, *Reducing suicide: A national imperative* (Washington, DC: National Academy Press, 2002).

4. Cacioppo, J., & Patrick, W. (2008). Loneliness: Human nature and the need for social connection. New York: Norton.

5. Gottman, J. M. (2011). *The Science of Trust.* W.W. Norton, New York: New York

6. Personal training with Rebecca Jorgensen at Emotionally Focused Therapy in Salt Lake City Oct. 2016.

7. Fraley, R. C., & Waller, N. G. (1998). Adult attachment patterns: A test of the typological model. In J. A. Simpson & W. S. Rholes (Eds.), Attachment theory and close relationships (pp. 77-114). New York: Guilford Press

8. Johnson, S. M. (2008). Hold me tight: seven conversations for a lifetime of

love. New York: Little, Brown & Co.

9. Granfield, R., & Cloud, W. (1999). Coming clean: Overcoming addiction without treatment. New York: New York University Press.

Chapter Eleven:

1. Myers, S. M., & Booth, A. (1999). Marital Strains and Marital Quality: The Role of High and Low Locus of Control. Journal of Marriage and Family Vol. 61, No. 2 (May, 1999), pp. 423-436. DOI: 10.2307/353759

2. Ibid. from 1

3. Shapiro, F. (1995). Eye movement desensitization and reprocessing: basic principles, protocols, and procedures. New York: Guilford Press.

4. B. A. van der Kolk, (2014). The Body Keeps the Score: Brain, Mind, and Body in the Healing of Trauma. Penguin Group. New York: New York.

5. B. A. van der Kolk, et al., "A Randomized Clinical Trial of Eye Movement Desensitization and Reprocessing (EMDR), Fluoxetine, and Pill Placebo in the Treatment of Posttraumatic Stress Disorder: Treatment Effects and Long-Term Maintenance," Journal of Clinical Psychiatry 68 , no. 1 (2007): 37–46.

6. Ibid from 3

7. Shapiro F. The Role of Eye Movement Desensitization and Reprocessing (EMDR) Therapy in Medicine: Addressing the Psychological and Physical Symptoms Stemming from Adverse Life Experiences. The Permanente Journal. 2014;18(1):71-77. doi:10.7812/TPP/13-098.

8. https://www.adaa.org/about-adaa/press-room/facts-statistics

9. https://www.adaa.org/understanding-anxiety/depression

10. Ibid from 7

11. Ibid from 3

12. Hase, M., Balmaceda, U. M., Hase, A., Lehnung, M., Tumani, V., Huchzermeier, C., & Hofmann, A. (2015). Eye movement desensitization and reprocessing (EMDR) therapy in the treatment of depression: a matched pairs study in an inpatient setting. Brain and Behavior, 5(6), e00342. http://doi.org/10.1002/brb3.342

13. Marcus, Steven V.; Marquis, Priscilla; Sakai, Caroline. Psychotherapy: Theory, Research, Practice, Training, Vol 34(3), 1997, 307-315. http://dx.doi.

org/10.1037/h0087791

Chapter Twelve:

1. Median, J. (2008). Brain Rules: 12 Principles for Surviving and Thriving at Work, Home, and School. Pear Press. Seattle, WA.

2. Dispenza, J. (2012). Breaking the Habit of Being Yourself : How to Lose Your Mind and Create a New One. Hay House, Inc. Carlsbad, CA.

3. Siegel, D. J. (2010). Mindsight: The New Science of Personal Transformation. Bantam Books. New York: New York

4. Siegel, D. J. (2016). Mind: A Journey to the Heart of Being Human. W. W. Norton: New York: New York

5. Hill, D. (2015). Affect Regulation Theory: A Clinical Model. W. W. Norton. New York: New York

6. Ibid from 5

7. Ibid from 5

8. Trauma Sensitive Yoga in Therapy: (Loc 471 of 2353)

9. Ibid from 7

10. van der Kolk, B. A. (2006). Clinical implications of neuroscience research. Annals of the New York Academy of Science, 1071, 277–293. van der Kolk, B., Stone, L., West, J., Rhodes, A., Emerson, D., Suvak,

11. Ibid from 8

12. Ibid from 10

13. van der Kolk, B. A. (2014). The Body Keeps the Score: Brain, Mind, and Body in the Healing of Trauma. Penguin Group. New York: New York.

14. Ibid

15. K. Hölzel, et al., "Mindfulness Practice Leads to Increases in Regional Brain Gray Matter Density," Psychiatry Research: Neuroimaging 191, no. 1 (2011): 36–43. See also B. K. Hölzel, et al., "Stress Reduction Correlates with Structural Changes in the Amygdala," Social Cognitive and Affective Neuroscience 5, no. 1 (2010): 11–17; and S. W. Lazar, et al., "Meditation Experience Is Associated with Increased Cortical Thickness," NeuroReport 16 (2005): 1893–97.

16. Ibid from 13

17. Ibid from 3

18. Kabat-Zinn, J. (2005). Coming to our senses: Healing ourselves and the world through mindfulness. New York, NY: Hyperion.

19. Shapiro, S. & Carlson, L. (2013). The art and science of mindfulness: Integrating mindfulness into psychology and the healing professions. Washington, DC: American Psychological Association.

20. Siegel, D. J. (2007). The Mindful Brain: Reflection and Attunement in the Cultivation of Well-Being. W. W. Norton: New York: New York

21. Desrosiers, A., Vine, V., Klemanski, D. H., & Nolen-Hoeksema, S. (2013). Mindfulness and Emotion Regulation in Depression and Anxiety: Common and Distinct Mechanisms of Action. Depression and Anxiety, 30(7), 654–661. http://doi.org/10.1002/da.22124

22. Witkiewitz, K., Marlatt, G. A., & Walker, D. (2005). Mindfulness-based relapse prevention for alcohol and substance use disorders. Journal of Cognitive Psychotherapy, 19(3), 211-228.

23. Wright, S., Day, A., & Howells, K. (2009). Mindfulness and the treatment of anger problems. Aggression and Violent Behavior, 14(5), 396-401.

24. Follette, V. M., & Vijay, A. (2009). Mindfulness for trauma and posttraumatic stress disorder. In Clinical handbook of mindfulness (pp. 299-317). Springer New York.

25. Siegel, D. J. (2016). Mind: A Journey to the Heart of Being Human. W. W. Norton: New York: New York

26. Siegel, D. J. (2007). The Mindful Brain: Reflection and Attunement in the Cultivation of Well-Being. W. W. Norton: New York: New York

27. Ibid Siegel (2007)

28. Ibid Siegel (2007)

Chapter Thirteen:

1. Hahn, T. N. (2002). Teachings on Love. Parallax Press. Berkeley California.

2. Ibid (Hahn 2002)

3. Neff, K (2011). self-compassion: Stop beating yourself up and leave insecurity behind. Harper Collins Publishers. New York: New York

4. Ibid

5. Neff, K. D., Kirkpatrick, K. L., & Rude, S. S. (2007). Self-compassion and adaptive psychological functioning. Journal of Research in Personality, 41(1), 139–154.

6. Neff, K. D., & Germer, C. K. (2013). A pilot study and randomized controlled trial of the mindful self-compassion program. Journal of Clinical Psychology, 69(1), 28–44.

7. Breines, J. G., & Chen, S. (2012). Self-compassion increases self-improvement motivation. Personality and Social Psychology Bulletin, 38(9), 1133–1143.

8. Davidson, R. J. (2012). The emotional life of your brain: How its unique patterns affect the way you think, feel, and live—and how you can change them. New York, NY: Penguin.

9. Ibid Davidson (2012)

10. Ibid Davidson (2012)

11. Harter, S. (1993). Causes and consequences of low self-esteem in children and adolescents. In Self-esteem (pp. 87–116). New York, NY: Springer.

12. Germer, C. K. (2009). The mindful path to self-compassion: freeing yourself from destructive thoughts and emotions. Guilford Press. New York: New York

13. Desmond, T. (2015). Self-Compassion in Psychotherapy: Mindfulness-based practices for healing and transformation. W.W. Norton Company. New York: New York

14. Bible. Matthew: 22:37-40. King James Version

15. Ibid Germer (2009)

16. Hahn, T. N. (2002). Teachings on Love. Parallax Press. Berkeley California.

17. National Institute of Neurological Disorders and Stroke (2007). Brain basics: Understanding sleep (NIH Publication No. 06-3440-c), Bethesda, MD: National Institutes of Health. Retrieved February 4, 2011 from http://www.ninds.nih.gov/disorders/brain_basics/understanding_sleep.htm

18. Puterbaugh, Dolores T. (2011). Searching for a Good Night's Sleep: What Mental Health Counselors Can Do About the Epidemic of Poor Sleep. Journal of Mental Health Counseling, 33.4 (Oct 2011): 312-326

19. Ibid same as 17

20. Adachi, Y., Sato, C., Kunitsuka, K., Hayama, J., & Doi, Y. (2008). A brief behavior therapy administered by correspondence improves sleep and sleep-related behavior in poor sleepers. Sleep and Biological Rhythms, 6, ! 6-21. doi: 10.1111/j. 1479-8425.2007/00329.x.

21. Lack, L., Wright, H., & Paynter, D. (2007). The treatment of sleep onset insomnia with bright morning light. Sleep and Biological Rhythms, 53, 173-179. doi: 10.1111/j.1479-8425.2007. 00272.x

22. Ebben, M., & Spielman, A. (2009). Non-pharmacological treatments for insomnia. Journal of Behavioral Medicine, 32, 244-254. doi: 10.1007/s 10865-008-9198-8.

23. Wickwire, E. M., Sehumacher, J. A., & Clarke, E. J. (2009). Patient-reported benefits from the presleep routine approach to treating insomnia: Findings from a treatment development trial. Sleep and Biological Rhythms, 7, 71-77. doi: 10.1111/j.1479-8425.2009.00389.x

24. https://www.mentalhealth.org.uk/a-to-z/d/diet-and-mental-health

25. http://www.webmd.com/mental-health/news/20150820/food-mental-health

26. https://pubchem.ncbi.nlm.nih.gov/compound/L-tryptophan#section=Top

27. Ibid same as 24

28. http://www.getselfhelp.co.uk/docs/healthy%20eating%20depression.pdf

29. Ratey, J. J. (2008). Spark: The Revolutionary New Science of Exercise and the Brain. Little, Brown and Company. New York: New York. You can find a fun podcast with John Ratey in the Apple ITunes store under Love Rice. It is titled, "New Brain Cells."

30. Ibid same as 28

31. Raglin, J.S. (1990). Exercise and mental health: beneficial and detrimental Effects. Sports Med, 9: 323. doi:10.2165/00007256-199009060-00001

32. Porges, S. W. (2011). The Polyvagal Theory: Neurophysiological Foundations of Emotions, Attachment, Communication, and Self-regulation (Norton Series on Interpersonal Neurobiology). W. W. Norton & Company. New York: New York

References and Notes:

Chapter Fourteen:

1. Siegel, D. J. (2010). Mindsight: The New Science of Personal Transformation. Bantam Books. New York: New York

2. Vanzant, I, (2015). Trust: Mastering the 4 essential trusts. Smiley Books. Carlsbad CA.

3. Seibert, A. (2005). The Resiliency Advantage: Master change, thrive under pressure, and bounce back from setbacks. Berrett-Koehler Publishers, Inc. San Francisco, CA.

4. Seligman, M. E. P. (2011). Flourish: A visionary new understanding of happiness and well-being. Simon and Schuster, Inc. New York: New York

Additional Support Resources:

Videos:

Treating Trauma from Sexual Betrayal: The Essential Tools for Healing (Video Package) as found on www.discoverandchange.com/tipsa/solutions

These 10 Videos are designed to support this book and can be purchased at a discounted rate by entering the coupon code: TTFSB

Other products by Dr. Kevin Skinner

Treating Pornography Addiction: The Essential Tools for Recovery (Book)

Strengthening Recovery Through Strengthening Marriage: Healing from Pornography Addiction (Audio CD's)

Websites:

1. www.discoverandchange.com (Online assessments and support for indi-

viduals and couples looking to heal)

2. www.bloomforwomen.com (Online programs and expert help for healing from crisis and trauma.)

3. www.addorecovery.com (Outpatient clinics for treating sexual compulsivity and sexual betrayal). You can find Dr. Skinner's video on accountability under resources.

4. www.rootwellness.co (Yoga and Mindfulness classes)

5. www.sexhelp.com (Find a certified sexual addiction therapist)

6. www.iitap.com (An organization that trains sex addiction therapists)

7. www.self-compassion.org (Self-Compasion)

8. www.brenebrown.com (Vulnerability)

9. www.tarabrach.com (Powerful meditation)

Books:

1. *Back from Betrayal (by Jennifer P. Schneider M.D.)*

2. *Disclosing Secrets (by M Deborah Corley Ph.D. and Jennifer P Schneider M.D.)*

3. *Facing Heartbreak (by Stefanie Carnes, Ph.D. and Mari A. Lee).*

4. *Mending a Shattered Heart (by Stefanie Carnes, Ph.D.)*

5. *The Body Keeps the Score (by Bessel van der Kolk, M.D.)*

6. *Your Sexually Addicted Spouse: How Partners Can Cope and Heal (by Barbara Steffens and Marsha Means)*

7. *Getting Past Your Past (by Francine Shapiro)*

Support Groups for Individuals whose lives have been changed by sexual compulsivity:

1. www.cosa-recovery.org (COSA) COSA is a Twelve Step recovery program for men and women whose lives have been affected by compulsive sexual behavior.

2. http://www.sanon.org (S-Anon) S-Anon is a program of recovery for those who have been affected by someone else's sexual behavior.

Support for Domestic Violence or Self-Harm:

Domestic Violence

1. The Intimate Justice Scale can be taken at http://discoverandchange.com/tipsa/assessments

2. http://www.thehotline.org (1-800-799-7233)

Suicide Hotline

3. Suicide Hotline: http://suicidepreventionlifeline.org (1-800-273-8255)

4. http://www.spsamerica.org

Appendix A:

Key Life Events Inventory

All of us have key life events that alter our lives for good or bad. In this assignment, your task is to identify the significant events that have changed your life. Take into account big events such as the death of a loved one, moving, your first sexual experiences, etc. Other things you might include: parents fighting or divorcing, a parent with mental health challenges or substance abuse problems, being bullied on a playground, difficult school or team experiences. Some of these events may have also happened in your adult years (e.g. Health problems, job loss, etc.). Don't think too much about it, just write down as many experiences as you can think of for the next few minutes. Once you are done, place your experience on the timeline.

Event: _____ Age: ____

_____

_____

_____

_____

_____

_____

_____

_____

_____

_____

Now place each of the events above on the timeline below:

Timeline:

| --- |

To review, respond to the following prompt in your journal: Now that you have identified key life events from the past, what sticks out to you the most? Identify any common themes throughout the timeline as well as the events that had the biggest impact on your life.

Appendix B:

Sharing Your Story

"For years I hide from the reality of what my partner was doing. I knew something was wrong, but who could I tell? The children would be devastated. My parent's and family would turn against my husband. Our neighbors would judge us. Who, who could I possible tell?" I receive comments or hear stories like this all of the time. Unfortunately, many who feel trapped by sexual betrayal don't realize that by holding in all of the hurt, pain, shame, embarrassment, and anger the issue doesn't go away. In fact, it often manifests itself in physically symptoms (e.g. headaches, IBS--irritable bowel syndrome, muscle tension. When trauma is buried we often develop physical ailments and emotional issues like depression and anxiety. Conversely, healing begins to occur when your difficult feelings and emotions can be shared in a safe place.

Furthermore, what you are feeling and thinking about matters. Your story truly matters and it is an important part of your recovery. This assignment is designed to help you give voice to your experience. While the focus of recovery can easily be turned to your partner, we want to validate your story. This is your story, your experience, your pain, and your hurt.

Each of the questions below are designed to help you think about your story.

Please describe how you found out about your spouse's behavior. Where were you? What time of the year was it? Describe what happened.

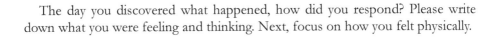

The day you discovered what happened, how did you respond? Please write down what you were feeling and thinking. Next, focus on how you felt physically.

Knowing what you do now is there anything you wish you would have said or done differently that day?

If you could go back in time and give yourself any advice, what advice would you give yourself?

As you reflect on your story, are you able to feel compassion for self or are you negative and critical toward yourself? Please write down your response and why you are responding the way you are.

As you reflect on these questions, there is a good chance that you will remember some of the hurt and pain associated with discovering your partner's addiction. However, as you write down your experiences and thoughts associated with what has been happening, your mind will begin to make sense of what you have been through. Hopefully, you will see areas that you have grown in and also find areas that you still need some healing.

Appendix C:

Support Resources for Couples Disclosures

Due to the difficult process of disclosures I encourage you to carefully review the following content. The information below is provided to help you understand the value of disclosures when done properly. However, because of the significant hardship of the disclosure process and the potential for harm when done improperly, this information should be used as a guideline. The best outcomes of disclosures usually occur in the context of a therapeutic process facilitated by a professional mental health counselor.

Disclosures Can Help You Heal

A disclosure done the right way can help you begin the healing process in earnest. Researchers who have studied couple disclosures have found that when done the right way can help individuals and couples heal. According to researchers Corley and Schneider, in their interviews with 80 self-reported sex addicts and their partners, 60% of addicts initially felt that disclosure was the proper course and in retrospect, 96% felt that disclosure was the proper course. In contrast, despite the pain of experiencing disclosure, 81% of partners initially felt that disclosure was the proper course and in retrospect, 96% felt that disclosure was the proper course. (1)

In additional research Dr. Schneider and her colleagues discovered the following in their work with couples trying to heal after sexual betrayal.

Key Findings on Disclosures:

1. Disclosure is often a process, not a one-time event, even in the absence of relapse; withholding of information is common.

2. Initial disclosure usually is most conducive to healing the relationship in the long-run when it includes all the major elements of the acting-out behaviors but avoids the "gory details".

3. Over half the partners threatened to leave the relationship after disclosure, but only one-quarter of couples actually separated.

4. Half the sex addicts reported one or more major slips or relapses, which necessitated additional decisions about disclosure.

5. Neither disclosure nor threats to leave prevent relapse.

6. With time, 96% of addicts and 93% of partners come to believe that disclosure had been the right thing to do.

7. Partners need more support from professionals and peers during the process of disclosure.

8. Honesty is a crucial healing characteristic.

9. The most helpful tools for coping with the consequences of sexual addiction are counseling and the 12-step programs.

I would strongly recommend reading the full article on this topic which can be found at:

www.jenniferschneider.com/article/surviving_disclosure.html

I would also recommend reading Dr. Schneider's book Back from Betrayal: Recovering From the Trauma of Infidelity.

Smart Ideas for Planning a Disclosure:

There are important principles behind an effective disclosure. They include:

• Self-disclosure is best done after deep self-evaluation and reflection by the offending party because it requires complete openness and honesty. This can stop staggered disclosures which has been associated with higher levels of trauma.

• Disclosures are more effective when the offending party has a period of sobriety.

• The spouse who was hurt needs to know how their partner acted out, for what length of time, and where it occurred (i.e. On the computer, while at work)

• While discussing the sexual betrayal, most couples are not prepared for the pain and intensity of the information being shared. As a result, fighting, yelling, and screaming are common. If you are at risk for high conflict, have a third party present (e.g. Religious leader, therapist).

What to Expect After a Disclosure

As a therapist trained in treating sexual betrayal I tell my clients who are doing a disclosure in my office that they need to: a) drive separate cars, b) have babysitters who can watch the children for an extended period of time--perhaps overnight, and c) they need to have an agreement on who will sleep where.

I also share that after disclosure it is not uncommon for there to be a worsening in the couple relationship. Additional challenges include: decreased ability to focus at work, feelings of shame and guilt, physical illness, and lack of sexual desire. (2) However, even after all of the challenges associated with disclosure, "Research confirms the benefits of going to counseling, having honest communication about the affairs and other sexual behaviors, and working on rebuilding the relationship. Disclosure of the addict's sexual acting-out behaviors is an important part of couple's counseling. (3)

Resources for this Appendix:

1. Schenider, J. P., Corley, M. D. (2002). Disclosing secrets: Guidelines for therapists working with sex addicts and coaddicts. *Sexual Addiction and Compulsivity 9: 43-67.*

2. Surviving Disclosure: A Partner's Guide for Healing From the Betrayal of Intimate Trust. By Jennifer P. Schneider and M. Deborah Corley. Recovery Resources Press, 2012.

3. Ibid

Appendix D:

Using Assessments to Guide Treatment

At Addo Recovery when a new client calls our center seeking help once we have identified their reason for seeking our help we invite them to take a battery of assessments. This information is very helpful and provides a good starting point for therapy. Early in my career I didn't have access to assessments that dealt with sexual addiction and sexual betrayal. As a result, I made mistakes because I didn't fully understand the extent of my client's problems.

Assessing Sexual Betrayal

At our center individuals who are experiencing sexual betrayal are asked to take the Inventory for Partner Attachment, Stress, and Trauma (IPAST). This battery of assessments includes the following:

- Trauma Inventory for Partner's of Sex Addicts (TIPSA)

- Depression, Anxiety, and Stress Scale (DASS-21)

- Partner Sexuality Survey

- Experience in Close Relationships

- And more

The IPAST can be administered by certified sexual addiction therapists (CSAT's). The value of the information gained in this assessment cannot be emphasized enough. It save hours of asking questions and provides valuable information to areas that need to be addressed in therapy.

Assessing Sexual Addiction

When we work with individuals seeking help for their sexual behaviors we begin by administering two validated assessments (Hypersexual Behavior Inventory--HBI-19 and Sexual Addiction Screening Tool-Revised--SAST-R). If their scores are elevated on these two measures we then administer the Sexual Dependency Inventory (SDI) which is a two hour assessment that has proven very valuable in helping us understand the depth of our clients sexually acting out behaviors. The SDI explores countless areas of sexually acting out behaviors (e.g. Phone sex, paying for sex, exhibitionism, etc.)

One of the most helpful aspects of the SDI is that it provides a look not only into the behaviors but it also offers insight into amount of sexual thoughts going on in the mind. This is referred to as Preoccupation in the inventory. The value of understanding the fantasy thoughts and mental aspect of what is happening in our client's mind is very helpful. By understanding our client's sexual behaviors and fantasy thoughts we gain a deeper understanding of their true challenges. This is essential for effective treatment.

Appendix E:

Assessing the Climate of Your Relationship

Here's a short quiz you can take to assess the climate of your relationship.

Please answer each question based on a Likert scale ranging from 1 (Never) to 7 (Always). Answer each question twice. Once for your behavior and once for your spouse.

Relationship Tension Scale

Question	Never	Rarely	Some-times	About half the time	Often	Very often	Always
I am critical of my partner.	1	2	3	4	5	6	7
My partner is critical of me.	1	2	3	4	5	6	7
I blame my partner for my behaviors.	1	2	3	4	5	6	7
My partner blames me for his/her behaviors.	1	2	3	4	5	6	7

I have lied to my partner to cover up my behavior.	1	2	3	4	5	6	7
My partner has lied to me to cover up his/her behavior.	1	2	3	4	5	6	7

Add your scores up for this section by summing the 1st, 3rd, and 5th questions together. This will give you personal score. Next sum the scores from the 2nd, 4th, and 6th questions together. This is your partner's score. Lower scores indicate less toxicity in your relationship while higher scores indicate that the climate of your relationship is difficult.

Scores below 7 generally indicate lower levels of conflict in relationships. Scores between 8-16 have some unhealthy behaviors, while scores above 18 are usually very toxic.

Relationship Attunement Scale

Question	Never	Rarely	Some-times	About half the time	Often	Very often	Always
I feel my spouse is aware of my hurt and pain.	1	2	3	4	5	6	7
I am aware of the hurt and pain my part-ner is feeling.	1	2	3	4	5	6	7
My spouse cares deeply about me.	1	2	3	4	5	6	7

I care deeply about my spouse.	1	2	3	4	5	6	7
My spouse makes it easy to love him/her.	1	2	3	4	5	6	7
I make it easy to love me.	1	2	3	4	5	6	7

Add your scores up for this section by summing the 1st, 3rd, and 5th questions together. This will provide you a personal relationship attunement score. Next sum the scores from the 2nd, 4th, and 6th questions together. This is your partner's score. Lower scores indicate less connection while higher levels suggest better levels of relationship closeness. Generally speaking individuals who score higher indicate that the climate of their relationship is caring, supportive, and likely safe.

If you or your partner's scores are below 9 your relationship is quite difficult at this time as there is very little closeness and connection. If you or your partner scored between 10-16 your relationship is not bad nor is it great. If you or your partner scored 17 or higher the more likely you will feel attuned to each other in your relationship.

Appendix F:

Questions to Help You Prepare for Change

As you prepare to make changes in your life it is valuable to take the time and reflect on the changes that you would like to make. The idea comes from the quote by the head of the Industrial Engineering Department of Yale University who said, "If I had only one hour to solve a problem, I would spend up to two-thirds of that hour in attempting to define what the problem is." (1)

Here's a list of questions for you to journal about as you prepare for making changes:

Getting to the Root of Your Problems

1. What is the root of the problem we are dealing with in our relationship?

2. Is my spouse showing addictive behaviors? (Compulsive behaviors, taking risks without thought, out of control behaviors?)

3. How have I changed as a result of what is happening in our relationship?

Self-Identity

4. How do I view myself now in contrast to how I viewed myself before marriage?

5. Am I taking my spouse's behaviors upon myself and blaming myself?

6. What has my spouse's sexual behaviors done to my perception of myself?

Boundaries

7. Have I tried to create boundaries with my spouse in the past? If so, what has been the outcome?

8. Am I comfortable creating boundaries with my spouse? If not, what is my biggest fear in creating boundaries with my spouse?

9. How has my spouse responded to my boundaries in the past?

Reference:

1. 1966, The Manufacturing Man and His Job by Robert E. Finley and Henry R. Ziobro, "The Manufacturing Manager's Skills" by William H. Markle (Vice President, Stainless Processing Company, Chicago, Illinois), Start Page 15, Quote Page 18, Published by American Management Association, Inc., New York.

Appendix G:

Self-Soothing Strategies

One of the most important things you can do for yourself if you are dealing with trauma is create a safe/calm place. This allows you to have a place to turn when you need to calm yourself down. One method to begin this process is to listen to the audio at www.discoverandchange.com/audio (see safe calm place.) Once you have created your safe/calm place, the next step comes from Dr. Francine Shapiro the author of *Getting Past Your Past*. In her book she offers a simple yet effective strategy for self-soothing. She suggests doing the butterfly hug, a technique developed in Mexico to help children following a hurricane. (1)

Here's a way for you to do it on your own.

Begin by crossing your arms in front of you with your right hand on your left shoulder and your left hand on your right shoulder. Then tap your hands alternately on each shoulder slowly four to six times. As you tap bring up the image you created in the safe/calm place audio. Allow your mind to connect with your safe/calm place. When you feel you are there and have the physical sensation inside continue tapping your shoulders an additional four to six times. Then stop and take a breath and see how it feels. Repeat this exercise at least one more time.

Reference:

Shapiro, F. (2012). Getting past your past: take control of your life with self-help techniques from EMDR therapy. Emmaus, PA: Rodale Books.

Appendix H:

5 Whys Exercise

This exercise is based on the model used by Toyota Motor Corporation to identify the root cause of problems encountered during manufacturing cars. Today more than 60 years after this model was created it is being applied to help individuals in various settings identify why problems occur.

This exercise can be used to understand many personal and relationship issues. While the process is basic, the awarenesses gained can be very valuable. You begin by identifying a problem that you are encountering in your life. The issue could be a personal problem, a relationship issue, a challenge with your child, a work problem, or something else you are dealing with.

Example of a problem:

I can't stop my mind from thinking about what my spouse did to me.

Now it is your turn. Identify a personal issue that you would like to understand better.

Issue I want to address: _____

_____

Begin by asking yourself why that issue is bothering you.

Why #1--Example: I feel betrayed. Like he only cares about himself. I am so angry at him.

Your turn:

Why #1: _____

Next, ask yourself why you are feeling the way you are based on your answer to "Why #1. Based on the example above the question would be, "Why am I so angry at him?

Why #2--Example: He only cares about himself.

Your turn:

Why #2: _____

Why #3--Example: He promised me I was his all. He lied to me

Your turn:

Why #3: _____

Why #4--Example: I don't matter to him

Your turn:

Why #4: _____

Why #5--Example: I'm not important

Your turn:

Why #5: _____

Appendix I:

Mindful Breathing Exercise

In this short mindful exercise the goal is to help you focus on your breathing.

Step #1: Please begin by doing a quick body scan. Notice any tension, tightness, or unusual sensation in your body. Just observe the sensation in that region of your body.

Step #2: Next turn your attention to you breathing. Your focus now should shift to your breathing. Notice your breathing as you inhale and exhale. Are your breaths shallow or are you getting deep breaths? Throughout this exercise one of the main goals is to help you establish deeper breathing patterns.

Step #3: Now begin focus on deep breathing as you inhale for about 4-6 seconds. Hold it for two seconds and then let out a powerful exhalation for about 6-8 second. Continue your breathing like this for three minutes. During the three minute period try to maintain your focus on your breathing. Don't worry if your mind wanders just notice that your mind has gone to another thought and bring your attention back to your breathing. Notice how your diaphragm moves as you breath.

Step #4: After completing the three minute exercise come back to your body sensations and again notice the sensations throughout your body. What are you feeling? Make note of how your body feels after this three minute exercise.

--

This simple breathing exercise is used by many people as they work through their stress and life challenges. It is recommended that you practice doing this breathing exercise three times a day. The more you practice this breathing exercise the stronger your capacity will be to calm yourself when you are feeling overwhelmed or stressed.

Appendix J:

Creating Your Emergency Self-Calming Kit

One way to help you establish more compassion for yourself is to find and do things that you enjoy. This exercise is designed to help you use your senses to calm down in difficult times. Below you will be asked to identify things around you that you enjoy. This exercise is designed to help you have compassion for self by doing things that lift your mood. This assignment will step you through creating your emergency self-calming kit.

When we are in crisis we often lose ourselves and behave in ways we didn't know were possible. In order to regulate our emotions and gain control of our lives, we need to access the solutions from within.

This assignment will assist you in creating a self-calming kit depending on your own unique likes, dislikes, and comfort level.

To create your kit, complete the following three steps:

Step 1: Make a list of items you enjoy from each of the 7 senses.

Here are some examples to help you begin thinking about what you enjoy:

Smell

- A favorite lotion or perfume
- A nostalgic smell
- Essential Oils

Taste

- Dark chocolate

- Honey sticks
- Gum

Sight

- Photos of family
- Post cards of places you have been or want to go
- Inspiring quotes

Touch

- Soft blanket
- Smooth stone

Sound

- Mix CD of inspiriting music
- CD of nature sounds
- Audio recording of positive self-talk

Kinesthetic

- Package of play-dough or clay
- Pen and paper for doodling
- Oils, makers, paints

Internal

- Crisis journal
- Scriptures/Quote

Step 2: Now, create your list:

Smell

_____

_____

Taste

_____

_____

Sight

_____

_____

Touch

_____

_____

Sound

_____

_____

Kinesthetic

_____

_____

Internal

_____

_____

Step 3: Find pictures that represent your self-calming kit and put them in a collage to remind you of each of these seven areas. This is a way to help you remember the importance of taking care of yourself.

CPSIA information can be obtained
at www.ICGtesting.com
Printed in the USA
FSHW02n2045071018
52836FS